Faith and Secularisation in Religious Colleges and Universities

There are almost 2,000 religious higher education institutions worldwide, 250 of which are in Europe. *Faith and Secularisation in Religious Colleges and Universities* is the first book to offer a comparative study of these institutions across many religions and countries including Christian, Islamic and Jewish universities in areas including the US, Europe and the Middle East.

Considering the current tensions and debates surrounding academic freedom, institutional governance, educational policy, mission and identity, this innovative and challenging book explores:

- institutions' relations with the state and their wider communities
- whether such institutions can be both religious and 'universities'
- the appropriate role of religious faith within colleges and universities
- academic autonomy and the role of religion in education

Faith and Secularisation in Religious Colleges and Universities offers some important ideas on how such institutions can be part of diversity and pluralism yet remain committed in a holistic and coherent way to their religious traditions. It will appeal to readers involved in higher education studies, religious study and the history of education, as well as individuals within religious institutions.

James Arthur is Professor of Education at Canterbury Christ Church University. He completed his doctorate at Oriel College in the University of Oxford and has written widely on the relationship between theory and practice in education.

Faith and Secularisation in Religious Colleges and Universities

James Arthur

Routledge
Taylor & Francis Group

LONDON AND NEW YORK

First published 2006 by Routledge
2 Park Square, Milton Park, Abingdon, Oxon OX14 4RN

Simultaneously published in the USA and Canada
by Routledge
270 Madison Ave, New York, NY 10016

*Routledge is an imprint of the Taylor & Francis Group,
an informa business*

© 2006 James Arthur

Typeset in Times by RefineCatch Limited, Bungay, Suffolk
Printed and bound in Great Britain by
TJI Digital, Padstow, Cornwall

British Library Cataloguing in Publication Data
A catalogue record for this book is available from the British Library

Library of Congress Cataloging in Publication Data
Arthur, James, 1957–
    Faith and secularisation in religious colleges and universities/
    James Arthur.
    p. cm.
    Includes bibliographical references and index.
    1. Church colleges.   2. Religious education.   3. Universities and
    colleges.   4. Education, Higher.   I. Title.
    LC421.A78 2006
    378.07—dc22
    2005036061

ISBN10: 0–415–35940–6 (hbk)
ISBN10: 0–203–00744–1 (ebk)

ISBN13: 978–0–415–35940–5 (hbk)
ISBN13: 978–0–203–00744–0 (ebk)

Contents

Foreword

In this innovative and challenging book Professor James Arthur has provided a remarkable examination of religiously affiliated higher education institutions that are linked to the Christian, Jewish and Muslim religions. Although he modestly claims this to be an introduction to the understanding of religiously affiliated universities and colleges it is much more. From considering the problem of definition, he considers the mission and identity of these types of higher education institutions and then goes on to consider their governance, funding, the issue of secularisation, academic freedom and the religious renewal or 'de-secularisation' within contemporary higher education.

What is impressive about this book is the range of knowledge about international higher education that it is based on and the author's sensitive and positive treatment of the three major religions and their relationship to higher education. His analysis of the effects of secularisation and the question of the continuing 'ambiguity and mission' of faith-based universities, especially some Christian universities, is well developed and is central to the book. Although I do not always agree with his conclusions, for example his critical treatment of Jesuit universities, I would still argue that his conclusions are balanced, fair and based on extensive evidence. His treatment of the ideas of John Henry Newman in his examination of the issue of the relationship between religious belief and knowledge in higher education is fascinating and surely the author should develop this more fully in an extended study of Newman's 'Idea of a University'. Another important feature of this study of the complex relationship between scholarship and religious faith is his treatment of academic freedom in an age of increasing religious fundamentalism. He firmly states that 'Religiously affiliated colleges and universities therefore have a role to promote the pursuit of truth, allowing question and debate, according to their traditions and in doing so they add a pluralism within higher education itself'.

An aspect of religiously based higher education institutions that James Arthur does not fully consider is the relation between their faith traditions and their engagement with the society that they are part of. What is particularly interesting about these institutions is their commitment to the ideas and practice of the 'engaged university'. It would be interesting to consider how this is based on a religious communitarianism that is linked to both theological views and a faith-based pedagogy.

In his insightful consideration of the religious renewal within higher education he offers some important ideas on how religiously affiliated higher education institutions can be part of diversity and pluralism yet remain committed in a holistic and coherent way to their religious traditions. He offers some interesting ideas on mission and identity, leadership and governance, the curriculum, the religious life and the ethos of the institution and the nature of the faith-based and academic community. This is a challenging view and readers will benefit from the author's scholarship, his cross-cultural sensitivity and honesty in developing his arguments.

Professor John Annette
Pro Vice Master
Professor of Citizenship and Lifelong Learning
Birkbeck College
University of London

Preface

My academic interest in the role of religion within higher education began in a serious way when I arrived to begin my doctoral studies at Oriel College, Oxford, in the late 1980s. On walking through the main gate into the first Quad I was struck by the large statue of the Virgin and Child peering down at me. The College is, of course, a fourteenth-century Catholic and royal foundation and is dedicated to the Virgin Mary. As a Scot, I was particularly interested in the reason given for the College's foundation: it was founded as the fulfilment of a promise to the Virgin Mary by Edward II for sparing his life at the disastrous English defeat at Bannockburn. It is therefore ironic that the first student to graduate from Oriel was a Scot! The College is famous, among many other things, for having John Henry Newman as a Fellow and for its pivotal role in leading the Oxford Movement in the nineteenth century. As a member of the College you hear Latin Grace said before Hall (dinner) each night and are aware of the variety of Christian symbolism contained in stained glass windows, portraits on the walls and statues around the College. You are also aware of the presence of an Anglican chaplain and are conscious that the chapel is actually used for religious services, which students and dons voluntarily attend on weekdays and Sundays. You notice that religious subjects are regularly and seriously debated by various Fellows and student societies and you observe that invited speakers to the College regularly come to discuss religious themes. There was and is a definite Christian ethos forming the backdrop to study at Oriel, which few can ignore. Indeed, Oxford University still offers and provides a wide range of religious activities for its students and retains many of the visible fragments of its Anglican and more ancient Catholic pasts. Many students at Oxford enter upon their studies with an interest in religion, if not a serious commitment to their faith. Nevertheless, I understood Oxford to be a 'secular' institution, even if the unspoken assumption among some was that it may not be in practice. I was also aware that religion in general and Christianity in particular were supposed to inhabit quite separate provinces in British higher education. The questions I asked myself as a Catholic were: What did all this mean today? Was there any current substance to this religious backdrop of fragmented Christianity? Did it actually influence anyone?

As part of my doctorate I spent a short time at Fordham University in New York in early 1990. I was accommodated at St John's Hall on the main campus in the Bronx, but on arrival I was not conscious of any religious atmosphere. I understood Fordham to be a Catholic university run by the Jesuits. It has a large chapel in the centre of the campus, but apart from this, I saw very few other specifically religious expressions in art or architecture, and practically none at the postgraduate centre in downtown Manhattan. There existed a chaplaincy that appeared devoted to social activism, counselling and imaginative liturgies. There were a number of organised meetings during my stay to discuss various contemporary ethical issues, but the intention, explicit or not, seemed to be aimed at developing a critical attitude to the teachings of the Catholic Church. The questions I asked myself as a Catholic included: Why does the Church invest so many people and resources in universities like this and what difference does it make? Why is this particular university listed as Catholic? What understanding of Catholicism does the institution attempt to promote?

In 1991 I was invited by the Abbot of Ampleforth, the Rt. Revd Patrick Barry, to attend an important meeting of the Catholic College Principals of Britain in Glasgow. This meeting had been called by one of the fourteen principals and was funded by a Catholic charity to discuss the possibility of establishing a national Catholic university. Recent government legislation on higher education had made this a potential option for these colleges of higher education, which were largely concerned with providing Catholic teachers, but had now begun to diversify their academic courses. Archbishop Thomas Winning of Glasgow (later Cardinal Winning) chaired the meeting and I was asked to act as secretary. Thomas Winning had been my parish priest and school chaplain when I was growing up in Scotland. Collectively, the colleges, or at least the religious congregations and orders that ran most of them, owned a great deal of property and the chairs of governors of these colleges were also present at the meeting. During the opening discussions the Jesuit Principal of Heythrop College in London declared that his institution was not legally a Catholic institution and that the recent document issued by the Vatican on Catholic universities (*Ex Corde Ecclesiae*) did not apply to Heythrop, which was a secular component of the University of London run and owned by the Jesuits. The reason why *Ex Corde Ecclesiae* did not apply to Heythrop was because the Jesuits did not publicly claim it as 'Catholic', but instead allowed the College to be secular in its legal and public character. He also did not think a national Catholic university was a good idea and distanced himself from the suggestion. The other Catholic principals began to record their excellent relations with their local secular universities, which validated their degrees, and praised their regional links with other Christian colleges with whom some were in the process of establishing joint agreements or amalgamations. There was certainly very little interest in founding a specifically Catholic university. The questions I asked myself of this experience were: What is a Catholic college or university? Who should control it and what public identity should it have? Does the Catholic Church seriously influence any of these colleges? Today, with less than a third of the original fourteen colleges still operating, the extent of their Catholicity is still a pressing issue for them and the Church.

The fate of St Andrew's College, Glasgow, where the original meeting was held, is worth recounting. The College had a number of incarnations from 1895, but all of them served by supplying teachers for Catholic schools. Indeed, the quality of these teachers, precisely as Catholic teachers, was so high that many were deliberately targeted for recruitment by English schools. However, the College was sold to the State by the Sisters of Notre Dame and the State subsequently undertook to continue to run it as a Catholic teacher training institution. In 1999 it was 'merged' with Glasgow University and became part of a new Faculty of Education. In order to preserve something of its Catholic identity, the Faculty established a Board of Catholic Education to offer advice on courses for teacher training for those who wished to teach in Catholic schools. The Catholic Church in Scotland opposed this 'merger' and Glasgow University Senate required assurances that the Catholic Church could not interfere in the internal decision-making processes of the University. In the end, the Faculty is a secular body and the Board of Catholic Education has merely an advisory function over a very limited area of the Faculty's work. Whilst the Faculty has subscribed to the International Federation of Catholic Universities, it is difficult to see how this Faculty is in any sense Catholic. It is therefore strange that the IFCU has allowed the Faculty to appear on its website.

On leaving Oriel College, I arrived at Canterbury Christ Church College (now Canterbury Christ Church University), an Anglican College that had just successfully hosted the first international gathering of the Colleges and Universities of the Anglican Communion (CUAC). Dr Edward Norman, formerly Dean of Peterhouse, Cambridge, was the active College chaplain and within a short time of my arrival I was being invited to various meetings with the local Anglican bishop to discuss how and in what ways the College was serving the Church of England and Christianity more generally. I was conscious that there was a renewed interest by the Church of England in trying to ensure that its colleges served Christianity in general. In 1995 I published my first academic book, *The Ebbing Tide*, which detailed from a huge range of documents what I believed to be the ebbing Catholicity in Catholic schools. Whilst the book received praise in public reviews it was not received well by some Catholic authorities in education. Some objected to aspects of the content of my book. It raised questions for me, including: What does academic freedom mean and how should it be exercised in the Church?

I was conscious throughout the 1990s that there were a growing number of people who wanted to reconnect religiously affiliated institutions of higher education more closely with their sponsoring religious bodies. I saw this within my own university and the Principals of the Association of Church and Affiliated Colleges asked me to organise an ecumenical conference on the theme of the Church Dimension in Higher Education. This conference was held in Canterbury in September 2000 and its purpose was to define the opportunities and challenges for Church colleges within the mission of the Church in education. The conference discussed the identity of Christian colleges and universities in Britain. In the same year I attended a conference at the Australian Catholic University in Sydney at which there were real tensions expressed about the nature and mission of a Catholic university – tensions which have since intensified for this particular University and which are discussed in this book. In Johannesburg, South Africa, I witnessed the establishment of the emphatically Catholic St Augustine's University (now St Augustine's College). In Chicago I met a young member of the faculty at Loyola University who described, at a conference, her institution's mission. Her definition was entirely framed in terms and in the language of social activism, freedom and transformation – no obvious religious content was even suggested. In visiting a number of religiously affiliated universities in Europe, the United States, Australia and South Africa, including the Catholic University of Nijmegen in Holland, the Catholic University of Lille in France, the Catholic University of Milan in Italy, the Universities of San Francisco, Georgetown, Marquette, Loyola, Notre Dame, DePaul, the Catholic University of America, Calvin College and Boston University in the USA, the Australian Catholic University and St Augustine's College in South Africa and the majority of Church higher education foundations in Britain, I have been struck in discussions with colleagues and students by the continuing ambiguity about identity and mission. These experiences have raised a wide range of questions for me. I was also conscious that almost all the literature in this field has been a product of the American context, which continues to have a huge influence on debates elsewhere in the world. I believe there is a need to widen the discussion, building on the work in America to include not only the experiences of Christians elsewhere but also some of the views and educational beliefs of Muslims and Jews.

In January 2005 I was appointed the first Director of the National Institute of Christian Education Research, based in Canterbury, UK. The Institute's remit is to conduct research into all aspects of faith-based institutions, including colleges and universities. The Institute was founded by Canterbury Christ Church University, the University of Gloucestershire, and St Martin's College, Lancaster, together with the Church of England. The Institute also seeks to conduct research and development in the theology of Christian education and explore the mission of Christian higher education. The Institute was launched in Canterbury at the CUAC conference in June 2005. This initiative represents another attempt by some of the Christian institutions of higher education in England to reflect positively on their mission as religiously affiliated colleges and universities.

This book serves as an introduction to those unfamiliar with the range of debates and issues surrounding religiously affiliated higher education institutions. It introduces some of the concerns and issues of the Jewish and Muslim communities in higher education around the world and attempts to widen the debate about Christian colleges and universities. However, the main focus will remain on Christian institutions of higher education as they represent by far the world's largest number of religiously affiliated colleges and universities. My purpose in this review has been a modest one – to illustrate some of the complex ways in which different religiously affiliated colleges and universities relate to some contemporary issues and questions in higher education. Whilst specific illustrations from my contact with colleagues in the colleges and universities I have visited are included in this review, to substantiate my broad assertions, I recognise that in-depth empirical research is needed. Consequently, I will be writing in general terms, as the breadth of the matter under consideration is huge. It is my view that ultimately the factors that secularise religious institutions are complex and need to be considered on an institutional and particular-faith basis in order to reflect this complexity. This book does not offer any specific models to follow, but suggests a tentative way forward for some religiously affiliated institutions. My evaluation and recommendations here are thus a dangerous undertaking, but serve as an introduction to an important area of higher education that is routinely neglected in the mainstream literature on higher education in Britain. My own personal stance is one that supports religiously affiliated institutions, because they ought to make a distinctive contribution to higher education.

James Arthur
Canterbury Christ Church University

Acknowledgements

In writing this book I have met and debated various themes with many colleagues from eminent academics to university administrators, together with a large number of other academic staff and students, both doctoral and undergraduate. These have included brief meetings with Professor Alasdair McIntyre and former university administrator Fr Theodore Hesburgh, both at the University of Notre Dame. There are clearly too many names and institutions to mention here, but I am thankful to them all for discussing with me many of the ideas contained in this review of religiously affiliated colleges and universities.

Nevertheless, I specifically wish to record my appreciation to the following who have read the early drafts of this book and have offered comments as well as to those who have offered support and encouragement: Professor Robert Benne, Jordan-Trexler Professor of Religion Emeritus and Director of the Center for Religion and Society at Roanoke College, Salem, Virginia; Professor Walter J. Nicgorski of the University of Notre Dame; Dr Simon Gaine OP, Vice-Regent, Blackfriars, Oxford; Professor Gerald Grace, Director of the Centre for Research and Development in Catholic Education, Institute of Education, University of London; Dr Gavin D'Costa, Head of Theology, University of Bristol; the Rt. Revd David Charlesworth, Buckfast Abbey, Devon; Dr Farid Panjwani, Aga Khan University, London; Dr Andrew Milson, formerly of Baylor University, Texas; Rabbi Dr Michael Shire, Leo Baeck College-Centre for Jewish Education; Dr Kenneth Wilson, former Principal of Westminster College, Oxford; Professor Tony d'Arbon, Australian Catholic University, Sydney; and finally to Canon John Hall, General Secretary of the Education Division of the Church of England. I am especially thankful to Professor John Annette, Dean of Education and Pro-Vice Master, Birbeck College, University of London, for providing the Preface to this book. Whilst I have warmly received and noted all these contributions, the views expressed in this book are my own, as are the mistakes.

Introduction

Scholarly interest in religiously affiliated higher education over the last decade or so has significantly increased as can be seen from the explosion of academic literature in the field (see Sack 1997 and, in Britain, Astley *et al.* 2004). Numerous books and articles are now available on various religious aspects of these colleges and universities, but they are still largely concerned with Christian developments and perspectives in the USA. This academic interest has coincided with religiously affiliated institutions working to renew and redefine their identities, as almost all have sought to rearticulate their mission after a long and serious process of reappraisal. A growing world resurgence of religious belief and practice among Jews, Christians, and Muslims has certainly aided this reappraisal. With a marked return to religion, there has been a rise of orthodox and fundamentalist religious forces around the world (Berger 1999). There has also been a new openness to issues in religion within higher education more generally. Since it is impossible to cover everything in the expanding literature, this book will consequently focus on the ideological/philosophical dimensions – on the broad underlying religious and cultural assumptions, ideas, attitudes and beliefs that have largely shaped the worldview and operations of Jews, Christians and Muslims in higher education. However, attention will be given to the methodological and institutional factors that have influenced the development of these colleges and universities. It is recognised at the outset that many of these religious colleges and universities are located within and influenced by the secular cultural climate of contemporary Western societies. In particular, this book seeks to discuss the process of secularisation that has been and is affecting these institutions, and their staff, students and courses. The intention of this review is to build on the work of scholars in the USA to provide a broader view beyond the boundaries of American higher education and beyond purely Christian institutions. Nevertheless, the principal focus will remain on Christian institutions and readers will see that this leads to some unevenness in coverage in each chapter. This book makes no pretence to be anything but an introduction to the area since it is practically impossible to deal adequately with the theological understandings in each of the great faiths discussed in the space allowed. This is clearly a complex and multifaceted task, especially as the contemporary debate can be confusing, with many publications that are both descriptive and prescriptive in tone and content. My aim will have been achieved if it leads those who have a limited knowledge of the area to read further in more detailed books.

This book examines contemporary religiously affiliated higher education institutions and aims to encourage people to seriously face this question of whether these institutions can be both religious and educational at the same time. Religious influence and involvement in higher education continues to be extensive and manifests itself through the presence of believing Christians, Jews and Muslims in almost all universities and colleges in the world. These three main religious faiths provide chaplaincies and religious associations in the majority of the world's secular universities and colleges. These religious associations of students and staff have experienced an increase in activity and membership within these secular colleges and universities in recent years. However, all three faiths also provide and sponsor institutions of higher education often in the form of large universities and colleges. These religiously affiliated institutions are on the increase today, as are the number of students who attend them. In this book the focus will be on higher learning institutions founded and operating under a religious mission or religious worldview. The book does not address seminaries, rabbinical schools or *madrassas* for the training of priests/ministers, rabbis or imams, but recognises that these types of institutions are also involved in higher education studies.

On a world basis there can be found organisations and networks of Jewish, Christian and Muslims representing faith-sponsored centres, college and universities. There are, for example, around 1,000 institutions of higher education federated to the International Federation of Catholic Universities in sixty countries, but 25 per cent of these universities are located in the USA which represents only 6 per cent of the entire Catholic world population. The colleges and universities of the Anglican Communion number over 60 and are situated in most continents in the world, including nine in Japan. Whilst the World Council of Churches numbers over 100 Protestant universities on its website there are many more, particularly in the USA. In 2000, the USA Higher Education Directory indicated that there were 4,077 institutions of higher education in the United States. The Directory also identifies those institutions with a current 'religious affiliation' as numbering 764. Of the 764 institutions listed, 235 are identified as Roman Catholic, the largest subset. The next largest subset is United Methodists, with 87 colleges, followed by Southern Baptists and Presbyterians, with 42 each; these are followed by the Baptists, with 39, Evangelical Lutherans, with 34, and Jews, with 26. These Churches have formed a number of associations and federations in the USA including the Christian College Coalition, the Council of Protestant Colleges and Universities, the Council of Christian Colleges and Universities, the

Association of Lutheran Colleges, the Association of Presbyterian Colleges and Universities, the Association of Jesuit Colleges and Universities, and the Association of Catholic Colleges and Universities to name but a few. The Russian Orthodox Church has two universities, but there are many Orthodox theology faculties in Eastern Europe and over 100 Orthodox chairs in theology and religion located in the world's secular universities. The number of Christian colleges and universities continues to grow in former communist states (see Petrenko and Glanzer 2005). There is also the International Forum of Associations of Christian Higher Education and a number of European, African, Asian and Latin American Catholic associations of colleges and universities.

The overwhelming majority of Jewish and Muslim universities are products of the second half of the twentieth century. There are seven Jewish universities in Israel. There are also Jewish colleges and universities in America and Europe, but overall these are small in number, serving the total world Jewish population of little more than fifteen million. Nevertheless, there are over 50 Jewish research centres attached to various universities in the world. The Organisation of Islamic Conferences, with over 56 member states, has, since the 1970s, encouraged the foundation of Muslim universities, especially in developing countries. Most Muslim colleges and universities are found predominantly within Muslim majority countries and they have similar associations such as the Islamic University League, which claims 120 universities as members, the Federation of the Universities of the Islamic World, claiming 193 members, and the Association of Arab Universities, with 16 member universities. Nevertheless, there are Muslim universities and centres existing outside strictly Muslim countries. Many Muslims have also followed the Jewish practice of establishing a large number of centres for Islamic studies within Western universities.

All of these religiously affiliated institutions and organisations face very similar problems. They include rising costs, lack of endowments and increasing external regulation. There is growing student preoccupation with future careers and of course the attempt by religious bodies and communities to address the more complex world we live in. Sometimes these colleges and universities play down their religious identity in the belief that this might possibly attract funding, students and academic staff. A small number instead emphasise their religious identity in order to attract students and staff of a particular mind set within their particular religious faith community. It should also be noted that some of these religiously affiliated colleges and universities can often be peripheral to the larger higher education systems in many countries. In the West religiously affiliated institutions are not generally a major part of the higher education establishment. Perhaps one of the most pressing background issues that they all face is whether or not they are being authentic in regard to their religious tradition. It is this concern with religious authenticity that this book principally addresses. In particular, there is the question of how these religiously affiliated colleges and universities have become more identifiably secular and less identifiably religious.

Outline of chapters

Chapter 1 reviews the definition of religiously affiliated higher education institutions and traces the broad development of these institutions. This chapter will provide the context for the current debate about the presence of religious institutions within higher education and offer an explanation of what is meant by secularisation within this context. There follows in Chapter 2 a discussion of the mission and identity of religiously affiliated colleges and universities. Do religiously affiliated colleges and universities have a distinctive character that distinguishes them from other institutions of higher education? Do they have a character that makes a difference to their educational enterprise? This chapter will consider how these institutions view themselves and wish to be viewed by others.

Chapter 3 examines how religiously affiliated universities are governed and the different kinds of relationships they develop with their sponsoring religious or government bodies. It explores some issues of secular government funding of religiously affiliated colleges and universities and examines how this funding involves control and whether it can reduce religious emphasis or mission. This chapter also considers how religious sponsoring bodies influence the governance of these universities. In particular it will look at how Islamic and majority Muslim governments control the identity and mission of their universities and how the Vatican has used *Ex Corde Ecclesiae* to exert influence over governance as a way of influencing identity. What role does the state play in relations with religiously affiliated universities in different cultural and political contexts? In Israel and Muslim countries, universities are often established by states that have a religious basis or bias – how does this influence their higher education institutions? Chapter 4 explores how religion and religious expression is thought by many to be unscientific and inappropriate in higher education. For others, the purpose of a religiously affiliated college or university is to provide knowledge within the ethos of Judaism, Christianity or Islam and therefore religious belief does not limit inquiry. Many secular universities have largely eliminated religious elements from their overall mission, proclaiming themselves to be open to all, free and non-sectarian. How does secularisation challenge the religiously affiliated college and university? Are there differences between Jewish, Christian and Muslim models? How do they understand secularisation and how do they respond? How can religiously affiliated colleges and universities pursue a holistic view of knowledge? How do the ideas of John Henry Newman assist us in understanding this complex area? The chapter reviews the connection between religious belief and knowledge, but does not address the question of theology in the university as a discipline – readers who are interested in this area are recommended to read Gavin D'Costa's book *Theology in the Public Square: Church, Academy and Nation* (Blackwell, Oxford, 2005).

Chapter 5 will make clear the difference between individual academic freedom and institutional academic freedom. It will discuss the meaning and operational use of academic freedom through a number of examples. Are all ideas and people welcome in religiously affiliated universities? The many tensions in outlining what academic freedom is within the context of a religiously affiliated university will be explored. What is the current state of academic freedom within the different faiths? The notion that the personal beliefs of scholars are compatible with their academic interests has long been questioned – but almost exclusively in the religious domain, since the personal beliefs of Marxists and feminists, etc., are largely respected in modern universities. More fundamentally, the idea that religion can somehow provide the necessary context for the conduct of all other disciplines within the university is certainly not accepted in the modern secular university. The very idea that any authority higher than the human mind should be considered is banished from the modern university. This chapter examines the tensions resulting from a religious university's recognition of, and desire to incorporate in its curricula, the truths found in its religious mission. Chapter 6 explores the secularisation process, how a religiously affiliated higher education institution becomes almost wholly indistinguishable from secular institutions through a number of steps, which are outlined.

Finally, in Chapter 7 the religiously affiliated college and university appears to challenge the modern secular university with a religious rhetoric. This chapter will examine what may be understood as religious renewal or 'de-secularisation' within higher education. It will also explore the future case for religiously affiliated higher education by setting out some of the steps they might take to make their declared mission a reality. Chapter 8 provides a short summary of the content of this review and make a brief case for religiously affiliated higher education institutions.

Chapter 1

Religiously affiliated higher education

Introduction

For the purposes of this book higher education refers to education beyond the secondary level and is provided by universities and colleges together with other institutions that award academic degrees. Therefore it refers to academic activities that are designated to be at degree level and above and includes teaching, learning, scholarship and research. It also includes professional training conducted within universities and colleges. There are significant differences between institutions of higher education. Institutions of 'higher education', 'universities' and 'colleges' have different meanings as not all institutions of higher education are universities or colleges. Higher education can therefore take place outside universities and colleges, but in this book the boundary is set with recognised universities and colleges. In some countries the title 'university' is in the gift of the state, whilst in others any academic organisation can call itself a university. The aims of universities are increasingly complex, but normally revolve around the needs of individuals and society. However, before a definition of a religiously affiliated institution of higher education is offered it is necessary to say something about religion in the context of education more generally.

The monotheistic faiths and education

There is a need to identify at the outset some of the characteristic features of Judaism, Christianity and Islam by way of an introductory sketch to understand what motivates the foundation of religious universities and colleges. All three faiths share much in common, including a belief in one God who Judges. All three of these major world Faiths represent a meta-narrative of ideas, visions and concepts that are fundamental in each religion to understanding human beings and the destiny of life. They offer a standpoint from which everything else can be seen. Therefore, at the core of education for each of these faiths there is a transcendent, spiritual idea that can give a particular purpose and clarity to learning. The narrative in each constructs ideals and provides a source of authority, and above all, gives a sense of continuity and purpose – a purpose that gives meaning to education through a sense of personal identity and community life and offers a basis for moral conduct. Judaism, Christianity and Islam have had from the beginning a written orthodoxy as religions of the Book. Each religion is described both as a set of beliefs and as a practice. Each believer believes certain propositions to be true and subscribes to a code of moral beliefs that is closely related to the set of beliefs. Education for all three religions includes the aim to encourage participation in the faith by engendering belief in the tenets of the religion through full-hearted participation in religious practices. Simply teaching about the beliefs and practices of one of these religious communities without engendering belief or a desire to participate is not considered to be authentic by any of these religions. Each in turn claims to have superseded what went before, and both Christianity and Islam have universalistic claims, whilst Judaism views both Christianity and Islam as derived from Judaism. Another important point is that Christianity and Islam seek to proselytise whilst Judaism does not. A brief description of the particular beliefs of each religion and their general implications for education is a useful starting point for this study.

The Jewish experience of living in the Diaspora lands for nearly 2,000 years ensured that the Jewish community was always a minority. The Diaspora marked the end of independent national life for the Jewish people until the establishment of Israel in the middle of the twentieth century. Education was vital for the continuing existence of the Jewish religion and a range of educational institutions was established, normally in connection with the synagogue, in order to transmit Judaism to the next generation. The synagogue was a place of learning that preserved the teachings and values of Judaism. With the study of the Torah, normally in the home, there was an emphasis on basic literacy as the Torah was taught to Jewish children. Education has always been highly honoured in Jewish culture and is the reason why so many Jews have made an outstanding contribution to learning in many fields of study in the world. However, Jews were generally unable to establish universities or colleges of their own, either because of the small size of their communities or because of persecution. Higher education was restricted largely to the study of the Torah in rabbinical schools.

Judaism affirms a number of basic principles of faith that one is expected to uphold in order to be said to be in consonance with the Jewish faith. However, there is no set outline of beliefs or statement of principles similar to what you would expect in a Christian catechism. Nevertheless, an understanding of Jewish education can be obtained from an understanding of the Jewish experience in history. Judaism remains the particular heritage of the Jewish people, which was born out of the history of a people. This experience or tradition is based upon two central features: first, the Jewish understanding of the creative work of God found in the Hebrew Scriptures, and second, the Covenant relationship between God and his chosen people. The knowledge and understanding of these aspects of divine activity are essential parts of the Jewish religious experience. Consequently, the transmission of the knowledge to succeeding generations and developing an understanding of them is what it means to be a religious Jew and is an essential part of Jewish education. Jewish education is based upon the belief in the unity of God, of the value of community and the unique value of every individual within it. God is eternal and the creator of the universe and the source of morality. Jewish education will thus emphasise keeping the commandments, prayer and participation in the life of the synagogue, and studying the Torah, together with classic Jewish homiletic literature.

The Jewish faith emphasises the freedom of Jews to follow the will of God and their responsibility to others. Ultimately, it is about affirming the identity of Jews and binding them inseparably to other Jews in order to ensure the continuity of Jewish heritage. This heritage is understood differently by each of the denominations comprising the Jewish people – divided between orthodox, liberal and secular. The first two seek to continue the tradition of studying the Torah and living their lives according to Jewish teaching. The liberal subset also composes conservative and reform Jews who, whilst accepting the essential principles of Judaism, seek to reinterpret them and apply them to the modern world. In relation to higher education, there are essentially two views within Judaism. First, there is the modern approach, which has a relationship with the idea of the university and is born out of the 'Torah with secular knowledge' movement of the nineteenth century. Second, there is the medieval approach that has no relationship with the idea of the university, because learning takes place in *Yeshivot* – academies of learning that pre-existed the Christian universities. This *Yeshiva* system of academies is still very much alive within modern Judaism and explains the ongoing endeavour of Jewish higher learning, criticism and interpretation (see Abramson and Parfitt 1994). It is also the case that ultra-orthodox Jews do not approve of secular colleges and universities and only use them when there is some overriding utility to be derived from engaging in secular learning, but generally ultra-orthodox Jews avoid such institutions. Secular knowledge is simply kept segregated from the religious.

Alexander (2003) describes three ways in which liberal, conservative and reform Judaism responds to education. First, some attempt an approach that seeks to synthesise non-Jewish knowledge with the Torah. Second, some believe that modern scientific and political knowledge and ideas should be studied only to the extent that they do not contradict Torah Judaism. The Jewish portion of the curriculum should thus take priority over the secular portion. Third, some believe that equal weight should be given to Torah and secular knowledge, and whilst there is not a total harmony between them the 'educational task is to equip students with enough knowledge of Jewish tradition and modern civilisation to enable them to identify conflict and tensions within and between these complex cultures, and to address them as they see fit'. Secular Jews reject the religious aspects of Judaism, but seek to remain ethnic Jews.

Some have argued that religious liberalism within Judaism has largely failed to retain the loyalty of Jews to a specific religious tradition. Ultra-orthodox Jews, by isolating themselves, have failed to address modernity. Despite the success and continued expansion of Jewish schools and higher education institutions, which some believe is a result of a spiritual renaissance within Judaism, many other Jews have opted out of organised Jewish religious life. Jewish religious scholars and leaders have, despite providing institutional and ideological frameworks for meaningful adaptation of religious Judaism to open, liberal and democratic society, failed to preserve Jewish identity intact. This book is concerned with religious Jews in higher education (as distinct from Jews as an ethnic group) who attempt to apply a Jewish religious worldview to higher education. The majority of Jewish universities and centres are recent foundations and their growth coincides largely with a few early centres of Jewish learning in the USA and more recently with the foundation of the State of Israel.

Outside Israel there is deep anxiety within the Jewish community to maintain traditions and ensure Jewish survival. In the USA and Europe intermarriage between Jews and non-Jews poses a threat to the long-term survival of American and European Jewry. In other countries the situation is often more perilous, with the threats of assimilation, erosion of Jewish identity, and vanishing knowledge of Jewish tradition, history and culture. Many Jews therefore believe that there is a need to shore up the Jewish identity of the young through the provision of Judaic studies in higher education. To this end, institutions such as the Hebrew Union College, in Los Angeles, founded in 1875, and the University of Judaism in California, founded in 1947, have been established for the advancement of the Jewish community and culture, as well as the training of aspiring rabbis. Members of the Jewish community have also helped to promote Judaic studies by financing the creation of Jewish Centres and Institutes within mainstream universities. All these institutions have a distinguished academic record.

Christianity is a faith that also believes in a living God, but specifically in Jesus Christ in whose life God was made known and was present in a unique way. Christianity also claims to be in possession of an exclusive body of knowledge or revealed truths which explain our place in creation and our relationship with the Creator. This relationship is in and through Jesus Christ, whose life and work can alone lead us to God. The life of faith on earth is therefore a preparation for our eternal destiny with God. Christianity is not a monolithic faith and has many divisions within it as represented by Catholic, Protestant and Orthodox Christians. Nevertheless, each of these communities are well organised and they seek to conserve, teach and promote their own understanding of the revelation of Christ. Indeed, Christianity has always had a strong conservative element within it which emphasises custom and tradition, slow incremental change and a sense of hierarchical order. The Christian doctrine of original sin also provides a kind of pessimism about human nature, which is considered imperfect and therefore in need of the services of the Church to prevent it becoming totally corrupted.

Christianity has not traditionally espoused the principle of the separation of religion and politics, of Church and State. The Catholic Church condemned the principle of Church and State separation explicitly and repeatedly until the Second Vatican Council. So did virtually all Protestant Churches until the eighteenth century. The ideal was the 'Christian State', sometimes with Church and State headed by the same person; such as in Byzantium, or within Anglicanism, in the Papal States, etc. Conservative Christians often base their political thought on the work of God of which, they believe, human laws can only be an imperfect manifestation. In Christian societies, religious and political leadership was in the hands of the same people. Traditional Christianity did not therefore have a tendency towards secularisation of the political sphere. It could be argued that there are generally three types of Christian theological thinking on higher education issues that can be identified as Catholic, Liberal Protestant and Conservative Protestant. Conservative Protestantism has several strands, including within it fundamentalists and evangelicals. Catholics are also divided between more conservative and more liberal strands and consequently the various visions of Christian education vary considerably. However, liberal or mainstream Protestantism has always been a more individualising faith than Catholicism or Evangelical Protestantism. Christian denominations have established a huge range of educational institutions including large numbers of universities and colleges around the world. Christians have traditionally used their educational institutions as vehicles to nurture their faith and ensure its expansion through conversions. They have also viewed them as making a positive contribution to civic society.

Finally, within Islam we find, like in Judaism and Christianity, a significant degree of diversity of belief and practice among Muslims which results in different interpretations of Islam. For example, whilst Muslims seek to achieve coherence and meaning in their lives by bringing their lives in line with what they understand to be the Will of God, this is achieved in many different ways. For some it could mean trying to follow the words of the scripture, the Koran, to the letter; for others, to understand the spirit of the scripture and apply it to their lives; for some others to re-interpret the scripture in light of changing circumstances; and, for still others, a mixture of all these possibilities. More generally, Islam, which views itself as being in continuity with the Judeo-Christian tradition, seeks to promote a coherent way of life by means of submission to God. It expresses a specific disposition of the mind, will and intellect – every Muslim voluntarily submits or surrenders their will to God, which is, as I have said, understood in different ways. Whilst

'Islam' means submission to God, 'Muslim' means one who, through submission to God, enters into peace. From a Muslim worldview, education can be seen as instrumental in bringing succeeding generations to the knowledge of God. Education begins and ends with the revealed will of God. Education cannot be an end in itself, but is a means to an end – submission to God. Adherence to Islam requires submission and obedience, which would appear, for some, to suggest a limitation to speculation and critical inquiry. The aims, therefore, of a Muslim education include the transformation of the person – their beliefs, actions, thoughts and expressions. Islam is not merely one among many religions, like Christianity, it is considered by Muslims to be the only one true religion. It does not accept any other belief system, whether religious or not, except in a subordinate way. The Muslim community, which is conveyed by the Arabic word *ummah*, emphasises unity and brotherhood. The *ummah* is an organised community, to which loyalty is always due. A clear line of division exists between those who are members of the *ummah* and those who are not. Individuals exclude themselves by not accepting the claims of Islam or rather not submitting to the will of Allah.

Islam therefore denotes both a religious system of beliefs and a way of life that has grown up around the religion. The claim that there is a secular and a separate religious world has traditionally or theoretically had no place within traditional understandings of Islam, but in reality we see that, for instance, in the sphere of law, Muslim rulers regularly made laws that fell outside the scope of Muslim law (Shariah). Islam is also about identity and loyalty as well as faith and practice. As Sarwar (1997: 91) says: 'The Islamic view of life is holistic, and rejects any separation between this life, which ends with death, and the eternal life, that begins after death. In Islam, mundane, empirical, metaphysical and spiritual matters are interconnected and inseparable.' Sarwar speaks as if there is only one uncontested 'Islamic view', he ignores other Muslim critics (see Panjwani 2004). The Muslim world is not ideologically monolithic and there is no single homogeneous group. There is no single uncontested definition of Islam and its precepts. Whilst the *ummah* is ideally made up of equality among all believers, it is in practice divided by racial, linguistic and national identities with their corresponding particular interests. The difference between Shia and Sunni is paralleled by differences between the various schools of thought in both groups. Consequently, there are serious differences of interpretation of political and religious issues. Some Muslims deny a connection between Islam and democracy, whilst others argue that Islam requires a democratic system. It is not surprising therefore that there are many different interpretations of Islam, so it is difficult to generalise about Islam, but generalise we must in order to make sense of education within Muslim contexts. When scholars speak of Islamic or Muslim education we need to ask whether this is confined to one subject in the curriculum or whether it implies the outlook a Muslim may have to the whole education system. The language of the nation-transcending Muslim community can be misleading, as it is often little more than an ideal espoused by some Muslim academics. Only Turkey has adopted full scale 'secularism' whilst almost every other Muslim country gives some constitutional status to Islam, but this status is often limited and has failed to provide, for example, a model for Muslim education.

The religious commitment of all three faiths can flow from an identity that is clear, rooted and particular. From people who know who they are and know what their tradition impels and compels them to do and why. Judaism, Catholicism and Islam have identities rooted in collective rituals and traditions, and together with some evangelical strands of Protestantism, have a deeply embedded historical self-understanding. These religions should provide their institutions with their real significance and coherence. Consequently, their colleges and universities have a potential to operate within a communal narrative which is perhaps more resistant to the influence of contemporary Western culture than is mainstream Protestantism. This book respects each of the three faiths and treats each as religions – *sui generis*, with their own integrity. Only Christianity has developed a distinctive idea of the Church as an institution with its own laws, hierarchy, clergy and authority structures separate from the State. Islam has never created an institution corresponding to the Christian Church, as in Islam the political and religious are themselves deemed to be one. However, it should be noted that in all three of these world faiths there is a progressive–conservative divide within which there is also a proliferation of divisions between fundamentalists and liberals, traditionalists and dissenters, neoconservatives and left-wingers, orthodox and pro-changers, to name but some of the descriptions given to these divides. All three of these monotheistic traditions assert their exclusive claims for the religious allegiance of each and every individual member of their faith.

The religiously affiliated institution of higher education

In concluding our brief description of each faith I must now give some understanding of what I mean by 'religiously affiliated' institutions of higher education. One could talk of the religiously controlled, sponsored, inspired, founded, or related college or university, but for inclusive reasons the term 'religiously affiliated' has been used in this book. Therefore, for our purposes the term 'religious' refers to an association with any recognised entity, group or organisation whose reason for being is primarily spiritual and moral, based upon an acknowledged faith in God. Given the diversity of existing religions, this book restricts itself to the three main monotheistic religions in the world – Judaism, Christianity and Islam. The term 'affiliated' should be understood in connection with those institutions of higher education that exist where the religion of the founding or sponsoring association or group has some direct influence upon the institution itself. It follows that an institution is not affiliated to a particular religion simply because its legal or cultural origins were religious, or its founders were religious men or women, or because it has a chapel, mosque, synagogue or religious symbols on the campus. There needs to be a direct and continuing influence on the institution by the sponsoring religion that can be clearly observed in some way in the governance, community, institutional identity or strategic operations of the university or college. Such religiously affiliated higher education institutions will also be identified by an institutional imperative within them to continue the direct influence of a particular religious body or faith tradition in their mission and policies. A religiously affiliated university or college will consequently develop a sense of its own distinctiveness and difference from others. Therefore, universities like Duke, Boston, Northwestern and Vanderbilt that maintain only a symbolic connection with their founding religious sponsor (Methodism) are not a major part of this review. In contrast, state universities in Muslim countries can be viewed as loosely 'religiously affiliated' in some respects, particularly because of the pervasive influence of the persons who overwhelmingly make up the community of these universities. A college or university can therefore be deemed in some ways 'religiously affiliated' even without being owned or run by a formal religious organisation. Nevertheless, if it is possible for Muslim majority countries to be secular despite their populations being largely Muslim, the question arises: can universities not be secular regardless of the beliefs of their students.

In regard to religiously affiliated institutions this study recognises all colleges and universities as part of higher education, whether they conduct research or not and irrespective of student numbers and range of subjects offered and taught. Indeed, many religiously affiliated institutions of higher education are small liberal arts colleges or specialise in a limited number of disciplines, but there are a significant number with international reputations in research and development. The overwhelming majority of religiously affiliated (and indeed all mainstream colleges and universities) institutions are creations of the late nineteenth and twentieth centuries – they are largely creations of modernity. Only about 60 universities have survived the medieval period into contemporary times and almost all of these are now secular in orientation. To illustrate how the different forms of higher education over the last 1,500 years had a religious foundation and affiliation it is necessary to provide a brief historical account of their foundation and development.

The origins of the religiously affiliated university and college

Higher education has many historic ties to religion and to religious instruction in particular. The foundation of the first colleges and universities were largely directly linked to religious motivations, and the spread of universities in Christian Europe was certainly heavily influenced by the Church. Some argue that Christianity's engagement with higher education began with the school at Alexandria in the third century. However, it is increasingly argued by some Muslim scholars that the Christian medieval university was inspired by the colleges found in Muslim culture. Their argument could be summarised in the following way. Muslim colleges were institutions that were dedicated to teaching and research and they existed for at least a century before universities and colleges appeared in Western Europe. The inspiration for them was found in the Koran, which explicitly states that God revealed to humankind knowledge and the use of the pen. With the spread of Islam there was a demand for grammars and dictionaries, since it was only permissible to read and study the Koran in the original Arabic. Consequently, there followed the spread of literacy in Muslim lands with an emphasis on reading and writing. Muslim colleges grew out of *madrassas* (literally a 'place for giving lectures') and were established under the patronage of Muslim rulers and wealthy individuals for the benefit of the whole community. It is argued that some of these colleges possessed large libraries, had elaborate buildings specially constructed for them and that they became a model for many Christian universities that followed. Further, whilst these Muslim colleges owed much to Greek science and philosophy, they quickly developed their own devotion to the study of science, astronomy and mathematics, and significantly developed Western ideas of scientific inquiry and experimentation. They had specialist schools of Islamic law and an interest in philosophy and theology as well as geography and history. Over time, it is claimed, they developed medical schools that were far in advance of any knowledge that existed in Europe at the time (see Hossain 1979: 1901–102 and Makdisi 1981).

In conclusion it is argued that Europeans were consequently strongly influenced by Muslim culture as they learned their language in order to read Arabic books, because Arabic in the tenth and eleventh centuries was the language of progress and scientific ideas. Europeans also attended Muslim colleges, especially in Muslim Spain, to study physics, chemistry, mathematics and medicine. In the eleventh century Alfonso the Wise, Spanish King of Castile and Leon, together with Archbishop Raymond of Toledo, established and expanded colleges in Seville, Murcia and Salamanca for the explicit purpose of making Arabic learning available to Europe. Indeed, the Scottish linguist, Michael Scot, working in the Toledo College of Translators translated Aristotle from Arabic into Latin. With the foundation of the universities of Paris and Bologna in the twelfth century, many of Scot's translated Arab texts remained standard reading within them for centuries. Indeed, in terms of organisation, teaching and assessing, these new Christian universities followed many of the features characteristically found in the Muslim colleges. For example, they adopted similar terms, such as 'reader', which is related to an Arabic term. The new European universities adopted assessment techniques from the Muslim colleges, including the oral defence of the thesis and the moot court in legal schools. European universities also adopted the wearing of distinctive dress for teachers and the award of a licence to students who completed a course of study with them. There are clearly many resemblances between European universities and Muslim colleges of an earlier period, but the question is whether these similarities are a result of Muslim influence or are simply a series of parallel developments?

The difficulty in deciding this question one way or the other is largely a consequence of the lack of documentary evidence. Nevertheless, some significant Muslim influence on European universities is certainly the case as described above and this is often ignored by Western scholars, but it has also to be said that elements of this Muslim influence is also misleading in a number of respects. First, many Western scholars argue that whilst there may have been some parallels between Christian universities and Muslim colleges, there is no physical continuity between them. Indeed, as 'universitas' is a Latin word, the 'university' was an indigenous product of Western Europe with no lineal descendents from either Greek, Graeco-Roman, Byzantine or Arab schools. Second, the Muslim colleges were linked or housed within a mosque and the teaching of subjects like medicine, astronomy and mathematics was often conducted in the homes of Muslim scholars, not within the colleges. The Muslim colleges were dedicated to religious themes, especially the duty in the Koran to educate in God's law. Many Muslims were also suspicious of new knowledge derived from sources other than revelation and tradition. Nakosteen (1964: 42) describes how these colleges became intolerant of new knowledge and essentially became institutions for dogmatic theological instruction controlled by various Muslim factions and closed to the majority within the Muslim community. A tradition of writing commentaries and then commentaries on commentaries on the Koran grew up, which effectively destroyed original thought. We also know very little about what was taught in these colleges. Third, Muslim institutions of higher learning were religious and privately established and organised by individuals from within the Muslim community. They also benefited from the cross-fertilisation of ideas from Greek scholarship (Watt 1945) and the classification of knowledge they used was of Greek origin. Muslim scholars established an institute in Baghdad for undertaking translations and copying Greek manuscripts, which directly led to the development of various disciplines like philosophy, mathematics, physical science and geography. Islamic learning in Baghdad and Cordoba was itself originally inspired by the Western Greek tradition. Rosenthal (1975) has gone so far as to say that Islamic civilisation would not have existed without the Greek heritage. Nevertheless, it has to be acknowledged that these early Muslim colleges were some of the very first religiously affiliated institutions of higher education.

Early Christian colleges and universities in Europe were 'privileged corporate associations of masters or masters and students with their statutes, seals and administrative machinery, their fixed curricula and degree procedures' (Cobban 1975: 21). 'Universitas' in Europe meant any body of defined persons with common interests and an independent legal status. When applied to education it referred to the body of masters and/or students, depending on how the body was organised. It was only in the fifteenth century that the word 'university' was more commonly applied to academic corporations. Before this date the medieval term that corresponded most to our concept of a university was '*studium generale*', most universities were simply called *studia*, by the students and masters. There was no exact equivalent of this in Muslim culture, but the knowledge obtained from the Muslim world was certainly a great boon to the medieval European university (Makdisi 1981: 105–52). It might be argued that the Muslim colleges anticipated the Western university in some respects, as there are a number of similarities, but the terminology used by scholars relating to colleges and universities together with the contemporary definitions of higher education often obscure the picture. For the purposes of this book, the origins and expansion of the *studia*/university are considered to be a thirteenth-century product of the Christian West (see Dunbabin 1999). The story of higher education in the West is the story of a Christian academic tradition that has played a vital role in Western and world history. It is interesting that the Muslim colleges began to fall behind academically by the thirteenth century, just as the new European colleges began to be established. Makdisi (1981: 290) suggests that this was directly a result of a new restriction imposed on thought and debate within the Muslim world. Rulers began to appoint experts in Islamic law (Mufti) as heads of these colleges, and these government officials restricted the independence of the colleges to pursue knowledge freely. Religious law and theology formed the central part of the higher education system in the *madrassas*. Bilgrami and Ashraf (1985: 13) suggest that this decline was due to the loss of the Muslim centres of learning at Cordoba in Spain to the Christians and to the fall of Baghdad to the Tartars. However, it is more likely that knowledge from the West was not appreciated and Muslim scholars focused their attention on the past glories of Muslim civilisation. Emphasis was now on revealed knowledge from the Koran, and this period of academic insularity and rigid religious orthodoxy lasted until the end of the nineteenth century when some Muslim governments began to introduce the Western system of university education.

The first European institution of higher learning was the Sorbonne in Paris. It first appeared in the second half of the twelfth century, but was only formally established in 1257 and received papal recognition in 1259. A whole series of European universities was then founded in the thirteenth, fourteenth and fifteen centuries and all received papal recognition including Bologna, Rome, Oxford, Cambridge, Salamanca, St Andrews, Aberdeen, and Glasgow. The recognition of the Church was essential and they were seen as integral parts of the Church. These Catholic universities flourished and advanced scholarship and knowledge. Mention has already been made of the Jewish academies that pre-dated these Christian universities. The

Reformation broke the Catholic Church's monopoly of religiously affiliated universities in England, Germany and Scotland. The ancient Catholic universities were now to serve the version of Christianity proclaimed by the new Protestant Churches of England, Germany and Scotland. The connection between the Reformation and religion was strong, and the purpose of some universities was now to provide qualified leaders for the Church and nation. The same divisive process in higher education also occurred in other parts of Northern Europe, particularly in Germany. Protestants either transformed older Catholic universities or founded new institutions of higher learning in Protestant areas. In order to teach or learn in England you now had to belong to the Anglican Church, and in Scotland every professor now had to subscribe to the doctrines of the Church of Scotland. It is also the case that a number of national Protestant Churches, created at the Reformation, became subservient to their respective nation-states. Nevertheless, universities continued to be controlled by religious motivations, whether in Catholic Europe or Anglican and Presbyterian Britain. In the newly discovered Americas, the Catholic Church established the first universities by founding the University of Mexico in 1551 and the University of San Marcos in Peru in the same year.

In North America the first universities began as small colonial colleges for the training of Protestant or Catholic clergymen. Harvard College was founded in 1636 by the Puritans, whilst the *Seminaire de Quebec* was founded in 1663 by the Catholic Church. It should be noted that the early Protestant colleges and universities were barely distinguishable from seminaries. Yale followed in 1701 and was established by Congregationalists, Princeton by Presbyterians in 1746 and Columbia was founded in 1754 by Anglicans. Georgetown, the first Catholic university in the USA, was founded in 1789. Different Protestant denominations and Roman Catholic religious orders and congregations actively engaged in founding a whole series of colleges in the nineteenth and twentieth centuries, adding to the rich diversity of religiously affiliated colleges and universities. The common characteristics of these colleges and universities were that they were generally small liberal arts colleges that required staff and students to attend chapel services and that they provided compulsory courses on the Bible or Christian doctrine for students. They had explicit rules for behaviour, were devoted to character building and had principals or presidents, often clergymen, who were appointed by a board of trustees or governors appointed in turn by the particular sponsoring denomination. It is also interesting that the public universities founded in nineteenth-century America, whilst claiming to be non-sectarian, were, in practice and ethos, distinctly Protestant institutions, often headed by clergymen. American Catholic universities were largely founded as a reaction against the prevailing Protestantism found in higher education.

However, in Britain the educational monopoly of the Churches in England and Scotland was challenged by the foundation of University College London in 1827 as a new non-denominational institution. The only other non-denominational institution of higher education prior to this date was the University of Pennsylvania, founded in 1740 as a non-sectarian college. The University of Edinburgh, of course, was founded much earlier as a civic university by the town council of the City, but it could be said that it was partly influenced by the Church of Scotland even though the university charter expressly disallowed the establishment of a college chapel. The aftermath of the French Revolution together with European anti-clericalism, resulted in the Catholic Church losing control over a number of universities. The Enlightenment in Europe produced a series of intellectuals who did not identify with the Christian tradition, and it was in this that the antithesis between learning and faith was born. The characteristics of the Enlightenment included a respect for reason together with the search for objective truth, an emphasis on individual freedom and a pronounced scepticism towards authority. Nevertheless, some universities remained nominally Catholic, such as the University of Leuven in Belgium, which had been founded in 1425. The majority of universities in Europe began to formally 'disaffiliate' themselves and secularise in the nineteenth century, such as the University of Paris in 1888. Christianity tried to regain ground by fighting the Enlightenment, and the Catholic Church continued to promote higher education and established the Catholic Institute in Paris in 1875 because it saw how other universities had embarked upon disaffiliation. The Catholic Church also founded new universities in the nineteenth and twentieth centuries, such as Lublin in Poland, Nijmegen in Holland, Milan in Italy and Lille in France, to mention just a few. These new European Catholic universities were deliberately founded by the Church against the rise of secular thought within the older universities. The Church realised that it had lost influence over its older foundations and that national governments increasingly sought the establishment of universities divorced from the influence of religion. In Britain, new universities established at the beginning of the twentieth century were perceived as secular institutions and the University of Liverpool would not allow the study of theology in its founding charter. At Manchester University a department of theology was established but was not allowed to teach doctrine and the prospectus of the department stated that nothing would be taught that offended the conscience of students. In contrast, at Oxford University chapel services continued to be compulsory and except for the Master of Balliol College all the heads of colleges were clergymen up until the 1930s. Today, most countries in continental Europe continue to have a small number of Catholic universities within their borders, whilst there are also a larger number of Catholic and Protestant Faculties of Theology in a number of secular universities. For example, the Catholic and Protestant Churches in Germany run over 40 institutions of higher education which are attached to large state-funded universities. The government completely funds these confessional faculties and this arrangement exists in other European countries such as Lithuania. The arrangement provides for the university and the local Catholic bishops or Protestant Churches jointly to make the appointments to the faculty.

Since the 1960s there has been a remarkable growth in the provision of Jewish studies in the curriculum of colleges and universities in the USA and elsewhere in the world. Until 1965 there were only two places in the USA that had professors of Jewish history, namely, Harvard and Columbia universities. Since 1965, there are now over 150 endowed chairs in Judaic studies in over 300 colleges and universities, which include Christian institutions. There are over 600 courses in Jewish studies on offer at these colleges and universities, and many are now funded by the state as Judaic studies have increasingly come to be recognised as respected academic disciplines. Following this example, there has also been a large increase in recent years of Catholic and Muslim studies taught within new centres and institutes based within secular universities. Chairs in Catholic studies have also been established at Harvard, Illinois, Vanderbilt, Kansas and Tulsa universities. The Hebrew University of Jerusalem seeks to promote Judaic studies around the world, and has founded the International Centre for University Studies in Jewish Civilization specifically to promote this kind of research and scholarship in Russia. As a result a number of Jewish research institutions have been founded in Eastern Europe assisted by the Fund for Jewish Higher Education. Israel and many within the Jewish Diaspora are interested in forming a broader philosemitic intelligentsia. The practice within the Jewish community of founding religiously affiliated institutions together with establishing Jewish centres and institutes within secular and religious universities has been remarkably successful in promoting Jewish civilisation.

Muslim colleges or *madrassas* remained as private institutions dedicated to Muslim religious studies throughout the Middle Ages, but there was little or no development of them as specifically higher education institutions. Universities were largely a nineteenth-century European introduction into Muslim lands, which raises the question: what is an Islamic or Muslim university? Certainly the type of university established in the Middle East during the European occupations of Muslim lands in the late nineteenth and early twentieth centuries was secular in tone and organisation. The National University of Egypt (founded by the British in 1908) and the University of Istanbul in Turkey were secular universities in which Muslim education was secondary or non-existent and consisted of teaching some religious subjects. The Osmania University was founded in Hyderabad in 1917, and whilst students did study the Muslim religion and law, their treatment was rather superficial compared to the Western subjects that were introduced. The British also established secular universities in India, such as the University of Lahore, which added an Islamic Department in 1950. However, most colonial governments allowed the old traditional system of Muslim education to continue in parallel with the new largely secular universities (see Fortna 2002). Consequently, *madrassas* continued to serve as theological seminaries and they retained within them a curriculum that remained unreformed. In India there were also a number of Muslim attempts in higher education, both conservative and moderate, to try and co-exist with the Indian brand of secularism that the British encouraged (Hashmi 1989).

Governments within Muslim countries largely controlled the teaching of religion in their own universities. For example, the secular Turkish University of Ankara eventually secured a Divinity Faculty but its academic staff had to be approved by the Turkish government (Kazamias 1966). Indeed, it could be argued that the majority of modern universities in the Muslim world are largely secular in inspiration and have no direct religious affiliation. Western influence on the Muslim world was and continues to be strong, and the overwhelming model of university education adopted in the majority of Muslim countries is a Western secular system. Many Muslim countries have been wholly concerned with supplying their society with the technological and scientific skills associated with Western progress (Husain and Ashraf 1979: 56). There has been a rapid expansion of universities in all Middle Eastern countries since the 1960s with the expectation that these institutions would help Muslim societies modernise. Therefore, these countries' economic needs have come before a stress on Muslim education as the principal motivation for establishing a university. Courses in Islamic studies have been provided in these new institutions, but they are almost always secondary considerations. Turkey adopted an overtly secularist position and viewed Islam as a stumbling block to progress and modernisation. Nevertheless, after colonial rule in many of these countries, there was some resistance to Western models of education and a strong defensive attitude towards Muslim traditions which has increased in intensity over the years. Many Muslim scholars believe that some governments in Muslim countries are excessively dependent upon Western models of educational provision and impose these systems by authoritarian means.

A number of Muslim countries have experienced a complete rejection of the Western model of university education, such as in the more extreme examples of Afghanistan and Iran. In Afghanistan the University of Islamic Studies in Kabul was established by the Taliban principally to promote Islamic studies, whilst after the Khomeini Revolution in Iran the government's Ministry of Culture and Higher Education rejected foreign and secular influence over its universities and placed them under religious authority – a situation which is being replicated in the Sudan. At a more moderate level, the University of Medina in Saudi Arabia is regarded as an Islamic university, but there is no unity of purpose concerning higher education within the Muslim world. The designation of 'Islamic', as opposed to 'Muslim', for universities suggests a more fundamental religious approach to the education provided within it. In 1977 the First World Conference on Muslim Education was held at King Abdulaziz University in Jeddah, and encouraged the setting up of specifically Islamic universities in Pakistan, Sudan, Nigeria,

Malaysia and Bangladesh. The conference marked the beginning of the Muslim educational response to Westernisation or modernisation. In Pakistan the attempt to establish an Islamic university in 1963, based on a *madrassa* and following the model of Cairo's traditional Al Azhar University, suffered from a lack of government funds and support. There had previously been an attempt in 1920 to establish a national Islamic university in Delhi, but this was also not achieved. Of the four Islamic universities established as a result of the conference in Jeddah only two are considered to have been successful – the international Islamic universities in Malaysia and Islamabad, Pakistan. It needs to be stated here that Muslim countries, and particularly their governments, are divided in their attitudes to Western education and not all, by any means, seek the establishment of Islamic universities. However, we need to turn to the sociologists of the latter part of the twentieth century who introduced the term 'secularisation' to account for the broader process of which the disaffiliation of religious affiliated institutions of higher education and the establishment of non-affiliated institutions of higher education is part.

Secularisation

What do we mean by 'secularisation' within the context of religiously affiliated universities and colleges? There is a clear clash between worldviews that presuppose God and those that do not. Secularisation's historical impact on universities which were founded with a religious mission is well documented, especially in Protestant universities, and can be seen in the fact that all the medieval universities which were founded or confirmed by Papal decrees (Paris, Oxford, Cambridge, Salamanca, Glasgow, St Andrews, etc.) are now largely modern secular universities. They all began as institutions of the Catholic Church. Indeed, more recent religious foundations (Harvard, Yale, Princeton, Kings College, London, etc.) have responded to social changes by distancing themselves from their particular religious pasts and also by becoming large secular research universities. For some reason their religious affiliation became less important to their participation in higher education with the passage of time. They have disengaged from their religious affiliations to such an extent that Sawatsky (2004: 5) believes that the transformation of such USA universities is 'one of the clearest examples of secularisation in American history'. The Lutherans in Germany established the University of Halle in 1694 but it soon became the pioneer among higher education institutions in renouncing religious orthodoxy in favour of 'rational' and 'objective' thinking – in other words of separating reason and faith. Manet (1994), in his *Intellectual History of Liberalism*, locates the history of modernity in the Enlightenment thinkers' determination to divorce everyday life from the influence of the Catholic Church. Chadwick (1990: 26f.) provides a similar analysis in finding in 'the declining hold of the church and its doctrines on European society' the origin of 'a major shift in Western life and thought'.

This understanding of secularisation is therefore seen as a movement away from traditionally accepted religious norms, practices and beliefs. Nevertheless, some institutions have remained connected with their religious affiliation, which provides us with two models of and approaches to higher education: the purely secular model/approach and the religious model/approach. Catholics in particular saw secularisation or the ideology of 'secularism' that it produced as a threat in the 1950s and Gleason (1995: 265) details how it came to be seen as the principal threat to their future survival, but only up until the 1950s, as it was later eagerly embraced by many as conferring some 'value-neutral' stance in meeting the demands and challenges of the modern world.

Writing forty years ago, Harvey Cox (1965: 217) commented on the Christian Churches within American higher education thus: 'The churches have never quite been reconciled to the fact that they no longer have a parental responsibility for the university. The daughter has grown up and moved out – for good.' Cox argued that the institutional Christian Churches ought not to have a place or role within the modern university and that the establishment and maintenance of their own universities and colleges is simply 'medievalism' – using the term pejoratively of course. Cox's rhetoric would suggest a greater degree of ideological commitment to secularisation than any concrete scientific evidence in support of it. He believed a secular age lay ahead and it was only a question of time before the complete elimination of the belief in God would occur, leading to a more peaceful and stable world. Cox rightly observed, in the days before mission statements, that few of the colleges could give a 'very plausible theological basis for retaining the equivocal phrase *Christian college*' (1965: 221). Discussions within higher education in the two decades since Cox made these comments would seem to confirm Cox's thesis that religious affiliation signified very little in higher education. Nevertheless, with a renewed interest in religion within higher education across the world, Cox's early comments (he later changed his mind) would, at first sight, seem out of place today with the resurgence of religious orthodoxy.

The ideological advocates of secularism were based in the West and simply assumed that the pattern of secularisation they claimed to detect in the West would be replicated globally. But interest in religion has grown globally since the high water mark of secularism in the late 1960s. Since the 1990s there has been widespread academic and professional interest in religion within higher education, particularly in regard to the role of religiously affiliated universities (see Mahoney 2001). Growing numbers of American students are attending religiously affiliated universities and these colleges and universities are growing more quickly than secular higher education institutions. How these faith-based institutions survive, far less proliferate, in a liberal secular higher education culture that is largely hostile to them is worthy of study. With this renewed interest in religion, at all levels, many colleges and universities have been working to renew and often to re-define their identities and mission.

Sawatsky (2004: 5) even suggests that American mainstream universities are becoming more Christian or religious. This is a phenomenon not limited to the USA, where most of the writing on this topic has been conducted, but is indeed a worldwide occurrence, particularly in Jewish, Christian and Muslim higher education institutions.

Originally the word 'secularisation' had a juridical meaning that referred to the forcible appropriation of Church property by the secular State. Today the word is used to describe a theory that comes in hard and soft varieties and was mainly promoted by sociologists in the 1960s and 1970s. It has also become an ambiguous concept that poses problems of definition and usefulness because it carries different emphases and meanings. The meaning given to the concept by Wilson (1966) and Berger (1969) refers to the process by which religious thought, practices and institutions lose social significance and how religious activity declines progressively over a period of time. It can be seen as simply the decline of religious beliefs and practices or the marginalisation of religion to the private sphere. Wilson and Berger believed that the decline in religion was an inevitable consequence of the process of modernisation. There are many methodological problems with these descriptions of the theory, not least whether the theory can be adequately tested. How do you measure the decline of religious activity when some will argue that it does not denote 'religious decline' but 'religious change'? Does secularisation comprise the demise or marginalisation of religion or rather its mutation into less homogenous and empirically verifiable forms? The work of Conrad *et al.* (2001) challenges some theories of secularisation in higher education with their study of *Religion on Campus* as does Martin (1969: 9), who no longer believes it to be an adequate category for social analysis, although it is still used by political scientists. Secularisation and secular learning seem to have lost all precise meaning as there is no consensus on the use of the terms (Stark 1999). The fact that the number of religiously affiliated institutions is increasing in the world is another factor that Wilson and Berger did not envisage in the 1960s. Consequently, Hadden and Shape (1989) conclude that secularisation is 'a hodgepodge of loosely employed ideas rather than a theory' and that 'existing data simply do not support the theory'. Some have dismissed the term as a sociological 'myth'. In addition, Berger (1999: 2) has withdrawn his advocacy of secularisation theories and has recently concluded that the 'assumption that we live in a secularised world is false'. Casanova (1994) argues that in the 1980s religion reversed one of the presuppositions of secularisation theory by refusing to be privatised and marginalised. He draws our attention to the 'deprivatization' of religion, which encourages religiously inspired movements, which in turn challenge the secular dominance of the public sphere in the West. Whilst this may be the case overall, within higher education the secular humanist ethos still largely predominates even with the persistent renewal of religion.

Nevertheless, the theory of secularisation can be useful at the level of asking questions, particularly concerning the religious significance of religiously affiliated universities and colleges today. Secularisation is not a uniform theory of social change as there are many models of secularisation that need to be understood within the context of the various interpretations given it. Secularisation in the context of this book examines the pressures that attempt to remove religious authority and influence over higher education. It recognises that many definitions of 'secularisation' hide the anti-religious dimensions to *secularism* by describing only the outcomes of secularisation. In this context this book views secularisation as the erosion of the religious identity and mission of religiously affiliated institutions. It asks whether religious groups have a diminished role in higher education and whether the bonds between religious sponsors and higher education have or are being loosened. What were the forces or pressures which sought greater independence from religious authority in the field of university governance and scholarship? For the purposes of this review, secularisation is seen as a process of reducing the influence of religion in higher education which renders the application of all or some religious beliefs and practices within higher education meaningless. This book also understands 'secularism' to be the attempt to exclude all considerations drawn from belief in God in the activities of the academy. This includes the exclusion of the view that theological commitments can be integral to academic goals. Education should therefore be secular, and not religious, and morality should be based on exclusively rational considerations and not religious ones. As Gates (2004) notes, 'secularism closes down all argument and simply asserts both the non-necessity and empty falsehood of religion'. This book does not address the question of secularisation in any systematic sociological way but includes alongside and within secularisation the influence of the ideas and core concepts of pluralism, relativism, modernity, and post-modernity on religiously affiliated colleges and universities. What we can certainly say is that the secularisation of higher education has not resulted in total secularism. Secularisation is certainly a more complex thesis than the above sketch allows (see Taylor (1998) and Martin (2005) for a description of the kinds of secularism and their implications for religion).

It needs to be recognised more widely that the secularisation of culture itself has led to the diminution of the sacred and an increase in so called 'rationality' in the thinking of men. Many universities in the West have large chapels that are often merely 'cultural spaces' today. These universities once had religious seals such as Harvard, which had a seal with *Veritas* (truth) in the centre and *Pro Christo et Ecclesiae* (for Christ and the Church) surrounding it. However, this was changed to reflect its more secular orientation. In the changing of Harvard's seal, Neuhaus (1996) notes that Harvard University did not become more of a university, but simply a different sort of university. For example, the academic departments in universities pursue their disciplines without reference to religion. The traditional religious framework which once underpinned our universities has largely dissolved, whilst in some religiously affiliated universities it is being rejected or ignored by academic staff to be replaced by a secular academic ethos. Modernity is really the emergence of a secular consciousness which excludes God and consigns religion to the realm of personal belief and private practice. We have clearly seen a decline of religious authority within many Western societies and the replacement of religious definitions of reality with secular definitions. These definitions are not 'neutral' with respect to religion since they generally act against religion. The plurality of ideologies that result from this situation compete with each other for our loyalty. As Plantinga (1994: 282–3) argues there is no such thing as an uncommitted or neutral university.

There appear to be two responses to secularisation, usually termed conservative and liberal. The conservative view seeks to defend traditional beliefs and structures. However, a more rigorous form of this conservative response, where there is deep anxiety and uncertainty, may lead to a more fundamentalist approach which is opposed to any accommodation with the secular world except at the practical and instrumental level. We can see this at work in Christianity (both Catholic and Protestant), Judaism and Islam (Kepel 1994). The religious group will state the fundamentals of their religion and seek to protect or establish institutions that are relatively exclusive and opposed to the secular viewpoint. They work to deny any religious legitimacy to certain other institutions which claim to be Catholic, Protestant, Jewish or Muslim on the grounds that they have compromised themselves with the forces of secularisation. Whilst Western progressive movements have had a secularising effect on religion, it has also provided a reaction that sometimes strengthens religion and leads to a non-liberal fundamentalist stance. As Berger (1999: 6) says, this counter-secularisation is at least as important as secularisation in the world today.

Secularisation and fundamentalism

Some would view Opus Dei, Evangelicals, Chabad Chasidism and the Muslim Brotherhood as examples of this appeal to non-liberal religion. They may also view these conservative religious groups as fundamentalist movements opposed to modernity, which make strict distinctions between themselves and 'non-believers' within and outside of their faith. Whilst Giddens (1999: 44–5) makes the point that religious traditions 'are needed and will always persist because they give continuity and form to life', he also claims that in a globalised world, tradition becomes more entrenched. Giddens (1999: 48–50) aligns fundamentalism with tradition and by fundamentalism he means a:

> call for a return to basic scriptures and texts, supposed to be read in a literal manner, and they [fundamentalists] propose that the doctrines derived from such a reading be applied to social, economic, or political

life. Fundamentalism gives new vitality and importance to the guardians of tradition . . . Fundamentalism is a beleaguered tradition. It is tradition defended in the traditional way – by reference to ritual truth – in a globalising world that asks for reasons. Fundamentalism therefore has nothing to do with the context of beliefs, religious or otherwise . . . fundamentalism isn't about what people believe but, like tradition more generally, about why they believe it and how they justify it . . .

Giddens is really saying that fundamentalism results in thinking and actions which are both uncritical and unquestioned – a kind of habit and routine of thinking and practice which lacks evidence. Academics who combine certain religious positions and methods with their academic pursuits are easily labelled fundamentalists, who are viewed as a threat to higher education.

Giddens seems to ignore the case that fundamentalism can be found at work in all spheres of life. There are indeed a wide range of economic, political, cultural and nationalist fundamentalisms and many universities have developed their own secular dogmas, rituals and professions of faith. These fundamentalisms also come in soft and hard varieties, with political correctness in the West often considered as a soft fundamentalism. Universities have their own normative account of what the university is and no university is neutral, and 'secular' is not a synonym for neutral. Barnett (2003) argues that universities are increasingly ideological in their approach to knowledge and he views as 'pernicious' approaches such as 'entrepreneurialism' and 'virtuous' such approaches as 'communicating values'. Secular academics espouse all kinds of extreme ideological and political ideas but seem to think that religious ideas should in some way be prohibited in the academy. The liberal humanist position is itself based on a presupposition that one can identify a pure rationality, free from the influence of cultural, religious and political assumptions. It is claimed that this rationality is universal rather than particular or partisan and thus the only proper object of academic inquiry. John Henry Newman recognised, much earlier, that a university's policy of non-commitment would turn out to be something else: as Ker (1999) says, the central insight in the *Idea of a University* was the impossibility of neutrality of the university. Giddens also seems to equate difference with division within society. It is interesting that many secular universities seek to diminish kinds of diversity in the name of diversity or alternatively in the name of diversity simply affirm nothing in particular. They appear to use the language of diversity, but in reality fear it. Diversity should not mean the eradication of difference, for the preservation of difference is essential within a pluralist society and is compatible with the promotion of diversity within a democracy. Colleges and universities which give pre-eminence to religious difference and distinctiveness are not therefore precluded from pursuing diversity. In a university the absence of diversity is often caused as a result of economic and peer pressures which ensure that funds are available for some kinds of research and teaching, but not others. Indeed, the mechanisms by which governments provide funding to universities often control the distribution of research funds. Consequently, academics are usually limited or not free to determine what ought to be researched.

Fundamentalism is increasingly the word used to describe Islam to the world by the Western media. The fear appears to be that Muslim or Islamic institutions of education are teaching extremist versions of Islam. This image of fundamentalism implies extremism, ignorance, bigotry, fanaticism and as a result is extremely misleading for it is used as a derogatory concept based on western stereotypes. It is vital therefore to understand what fundamentalism really means. It is perhaps more accurate to say that there has been a revival of conservative religious forces in all three main faiths against a backdrop of a crisis in modernity. Fundamentalism was originally a label to describe evangelical Protestants who held absolutist claims of religious truth and reacted against modernity. Many Muslims object to the word 'fundamentalist' on the grounds that it has Christian origins; however, others are happy to use it about themselves, seeing it as orthodoxy of faith in confrontation with modernity. Yet others prefer to call themselves Islamists or 'Islamic radicals'. Fundamentalism can be a particular interpretation of the Koran, and its legitimacy is often challenged by other Muslims. Forms of this fundamentalism can lead to an 'Islamic correctness' in which nothing is done that upsets Muslims. Fundamentalism therefore describes a host of disparate religious and political movements. These movements can be seen in all three religions and they can be aggressive and confident, with many led by a young intelligentsia. Fundamentalism can also be state sponsored or state tolerated. Kepel (1994: 191) argues that these conservative forces believe that they have a double task to perform. First, they need to explain to their constituents, in language drawn from traditional faith, the nature and causes of the crisis in modernity. Second, they plan to change the world, bringing social order into compliance with the commandments of the Jewish Holy scriptures, the Bible or the Koran. Traditionalist religious groups in all three faiths have been discontented about the development of their societies for some considerable time and now believe that they have reached a critical point in which decisions need to be made.

Searching for security in a time of rapid change is not extreme nor is the human urge for certainty in life. Those who freely submit to a system of religious beliefs and conceive of themselves as adopting the true religion are not necessarily extreme or fundamentalist in their expressions of their position in the public realm. However, it is recognised that those who do not tolerate legitimate dissent or difference are fundamentalist in the extreme understanding of this word. It is the kind of fundamentalism that is extremely harmful to religiously affiliated institutions of higher education because it demands uncritical adherence to a creed and generates a strong desire to suppress all other viewpoints. It enforces conformity and is authoritarian in its methods, leading to control and dominance over others. This kind of fundamentalism is inextricably implicated in politics and is really a search for power. It accepts no equal partners in a pluralistic debating forum and essentially denies that there are other valid viewpoints. All three faiths discussed in this book have elements within them that would correspond to this hard definition of fundamentalism, but few of these elements have attempted or been able to found fundamentalist universities.

In the Muslim world, some of these conservative forces have acquired political backing, which has resulted in increased government efforts to advance Islam. It is also important to note that anything separate from religious authority is alien to what some Muslims refer to as 'pure' Islamic thought and practice, and accordingly many Muslims will not compromise with secularisation, which in any case is seen as a Western disease. And yet, as has been noted, secular ideas are not new to Islam in any historic period of its development. There has been and is secular writing among Muslims, but it is difficult to determine how far they have been influenced by Western ideas. In 1925 Ali Abdul Razek, who was educated at the Azhar University, published *Islam and the Origins of Government* in which he argued forcefully against Islamic states and for the separation of religion and civil society. Abaza (2002: 197) cites S. Hussein Alatas as a contemporary Egyptian secular intellectual who also believes in and advocates the separation of religion and the state. Some Muslims have also formed the Institute for the Secularisation of Islam, but they are a very small minority. Muslim responses to secularisation are either to view it as an anti-religious ideology or as a Western-Christian form of organising the relationships between Church and State. Within Muslim countries it is seen more directly as the state controlling religious communities. However, Muslims, like Jews and Christians, have important internal differences resulting in a spectrum ranging from those who see no difficulty in simultaneously being secular and Muslim (in the sense of keeping their religious beliefs in the private sphere) to those who think it is their religious duty not only to have religion play a role in public life, but also to force the precepts of their religion on others.

The liberal response to secularisation has been largely to accept it as an accomplished fact of life. Instead of warding off cultural and social change, the liberal response has been to try and re-interpret the changes in the light of their implications for their faith. The liberal is open to changes and innovations and will willingly depart from traditional beliefs and structures. The liberal seeks to hold on to what he considers are the 'essential' or 'core' meanings of their religious tradition, whilst being prepared to integrate new insights and influences from cultural trends derived from outside their religious tradition. The liberal position therefore assumes that accommodation to new circumstances and ideas is absolutely necessary if religious institutions are not to be fossilised. The liberal may also 'suspend' his/her religious worldview when searching for objectivity, especially in the sciences, on the basis that religion only has an indirect role in the study of many subjects. This is a view that many within Christianity and Judaism and a few within Islam have supported. Secularisation can therefore be used in a number of senses here and not all secularisation processes are completely antagonistic to religion.

Often the secular attacks on religion have been attacks on religious authoritarianism as opposed to religious belief. Indeed, it has been argued that this separation of the religious and secular is a product of Christianity in practice. Ideas, such as Augustine's theory of the 'two cities' and the medieval conception of the 'two swords', it is claimed, have produced the conception of the state as an independent and secular jurisdiction. Thomas Aquinas, strongly influenced by the thought of Aristotle, saw each sphere of human activity as enjoying its own autonomy. Whilst the spiritual and the temporal are both derived from God, Aquinas believed they could be distinguished (Bigongiari 1953: 168f.). The Protestant Reformation also recognised the 'two Kingdoms' theory – the sinful secular world and the reign of God in spiritual matters. The conservative and liberal responses to secularisation normally represent two extremes, on the one hand embraced as a friend and on the other seen as a destructive force to be resisted. The Jewish faith has also had its secular movements and writers, and many Jews secularised themselves in order better to assimilate into European society. Many Jewish writers are also known to be deeply committed to principles of freedom of religion and thought and have adopted a positive stance to modernisation in education – modernisation and secularisation are often seen as synonymous. However, there are tensions between modernity and Judaism and some Jews choose to isolate themselves as far as possible from the effects of secularisation. Therefore, it is possible for higher education institutions to be marked by a strong tone of secularity, but without any strong connotation of negativity to religion. Some would argue that that this is because these institutions are simply indifferent to religion.

Models of religiously affiliated institutions

There are a number of different typologies or models of religiously affiliated institutions, but all are drawn from the Christian experience in higher education. Pace (1972), in an early study, provided four models of Protestant colleges. First, those colleges and universities that had Protestant roots, but are now no longer Protestant in any legal sense. Second, those that remain nominally related to Protestantism but are now on the verge of disengagement. Third, those that retain some formal connection with a Protestant denomination and fourth, those colleges associated with an explicit evangelical or fundamentalist version of Protestantism. He concluded that group two had clear academic identity, whilst group three had neither a strong academic nor religious identity. Group four would survive because of their clear distinctiveness and strong support from their Churches. This typology can also be applied to Catholic higher education but few institutions would be found exclusively in groups one and two at this stage. Wolfe (2002: 31) suggests three lines of development that religiously affiliated colleges and universities, including by extension Jewish and Muslim institutions, can take. First, they can return to orthodoxy and make an emphatic commitment to their faith perspective in education. Second, they can parallel the main-stream university in their approach to higher education. Third, and the approach that Wolfe favours, they can be pluralistic in a way that develops all kinds of visions of a university education. In practice all these lines of development have been adopted by different religiously affiliated institutions and the one that Wolfe favours could so easily be an open minded secular university.

It is very insightful to contrast two other typologies of religiously affiliated institutions, separated by a period of more than twenty years. In 1979 Henle (1979), a Jesuit priest, on behalf of the International Federation of Catholic Universities produced a four-part typology of Catholic universities in America. His first type concerned pontifically or canonically established universities or faculties directly answerable to the Holy See. Only a tiny minority of Catholic establishments in the USA would be listed under this classification. His second type concerned a model of Catholic higher educa-tion that was exclusive, sectarian and isolated, and again few institutions would be listed under this classification. His third type concerned Catholic universities that were open to all, pluralist in orientation, independent of direct Church authority and dedicated to academic excellence. Henle believed that the overwhelming majority of Catholic universities in the USA belong to this category. His fourth type concerned the 'Catholic secular college' which abandons any kind of Catholic character. It is perhaps the case that in con-temporary Catholicism a number of Catholic colleges and universities might be classified under this heading. Henle is clearly pejorative in his classification system as he questions whether an orthodox Catholic institution that is exclusive in any way can authentically be Catholic in the 'spirit' of the Second Vatican Council. He applauds pluralism in all its forms and clearly favours his open model of Catholic education. Henle, of course, represents one end of the spectrum in Catholic higher education as he spoke for the Catholic 'progressive' 'Land O' Lakes' group for which he had acted as secretary. In contrast, a more recent four-part typology by Benne (2001: 40–51) classifies religiously affiliated institutions of all Christian denominations in the follow-ing way: 'orthodox', 'critical mass', 'intentionally pluralist' and 'accidentally pluralist'. Benne believes that for religious institutions in higher education within the USA to be able to maintain a religious identity, they must have a theological vision and purpose which compels them to engage with and extend their founding heritage. Benne's tone is much more positive and less sceptical than Henle's as he describes his orthodox model (equivalent to

Henle's second classification) as an institution trying to assure a Christian account of life by requiring all its members to subscribe to a statement of belief so that there is a common commitment to the Christian faith. Under 'critical mass' Benne describes how Christian institutions need a critical mass of adherents to inhabit all the main constituencies of the university to define, shape and maintain its religious identity. This is often a majority of staff, but it can be a strong minority. This critical mass category is absent in Henle's classification.

Benne's 'intentionally pluralist' category is where Henle appears to place the majority of Catholic and a minority of Protestant colleges and universities. Benne describes this category as institutions respecting their relationship to the sponsoring tradition, ensuring that some members of this religious tradition are sprinkled around the institution, and ensuring that the main motivation of the institution is academic excellence and being inclusive of all. Benne's final category of 'accidentally pluralist' concerns an institution abandoning its religious mission and following a wholly secular approach without any real commitment to its sponsoring religious tradition. This last category corresponds to Henle's 'secular' model. Benne insists that his orthodox and critical mass categories, which insist on the public relevance of Christianity to education, are much closer to each other than they are to the intentionally and accidentally pluralist models. Henle's main pluralist model emphasises separation from the Church and is very much part of the 1970s culture that prevailed in Catholic higher education, whilst Benne emphasises strengthening the connections with the sponsoring religious tradition which many Protestant colleges and universities today are attempting to do. In contrasting these two specific models he indicates that there has been a marked shift in understanding religiously affiliated institutions. They are no longer attempting to become completely secular, and many Catholic institutions in particular are much less pluralist and secular today as Henle would have us believe they were in the 1970s. Benne's typology is an excellent way to understand religiously affiliated institutions, as it presents us with a continuum from being fully religious in orientation to being fully secularised. Benne believes that since nominally religious colleges and universities have so many grey areas in regard to their religious identity, there is scope for making re-connections with the sponsoring religious tradition. Benne emphasises that leadership is essential for this re-connection. This book expands on the usage of Benne's typology as offering the best way to understand religiously affiliated higher education institutions within all three faiths. I have added a fifth category or model of a religiously affiliated institution and have called it 'fundamentalist', meaning a university or college that tolerates no dissent and insists upon an uncritical adherence to a particular interpretation of faith and politics. Some religiously affiliated institutions of higher education will not fit neatly into Benne's typology as they will display aspects of a particular model in areas such as the curriculum, but perhaps not in other areas of university life. There is also difficulties applying Benne's models to Muslim institutions and so this is only done in a tentative way. The following chapters will employ Benne's typology in assessing how religiously affiliated institutions of higher education have responded to secularisation, beginning with their mission statements.

Chapter 2

Searching for institutional identity and mission

Introduction

The survival, establishment and expansion of all kinds of religiously affiliated colleges and universities have been accompanied by an ongoing discussion on the nature and identity of these higher education institutions. There is a great variety in the way that different faith traditions think about mission and identity. This discussion has arisen from within these religious institutions and from within the religious communities that own and sponsor them. The questions that are asked are essentially about *difference*. How is the religiously affiliated college or university different from others and what difference does it make? Should these religiously affiliated institutions have a distinctive character that distinguishes them from other institutions of higher education? Would this character necessarily make a difference to the educational enterprise in which they are engaged? In what ways do religiously affiliated colleges and universities serve as alternatives to secular universities? These are serious questions and different religious groups and bodies have different answers to them. Religiously affiliated colleges and universities do not represent a homogeneous group within Judaism, Christianity or Islam and their mission and purpose needs to be understood against the cultural, political and economic contexts of their regional and national communities. One of the first things one notices about the goals religiously affiliated institutions set themselves is that they are more complex and more numerous today because of the pluralism of society and the fragmentation brought about by increased academic specialisation. Mission statements of religiously affiliated colleges and universities can therefore appear ambiguous because of the vagueness of the language used and the lack of any substantive religious commitments made. This study is careful not fall into the error of equating official mission statements with actual representations of reality. Whilst these goal statements claim to provide the essential framework and direction of the college or university's operation they can often, it is recognised, be little more than idealistic rhetoric.

All institutions in higher education are concerned about their identity –

about how they wish to be perceived. Newman, in writing his *Idea of a University*, made it clear that he was 'investigating in the abstract' and that he was advocating a 'certain great principle' (in Ker 1976: 24). What he meant was that he was concerned with an abstract idea of a university often different from its real institutional and historical embodiment at any given time. In more recent times mission statements have become a relatively new device employed by all higher education institutions to provide themselves with a statement of purpose that distinguishes them from one another – even if the difference is minimal in their operational reality. This chapter will employ the term mission statements to cover all the different terms colleges and universities use to identify themselves, e.g. mission and values, institutional statement of mission, mission and goals, statement of purpose, character and commitment, vision and values, institutional declaration, founder's spirit, objectives and statutes, etc. Often the people most concerned with mission statements are the trustees, governors and senior administrative and management staff within a college or university, and, in the case of the religiously affiliated institutions, the wider religious sponsoring body and community.

The analysis of mission statements in the USA has been a well-trodden path, but none have been as detailed or thorough as James Burtchaell's. He argues (1998: 851) that the secularisation of many USA Christian institutions occurred through a confluence of many factors and concludes his massive study of the problem with:

> The elements of the slow but apparently irrevocable cleavage of colleges from churches were many. The church was replaced as a financial patron by alumni, foundations, philanthropists, and the government. The regional accrediting associations, the alumni, and the government replaced the church as the primary authorities to whom the college would give an accounting for its stewardship. The study of their faith became academically marginalised, and the understanding of religion was degraded by translation into reductive banalities for promotional use. Presidential hubris found fulfilment in cultivating the colleges to follow the academic pacesetters, which were selective state and independent universities. The faculty transferred their primary loyalties from the college to their disciplines and their guild, and were thereby antagonistic to any competing norms of professional excellence related to the Church.

This could clearly be read as a damning indictment of many Christian colleges and universities; it is certainly a very pessimistic statement about the future survival of these Christian institutions.

It is clear from the literature that many religiously affiliated colleges and universities had an isolated existence and were increasingly faced with demands for academic excellence and inclusion within the secular higher education sector, which accordingly encouraged them to relegate the institution's religious identity to largely extra-curricular activities. Burtchaell (1998: 851) concludes that 'the failures of the past, so clearly patterned, so foolishly ignored, and so lethally repeated' provide a warning to any contemporary religiously affiliated college or university. Burtchaell provides very detailed goals/mission statements for a number of Presbyterian, Methodist, Catholic, Baptist, and Lutheran colleges and universities that span up to 140 years from their foundations. From a first reading of these statements, there appears to an increasing secularisation of the language used to express the mission of these institutions. Above all, they illustrate that many religiously affiliated institutions have significantly departed from their original foundation missions. However, religious colleges and universities do not have the option of being hermetically closed to the modern world and it is therefore not surprising that their goals will alter over time. Indeed, modern universities of every kind are characterised by widely dispersed decision-making, fragmented professional structures and multiple goals. Within these considerable complexities many religiously affiliated institutions have found themselves stating the minimum level of religious specificity in order to satisfy certain perceived external demands. However, these demands are more usually concerned with the mediocre character of their academic work and much less to do with their religious affiliation. At this point, it is worth considering and reviewing the mission statements of some Catholic, Protestant, Muslim and Jewish colleges and universities to illustrate the multiple issues that have arisen.

Mission statements – Catholic

Any reading of the back issues of the *Journal of Current Issues in Catholic Higher Education* indicates that there is a real concern on the part of American Catholic higher education institutions for questions of institutional identity and mission. Issues of identity are repeatedly addressed in articles and 'mission' is presented as a contested concept which is endlessly debated and critiqued. It is certainly a confusing picture and there is no uniformity in position, with some goals of Catholic higher education emphasised whilst others are minimised. There is a lack of coherence in the way Catholic goals are employed and there is no unity of meaning nor any baseline of value priorities in Catholic institutions. This makes it difficult to classify Catholic colleges and universities and to judge whether they are genuinely religiously affiliated institutions. These multiple and complex identities result in varying degrees of intensity of religious affiliation. Nevertheless, there is a rhetoric which apparently seeks to preserve and intensify religious commitment, but in reality the language is generally secular. Whilst Catholic colleges and universities want to be seen as Catholic there is simply no agreement among them on how they should be Catholic or even whether this is their first priority in the policies they adopt and implement.

In order to illustrate this secularisation of language in Catholic mission statements, it is useful to employ the analysis of mission statements conducted by a Belgian Jesuit, Jacques Berleur, in 1995. Berleur studied 52 Jesuit university mission statements (25 from the USA; 27 from other countries) from a total of 190 worldwide Jesuit institutions of higher education. He concluded that the profile of Jesuit institutions, or at least what they say about themselves, is first and foremost a claim that they are rooted in the Jesuit tradition, with an openness to the world – whether religious or not – caring personally for each person in all his or her dimensions, developing an integral vision and fulfilment of the person and his or her liberty. He found that emphasis was placed on following academic excellence as well as promoting social justice, peace, a critical sense and other traditional humanistic values. He found that the 'preferential love for the poor' was also stressed in many mission statements.

However, what he did not find is also very significant. He did not find references to the formation of Catholics, which he says appears not to be a primary concern of Jesuit universities. There are no references to the explicit transmission of the Catholic faith and a specific place for theology is mentioned in only ten of the documents. Berleur asks whether this is so obvious a task of the Jesuit university that it does not need to be mentioned or whether it simply indicates that Jesuit universities are fully secularised. The former Jesuit President of Georgetown University, Fr Healy, claimed that the Church and university were essentially two radically distinct entities capable of coexisting in a mutually beneficial relationship but only if this mutual autonomy of mission was retained. He believed that his university had a secular job to do and could therefore only provide a secular education within a broad context of 'Catholic values' – an 'intentionally pluralist' model. The Catholic university, for Healy, was clearly university first and Catholic second. Today, some Jesuits believe that their higher education institutions are losing their Catholic direction and this is why O'Hara (1997) has stated that 'a renewal of Fordham's Catholic identity is necessary'.

Robert Harvanek (1989) of Loyola University, Chicago, has stressed the main characteristics of a Jesuit 'vision of universities' when he wrote that they are 'action-orientated, socially conscious, and concerned with personal growth and fulfilment, and religious'. The substantial evidence accumulated in Burtchaell's study would strongly indicate that these universities have become largely secular entities and have therefore less credibility as Catholic institutions. Many Catholic and Protestant universities are distinctive in the USA principally for their emphasis on service programmes, character and community building, and in trying to integrate certain values and practices – but the theological justification for this emphasis on distinctiveness is often lost. Buckley (1998: 6–9) examined three mission statements of Jesuit universities at random and discovered that they were generally vague documents that avoided mention of the Catholic Church. He concluded that there was no serious difference between them and many secular universities and that they had effectively dissolved, gradually and almost imperceptibly, their distinctiveness as Catholic institutions. He concludes, 'one can only read the mission statements of some Catholic universities with a sinking sense of regret. The very vagueness of their language and the indeterminacy of their acknowledged commitments can leave one with the sense that the decline in some institutions may be already advanced, that the conjunction between a vibrant Catholicism or a Catholic culture and these universities appears increasingly faint, that the vision is fading'. There is no doubt in the mind of Buckley, who is himself a Jesuit priest, that these universities have largely secularised themselves. At best they share the fundamental presupposition that the university should have a normative secular character along the lines of a weak 'intentionally pluralist' institution.

Norman (2001: 3) would perhaps propose that what the Jesuits are doing is providing a secularised version of 'love of neighbour', which in turn elevates human needs as a sovereign principle. As he says, 'Once Christianity has been represented as primarily concerned with justice and welfare, rather than with sin and corruption, the equation of his religion with the leading tenets of modern Humanism is easily effected.' This equation destroys, according to Norman, the Christian faith from within and makes humanism the probable successor of Christianity. Nevertheless, the Jesuit liberation theologian Jon Sobrino (1997: 153–4) would challenge Norman's conclusions. He believes that the Christian university, and presumably the secular university, do not question society's unjust structures because they simply produce professional persons who in most cases serve to support these unjust structures. Christian universities, by their silence, he claims, allow grave violations of freedom and fundamental human rights. Sobrino concludes that Christian universities have merely supported the evils of today's world. This kind of liberation theology has certainly inspired Jesuit universities in revising their mission statements, but in reality Sobrino may be right, for despite great efforts in promoting social activism, the results have been disappointing to many Jesuits who run some of the most prestigious and socially exclusive Catholic institutions in America, which tacitly side with the status quo and could therefore be accused of reinforcing injustice and exclusion.

Berleur compared Jesuit universities in Latin America, Europe, Africa and Asia to those in the USA and found that they generally had a greater emphasis on Christian vision and principles, had a more emphatic place for theology and philosophy, and a greater preoccupation with religious values. In the USA Jesuit universities were more sensitive to academic excellence, freedom of thought and research, global development of the person and service to others, together with collaboration with other religious faiths. Of course the majority of Catholic universities are outside the USA and are not controlled by the Jesuits. The La Salle University in Bogota, Colombia, for example, 'is engaged in the preservation, deepening and transference of

Christian Doctrine which illuminates all fields of knowledge', whilst its neighbour the University of Mariana stipulates that 'its orientation and inspiration is under the Catholic faith'. Latin American Catholic universities were largely a product of the Catholic Church, which controlled them until the early twentieth century when they were effectively secularised by the state. When the Church failed to exert sufficient influence over them, it began to establish a new generation of universities in the 1950s. With the pervasive influence of the American model of a university emphasising 'academic excellence' and with the strong encouragement of the Jesuits who advocated social activism, the traditional religious mission of these new universities was substantially diluted. Few offered or required students studying secular subjects the opportunity to take complementary religious courses and indeed Levy (1985) argues that some of these universities were never intended to function according to identifiably Catholic standards. The emphasis at the beginning of the twenty-first century is very different and Latin American Catholic universities, such as the Catholic University of Argentina, are increasingly emphatically Catholic in their mission. The majority of Catholic colleges and universities in the USA generally stipulate that they work within the Catholic tradition whilst some are more explicit, like the University of St Thomas, which seeks an active participation in the mission of Christianity as an 'orthodox' model a of religiously affiliated institution. It is clear that the majority of Catholic universities around the world have mission statements that seek to pursue Christian ideals and values and offer themselves as a resource to the Church, but fewer of them are explicit about how this will be carried out, which places them in the 'intentionally pluralist' classification.

The University of Notre Dame in the USA has a stronger religious mission statement than any of the American Jesuit universities and is certainly a 'critical mass' institution according to Benne's typology. The University of Notre Dame attracts some of the best Catholic students in America and its Catholic identity is often seen as its 'most enduring competitive advantage'. Its current mission statement was drawn up in 1993 and marked a departure from the degree of ambiguity surrounding the university's previous mission statement and practice. The President in his inaugural address stated that 'Notre Dame will continue self-consciously and proudly to proclaim itself to be a Catholic university' (Malloy 1992: 15). Previously, the university successfully expanded and grew in prestige, but its Catholic identity suffered. The new statement makes it absolutely clear that Notre Dame is 'a Catholic academic community of higher learning' and that it seeks to develop various lines of 'Catholic thought' so that 'they [the students] may intersect with all forms of knowledge found in the arts, sciences and professions'. It states that 'the Catholic identity of the university depends upon, and is nurtured by, the continuing presence of a predominant number of Catholic intellectuals'. The statement concludes that 'in all the dimensions of the university's work it pursues trying to promote its objectives through the formation of an authentic human community graced by the Spirit of Christ'. The university is clearly conscious of the fact that Christian academics depend on a larger Christian community, but it took care to consult its staff, knowing that some would have objections to a more Catholic identity for the university. Since the university has become increasingly aware of its intended Catholic purpose the former President of the university, Theodore Hesburgh (1994) edited a large collection of essays on the debate about Notre Dame's Catholicity.

Indeed, the university had collected together an unprecedented number of scholars who have written about and researched religiously affiliated institutions (Burtchaell, Gleason, Marsden). It could be argued that when characteristics such as excellence in research, teaching and quality take precedence over more religious orientated elements of the mission statement then the religious elements are minimised. When a university is not overtly concerned with producing future leaders of a particular religious body or developing them personally within a particular religious tradition, then secondary goals take precedence. When religiously affiliated colleges and universities are simply associated with service programmes or developing good moral character, then they do no more or less than good secular universities. Young (2001) in a survey of 73 Catholic universities in the USA found 'service' was mentioned more often than any other value. Notre Dame is clearly more distinctive in its mission than this and its mission statement has a number of potential practical outcomes, not least on who should be appointed to the staff. Indeed, it is a declared aim of the university to ensure a majority of Catholic faculty. The university fosters Christian humanism through its Erasmus Institute and strongly promotes theism by arguing for the rationality and coherence of theistic belief and action through its centre for philosophy and religion. The university also requires every student to complete two courses in theology and two in philosophy during their time in the university. These courses aim at introducing theology and philosophy, largely from a Christian perspective, but in reality the Catholic content of them can be minimal. The new President, Fr John Jenkins, in his inaugural address in September 2005 explicitly stated that the university was absolutely committed to cultivating the faith of the university community and seeking a synthesis of faith and reason. It is not surprising therefore that many Catholic universities in the USA and beyond look to Notre Dame as a model of what it means to be a Catholic university.

In visiting the University of Notre Dame you cannot fail to be struck by the Catholic symbolism found on the campus. From the Grotto of Our Lady to the Basilica, from the religious statuary to the hall chapels, there is a palpable Catholic atmosphere. Many of the students are devout Catholics coming from the best Catholic high schools in America and perhaps more importantly from practising Catholic families. Mass can be celebrated in many innovative ways but attendance is high and some student groups are active in promoting a wide range of traditional Catholic activities. The priests of the Holy Cross congregation, who founded the university, are active on campus and they are numerous enough to have a strong formative influence on the students. Indeed, the university trust ensures them a role in the intellectual, pastoral and academic functions of the university. In 2005 there was a Eucharistic Procession around the campus, a very traditional Catholic practice which has been restored in the university after forty years. However, many of the students who were not part of the procession did not know how to respond – they knew that they should do something, but were unsure what. Consequently, many simply stood or took pictures of the procession. This raises the question: to what extent have the students at Notre Dame been well catechised in the Catholic faith? The kind of Catholicism found at Notre Dame is outwardly traditional, but in reality it may be more cultural than overtly religious. It is not clear that the Catholic intellectual life is well integrated with the faith and practice of the students. Nevertheless, a number of well-organised student groups are asking the university to be more Catholic in its mission and to be less concerned about secular prestige. Many alumni, some trustees and a number of the younger priests in the Holy Cross congregation would agree with these students. There are tensions among the staff: whilst 50 per cent are nominally Catholic many do not subscribe to the Catholic ethos or mission of the university. Others, including many committed Catholic students, feel that the university is losing its Catholic identity. So concerned is the university about the current number of Catholic faculty that the administration is considering establishing a search committee in order to attract potential Catholic academics. There is no question that Notre Dame is unique, but it is difficult to see how it can be easily replicated, which raises the question of whether or not it is a realistic model for other established Catholic institutions.

Few other Catholic universities in the world could boast a nominally lay Catholic intake of over 85 per cent. Notre Dame also has the service of numerous priests and sisters; again few other Catholic universities could provide and sustain such service. The spiritual and residential life is potentially excellent for educating lay Catholics, but whether or not the compulsory courses in theology and philosophy aid the formation of Catholics is debatable. Nevertheless, the potential to educate a new 'missionary generation' (see Riley 2005) that will bring faith into the professional world is huge. The university administration is sometimes accused of being overly concerned with enhancing academic prestige and widening diversity at the expense of its core Catholic identity. Where other universities have followed the example of Notre Dame has been in establishing research centres for the study of Catholicism. This raises the question why a Catholic university needs a separate Catholic studies programme and research centre. As Notre Dame expands, it is increasingly likely that the proliferation of largely secular research centres of all types may eventually distract the faculty and administration from ensuring the Catholic identity of the university.

The USA Conference of Catholic Bishops (2003) has set out in a draft application of the papal document on the Apostolic Constitution on Catholic Universities entitled *Ex Corde Ecclesiae* (From the Heart of the Church) what it believes Catholic colleges and universities should do to safeguard their Catholic identity. The bishops say that Catholic mission and identity is freely chosen and that in a Catholic university's official documentation there should be clearly set out a statement of its Catholic identity and how this should be implemented in practical terms. The essential elements of this Catholic identity include:

- commitment to be faithful to the teachings of the Catholic Church;
- commitment to Catholic ideals, principles and attitudes in carrying out research, teaching and all other university activities, including activities of officially recognised student and faculty organisations and associations, and with due regard for academic freedom and the conscience of every individual;
- commitment to serve others, particularly the poor, the underprivileged and vulnerable members of society;
- commitment of witness to the Catholic faith by Catholic administrators and teachers, especially those teaching the theological disciplines, and acknowledgement and respect on the part of non-Catholic teachers and administrators for the university's Catholic identity and mission;
- commitment to provide courses for students on Catholic moral and religious principles and their application to critical areas such as human life and other issues of social justice;
- commitment to care pastorally for the students, faculty, administration and staff;
- commitment to provide personal services (health care, counselling and guidance) to students, as well as administration and faculty, in conformity with the Church's ethical and religious teaching and directives.

Catholic colleges and universities are therefore not only to be academically viable and competitive, but they are to be committed to maintaining a Catholic identity within an increasingly secular world. The bishops are demanding a far more explicit definition of the identity and distinctiveness of Catholic colleges and universities, which corresponds to the 'critical mass' model of an institution. *Ex Corde Ecclesiae* met with some considerable controversy among the majority of USA Catholic institutions and only a few embraced it. The official Jesuit journal *America*, on 14 November 1999, called the implementation drafts of the American bishops' version of *Ex Corde Ecclesiae* 'unworkable and dangerous' and the President of the University of Notre Dame called it 'positively dangerous'. The Catholic Theological Society of America produced a report on the *mandatum* in September 2000 and declared it to be a threat to Catholic higher education. In Catholic theology faculties within recognised Catholic institutions of higher education Canon Law (812) states, 'It is necessary that those who teach theological disciplines in any institution of higher studies have a *mandatum* from the competent ecclesiastical authority.' This *mandatum* will usually, depending on the local bishop, contain the words 'I am committed to teaching authentic Catholic doctrine, and to refrain from putting forward as Catholic teaching anything contrary to the Church's magisterium.' This means that theological academic staff must receive their local bishop's written recognition of their pledge to teach in communion with the magisterium of the Catholic Church.

No university today is Catholic in the pervasive way that many once were. For example, De Paul University in Chicago has a student body of 23,000 and claims to be 'urban, Catholic and Vincentian'. By urban it means it serves the community in Chicago; by Catholic it means it provides a service to the poor by facilitating volunteer programmes for its students; and by Vincentian it means it was founded by a religious order whose current version of its tradition emphasises respect for persons, human dignity, diversity and individual 'personalism'. Much of this is indistinguishable from De Paul's secular liberal counterparts in higher education. Indeed, De Paul University has perhaps kept its statement of values ambiguous and vague to maximise greater participation among staff and students in the core activities of the university. The Chancellor of the university even commented that, 'I have an awful lot of trouble with the Catholic values because I don't know what authentic values are.' Therefore, by presenting loosely construed values which are not tightly defined so that people can subscribe to them, the university can avoid specific Catholic issues which may be seen as divisive. The university has simply chosen its own way of expressing its mission, which fits perfectly with the individualism of the present age. Whilst Catholic bishops have no powers to decide who should be appointed to a Catholic university they can use other methods if they are unhappy with a particular institution, as the following example from Australia illustrates.

The Australian Catholic University (ACU) was founded in 1991 from four vocationally oriented Catholic colleges that had been established in the mid-1900s under Catholic trusts. Through a series of amalgamations, relocations, transfers of responsibility and government and diocesan initiatives, it became a public university in 1991, located on a number of campuses throughout Australia – in Sydney, Brisbane, Canberra, Melbourne and Ballarat. There are over 10,000 students and 800 staff in the university. The university is publicly funded and its mission statement makes clear that it sees itself as part of the 'Catholic intellectual tradition' and that it 'brings a distinctive spiritual perspective to the common tasks of higher education'. Most of the mission statement is essentially about being an excellent university, which ACU shares with any secular university. Nevertheless, there is a note by the Head of Theology in the university which gives some definition to this 'Catholic intellectual tradition'. It is stated that this tradition spans 2,000 years, and then the note links the tradition to the foundation of the universities of Paris and Oxford. The author claims that these universities 'functioned with a remarkable degree of independence in philosophical and theological investigations'. There is reference to following the way of Christ and a commitment to Christian values, together with participating in the mission of the Church and a continuing dialogue between reason and faith. There are no references to Catholic formation or providing a Catholic perspective in the academy.

The Vision Statement of ACU was the result of a long and vigorous series of discussions that still go on, starting in 1990. It was written by a group called the Goals Committee which began by comparing the vision statements of other Catholic institutions, particularly American Catholic universities. Then a smaller group distilled these vision statements and came up with a short three-paragraph statement together with a longer statement about the nature of the university. The process of developing both statements was concerned with the establishment of the identity and definition of the institution; first as a university and then with the unique identity as a Catholic university. In the process ACU was aided by *Ex Corde Ecclesiae*. The longer Statement on the Nature of the University attempts to follow the core elements within *Ex Corde Ecclesiae*. It is stated, for example, that as a university 'spiritual values are fostered in harmony with the beliefs and practices of the Catholic tradition. In this tradition people believe in and are committed to God and the reality of God fully manifest in Jesus Christ and they attempt to shape their lives in accord with that belief and commitment' and that integral to the university and its ethos are staff 'who espouse the Catholic ideals of the University'. Generous quotations are used from *Ex Corde Ecclesiae* and the statement concludes that the university 'is unreservedly Catholic in its determination to serve the Church'. Whilst there is a clear and unambiguous Catholic statement of the purposes of higher education in accordance with *Ex Corde Ecclesiae*, the difficulty remains that this statement is not on the university's website or in the student prospectus nor is there any indication of how the statement is to be implemented. Perhaps this is because the debate at ACU had moved on since both the Vice-Chancellor and Pro-Vice-Chancellor of the university have written extensively about the Catholicity of the university and these articles and lectures are on the website. The Vice-Chancellor, Professor Peter Sheehan, gave a public lecture in October 2005 in which he declared his belief in an 'expansive identification' of the term 'Catholic', principally by avoiding a narrow conceptualisation of 'Catholic' as 'one that fits a single mould'. Essentially, Sheehan sees 'multiple identifiers of a Catholic university', and argues that ACU continues to adhere to *Ex Corde Ecclesia*, as understood and interpreted by ACU.

In 2004 the university became embroiled in a rather public debate with the local bishop on two separate, but, some would claim, linked issues. The local bishop is Cardinal Pell, Archbishop of Sydney, who is the President of ACU Limited, the university's controlling company. Pell had also been Chairman of the committee which established the university and he served as its first Pro-Chancellor. However, Pell was dissatisfied with the university's religious programmes, particularly with the fact that the university does not have any compulsory religious courses for students. Despite the explicit Catholic statements in the statement referred to above, the university tends to emphasise that it offers an ethical value-based education rather than an overtly Catholic one. The university had also begun to advertise itself as ACU National which some believed played down the institution's Catholicity. It is also the case that some within and outside the university wrote to the Cardinal about their concerns for the university's Catholic nature.

The Archdiocese owns the land and buildings on the two sites in Sydney where the university is located and has levied a peppercorn rent on the university – of only $10 annually. These were former teacher training colleges run by religious communities – one is at Strathfield, founded by the Christian Brothers in 1908, and the other in North Sydney, founded in 1913 by the Sisters of St Joseph. The Archbishop has used the opportunity of the peppercorn rent agreement coming to an end after ten years to enter into negotiations with the university about paying commercial management fees. This could have significantly affected the university's finances and have had the further effects of raising fees for students and reducing staff. The Archbishop has also invited another Catholic university to open a campus in Sydney. The University of Notre Dame Australia is based in Perth and is clearly more emphatically Catholic in its mission statement and practices than ACU. Notre Dame Australia teaches and researches 'within a context of Catholic faith and values' and to this end requires all students to complete units in theology, ethics and philosophy regardless of the degree course they are undertaking. The university is a private institution, unlike ACU which is funded by the Federal Government, and it seeks to educate within the Catholic tradition which, it claims, dates back 800 years. The Archbishop of Sydney, who strongly supports Notre Dame Australia, has persuaded the Federal Government of Australia to support the opening of a campus in Sydney by providing $4 million for capital expenditure. The Australian Government amended the Higher Education Funding Act (1988) so as to allow funding for this private institution. The Archdiocese is to provide $20 million in land and property together with a further $5 million in cash. This new university will be in direct competition with ACU, as it will teach in similar fields, especially law, business, teaching and health-related areas, and it will also seek to open a medical school in 2007. Notre Dame University Australia was and continues to be inspired and supported by the University of Notre Dame in the USA, which was a founding partner and has two places on the Board of Trustees.

ACU sought legal advice about the actions of the Archbishop in regard to the legality of the demand for management fees, as it claimed that this demand went against the 'spirit and understanding people might have had, when the university was first formed'. The university believes that the Cardinal was attempting to 'interfere' in the curriculum of the university. The Archbishop has responded by saying that the question about compulsory religious units is totally independent of the management fee issue. The Archdiocese has decided that it is no longer appropriate to subsidise ACU's operations to the same level through a peppercorn rent. The university has responded by establishing a committee of inquiry to look at its own programmes of study and has repeatedly stated that the university has met the provisions of *Ex Corde Ecclesiae*. Some believe that the Archbishop is attempting to make changes to the curriculum of the university through the leverage of lower rents – an accusation the Archbishop denies. The Archbishop also claims to support the new Notre Dame University because it offers a further choice for the Catholic community in Sydney and that it will offer courses not on offer at ACU. Nevertheless, there appears to be a breakdown in trust, despite the inclusion in ACU's Statement on the Nature of the University of an extract from *Ex Corde Ecclesiae* stating that the relationship with the local Church 'will be achieved more effectively if close personal and pastoral relationships exist between university and Church authorities characterised by mutual trust, close and consistent co-operation and continuing dialogue'. It is interesting that the ACU adds 'Fruitful communication will follow with bishops expressing their pastoral concerns and the University's passion for new truths and old truths newly expressed'. After receiving and considering the implications of legal advice, the university has decided to enter into further discussions with the Archdiocese to attempt to resolve the matter and secure its tenure over the properties in dispute. By December 2004, the university had agreed to pay a 'substantial' amount in fees, $8 million, to the Archdiocese of Sydney to continue to hold the properties on behalf of ACU. There is still tension in the relations between the university's academic staff and the Archdiocese. It could be argued that Cardinal Pell was seeking to establish a 'critical mass' Catholic university in his diocese, as opposed to being satisfied with an 'intentionally pluralist' university in the form of ACU.

More distinctive than ACU is Aquinas University in the Philippines, which states that it is 'distinctly Catholic in mandate, Dominican in Charism and Filipino in Character'. It is interesting that some Catholic universities in the USA play down their Roman Catholic connection by declaring themselves first to be Jesuit or Franciscan universities, in the same way that Protestant universities increasingly refer to themselves as Christian as opposed to Baptist, Methodist, Presbyterian etc. Gleason (1995: 320) believes that the identity problem of most Catholic institutions has not been resolved and 'consists in a lack of consensus as to the substantive content of the ensemble of religious beliefs, moral commitments, and academic assumptions that supposedly constitute Catholic identity, and a consequent inability to specify what that identity entails for the practical functioning of Catholic colleges and universities'. It appears that many within Catholic higher education in America and elsewhere in the world are no longer sure what remaining Catholic means. In regard to the authority of the Church, Catholic colleges and universities often respond by asking for 'dialogue', which can simply mean the rejection of the authoritative teaching of the Church and replacing it with some other statement of their own making.

In Europe the goals of Catholic universities were generally set down in a Brief issued by the Vatican at the foundation of the university. The Briefs issued in the nineteenth century emphasised two central features: first, that religion is the soul of education, and second, that there is an essential unity of religion and secular teaching. The idea that all the subjects taught in university education must be illuminated by the light of Catholic principles was emphasised in these Briefs because of the denial by liberal philosophy that there was any relation at all between religion and the other subjects taught in a university. In almost every case the adjective 'Catholic' appeared in the title of European universities, and professors were appointed to give a good example in their teaching and conduct according to the traditions of the Catholic Church. Provision was always made for the teaching of sound Catholic theology and for the conduct of Catholic worship in the university. European Catholic universities were therefore once explicit about their religious goals.

Today, many of the Catholic universities in Western Europe say very little about their religious mission, other than a general claim on their official websites that they are Catholic or have a Catholic background. This contrasts sharply with American universities which invariably have publicly stated mission statements. Of course Western Europe is often considered far more secular than most other parts of the world. There are a total of 42 Catholic universities in 12 countries within Western Europe and all are very different in how they are linked to the Catholic Church. As Catholic institutions they are all rooted in different cultures and in different experiences and can be considered an extremely heterogeneous group. Nevertheless, almost all of them have large and important faculties of theology, with departments of dogmatic, moral, pastoral, and biblical theology or studies within them. However, even in terms of the publicly available documentation, many Catholic European universities say little about their Catholic foundation or mission. The Catholic University of Lille, for example, in its information guide for students simply states that the university was founded in 1875 'with the active support of the Catholic bishops and a group of Christian managing directors'. The charter statement notes that the community of the university is inspired by 'human and Christian values' and emphasises general personal competences and skills. Essentially, the university gives first priority to its academic pursuits and to complete openness to all cultures and spiritual differences. It has a Catholic theology department, but nothing is said about chaplaincy provision in the documentation, even though there is an active chaplaincy. There appears to be no overarching Christian framework in place and it is difficult to discern any Christian or Catholic input into most of the courses on offer. Whilst the university has a concern for ethics, this is largely viewed within a humanistic and secular framework. Despite this, the university has the approval of the local bishop to call itself 'Catholic'. The local bishop potentially has considerable influence over the university and has the power in his hands to veto the appointment of any president. Senior members of the university are also very conscious that the local bishop seeks a more explicit statement and commitment to the Catholic mission in the university. However, there are particular difficulties with the five French Catholic universities, not least the fact that as private institutions they are not significantly funded by the state. The secular nature of French government ensures that Catholic universities play down or eliminate any religious references in their literature in order to secure contracts for teaching or research at regional or national level. There is also the very conscious split between private and public, which is characteristic of the French academic elite; privately they may try to operate as Catholics, but publicly they subscribe to secular approaches in the academy. This makes the context in which French Catholic universities function problematic and makes for a less than explicit Christian mission.

In contrast, the University of Navarra in Pamplona, Spain, does not 'belong' to Opus Dei, but is run by members of Opus Dei and others, who are not necessarily Catholic. It has an explicit commitment to serve the Church and promote Catholic teaching – it can be considered to be an 'orthodox' university according to Benne's typology even though it is an independently owned university and is operated as a secular enterprise under a private trust. It is interesting that Opus Dei, as an organisation, does not own its 'corporate works' or projects, such as universities, of which its members run over fifteen with over 80,000 students (Allen 2005: 34). Since Opus Dei neither owns nor governs these universities it therefore does not have to register them as specifically Catholic institutions with the local bishop. Consequently, they are not subject to the provisions in *Ex Corde Ecclesiae*. The University of Navarra, the largest Opus Dei 'sponsored' university, has major faculties of law, medicine, theology, canon law, philosophy and letters, economics, natural sciences, communications and pharmacology. It is also academically respected and successfully combines its undoubted academic excellence with a strong Catholic mission. Indeed, it was founded by Saint Josemaria Escriva, in 1952, the founder of Opus Dei. Other universities run by members of Opus Dei attract some of the best minds in their countries, such as Strathmore University in Nairobi, Kenya, the University of the Andes in Chile, the University of Piura in Peru, and the University of the Isthmus in Guatemala. These universities all have generic names and secular academic aims, but whilst they are not technically Catholic, it is because they contain many members of Opus Dei and provide a Catholic formation for many of their students that makes them count as religious affiliated. They certainly provide an interesting model of a religiously affiliated higher institution.

There are also 157 university faculties of theology approved by the Holy See to award theological degrees attached to both secular and Catholic universities in Europe, especially in Poland, Switzerland, Netherlands, France, Germany, Belgium, Austria, Lithuania, Czech Republic, Slovakia, Spain and Italy. These faculties are supervised very closely by the Catholic Church and work under guidelines prescribed by the Vatican. There are similar theological institutes outside Europe, e.g. the Catholic Institute of Theology attached to the University of Auckland in New Zealand. The Flemish section of the University of Leuven, the oldest Catholic university still in existence, states in its mission statement that it is 'a Flemish university of Catholic signature' and is 'a critical centre of thought within the Catholic community, and as such it is deeply concerned with the relationship between science and faith, and with the dialogue between Church and the world'. It goes on to say that it has 'a Christian view of man and society'. Leuven is a university of nearly 30,000 students and the majority of staff and students, whilst baptised Catholics, are in practice largely cultural Catholics. The university is careful to nurture a good relationship with the local bishop and has recently elected a theologian President. The university is widely diverse in the courses offered, but has Pontifical Theology and Canon Law Faculties that come directly under the influence of the Catholic Church. The university appears to meet the criteria of a 'critical mass' religiously affiliated institution in some important areas, but also displays characteristics of the 'intentionally pluralist' university. Many of these diverse universities truly believe that they serve the Church in some way and that they share the conviction with the Church that faith and other knowledge converge, but they are all concerned to differing degrees that the epithet 'Catholic' could diminish the quality of their teaching and research. So whilst they consistently proclaim their Christian heritage and some even wish to retain the title 'Catholic', they in practice largely conduct a secular scholarship and are at pains to emphasise their academic reputation and also that they respect the secular notion of academic freedom. They are university first and Catholic second. Leuven is outwardly a Catholic university and still retains many important aspects of Catholic education, but it is a difficult university to place securely within Benne's typology.

One example to illustrate this secular approach is the development of the Catholic University of Nijmegen in Holland. The university was founded in 1923 from the Dutch Faculty of Theology of the University of Leuven. It was legally founded as The Roman Catholic University but the title in common usage was the Catholic University of Nijmegen. It opened with under 200 students and had a theology faculty that could award university degrees and ecclesiastical degrees of the Catholic Church. Today, the university has grown to over 13,000 students and its website simply states that the university has a Catholic 'background'. Indeed, in recent times many within the university dropped the epithet 'Catholic' and it was not unusual to see the title of the university as simply the University of Nijmegen in academic publications. The university authorities therefore decided, after consultation, to change the name of the university by officially dropping the epithet 'Catholic'. From 31 August 2004, the official name of the university was changed to Radboud University Nijmegen. The new title is named after St Raboud, who was a Catholic bishop and scientist who lived around AD 900. However, it is extremely unlikely that many will recognise Radboud as a Catholic designation, especially since the prefix 'Saint' has not been used. Nevertheless, the university is eager to retain Catholic recognition and so has developed a policy which attempts to meet some of the requirements of *Ex Corde Ecclesiae*. It states that the university seeks to promote its Christian identity through a number of institutes within the university, including the Heyendall Institute, a small Catholic Studies Centre, which was founded in 1999 to help define the relevance of the Christian tradition and contemporary culture to the Catholic university. The university's main activity in this regard is to promote links between scientific study and religion. It also continues to be a centre for training Catholic priests and for the study of theology. The university highlights Catholic interdisciplinary studies and appoints a number of professors to chairs in cultural and religious psychology, cultural and religious sociology, and the history of Catholicism. We are informed that the school of philosophy gives special attention to the Catholic tradition in ethics and metaphysics and that the theology faculty has a 'special attachment to the Catholic Church in the Netherlands' and also that there is an attempt to integrate the insights from theology across the academic work of the university. The are many parallels here with the University of Notre Dame in the USA.

However, in a study by Prins *et al.* (2003: 182), it is claimed that Nijmegen no longer has one identity for the university as a whole, that it is not a unified entity. Their research found a multitude of sub-identities and sub-cultures and this corresponds to the 'intentionally pluralist' university model. They found that only in the theology faculty did students differ so significantly that it counted as a separate culture and indeed the only culture that had a Catholic identity. As they conclude: 'Most of the theology students are Catholic, are interested in matters of religion, read about religious matters, speak about it and go to church.' Students in the other faculties are, they conclude, 'in a process of secularisation'. This research would appear seriously to question Raboud University's attempt to integrate Christian principles into all the areas of its activities. Raboud has followed the general recommendation of O'Brien (2002) by developing a small institute to study and reflect on the basic university mission. Also in Holland, the Catholic Theological University at Utrecht has merged with the Protestant Faculty of Theology at Utrecht University with government encouragement through financial assistance. Whilst there will still be an opportunity for the new Catholic section of the faculty to teach and research what it likes, there is clearly a reduction in the autonomy that the previous Institute enjoyed. The Dutch government has recently decided to provide state finance for Catholic theology faculties within state universities. This comes at a time when the number of students studying theology across Europe is in serious decline.

It is in the new Catholic universities currently being established in Eastern Europe that we see more emphatic assertions of Catholicity. Indeed, the older Catholic universities, such as the Catholic University of Lublin, survived over forty years of repression and lack of material support under communism to emerge as a large and academically successful 'orthodox' model of a Catholic university: precisely the kind of model of a university that many within American Catholic universities said was impossible in the 1960s. These universities have an explicit Catholic identity and attempt to have a culturally unifying effect across all members of the faculty as a counterbalance to fragmentation in the curriculum. The Peter Pazmany Catholic University in Budapest in Hungary was founded in 1992 and makes clear that it conforms to *Ex Corde Ecclesiae*, 'staying faithful to the Christian message conveyed by the Church'. It provides a Catholic education and teaches the 'secular sciences in the light of the Catholic Faith'. It also works closely with the local bishops. The Ukrainian Catholic University was founded in 2002 and again emphatically states that it is a Catholic university and a centre for Christian thought and values. In Poland, the recent foundation of the Cardinal Wyszynski University is another example of an explicitly Catholic institution. The Legionnaires of Christ, a Catholic religious order, established a university in Rome in 2005 called the European University, Rome, which is again emphatically Catholic in its orientation. It is interesting that in America the establishment of Ave Maria College as an orthodox Catholic institution has attracted considerable funding from lay Catholic sponsors, including over $340 million from Tom Monaghan of Domino's Pizzas. This college, soon to be called a university, is being established in Naples, Florida, and is intended to house over 5,000 students. Ava Maria University will follow the examples of Christendom and Steubenville universities with dress codes, single sex dorms, and compulsory religious courses – identifying with the 'orthodox' model of religiously affiliated institutions.

These kinds of Catholic university are responses to the secularisation of mainstream Catholic institutions and their perceived loss of a distinctly Catholic religious ethos and identity. The foundation of the International Catholic University in 1994 is another response to this general secularisation process. This is an 'orthodox' American-based university that was founded by Ralph McInerny, a philosophy professor from Notre Dame University. The Jesuits at Boston College established the Jesuit Institute to explore relations between faith and scholarship. Another such institution has been created at the Catholic University of Dayton. Indeed, there has been some expansion of chairs in 'Catholic Studies' and interdisciplinary religious studies within Catholic universities which strangely appears to replicate the expansion of such chairs in secular universities. Roche (2003: 168), at the University of Notre Dame, argues that if we can define what Catholicism is, then it is this that a Catholic university should be. Roche offers a theology of higher education and indicates four different ways in which a Catholic university can demonstrate its distinctive 'Catholicity': by adopting a universalistic approach that encourages a concern for love and justice; by espousing a sacramental view that enables students and faculty to ask deeper questions; by blending reason and faith in such a way that places theology and philosophy at the heart of the university; and by emphasising the unity of knowledge. Roche believes that Catholic universities should assimilate the best aspects of secular culture, but that Catholic universities should be places where Catholic scholarship can flourish. He uses the example of the University of Notre Dame to illustrate this. However, do Catholic colleges and universities demonstrate what Roche says they should? It could be argued that there is a pattern of religious renewal taking place in a minority of Catholic colleges and universities, or at the very least that there is recognition that secularisation is not irreversible as some thought. In the last ten years over 150 centres and institutions dedicated to religion have been established in higher education and 10 per cent of Catholic colleges and universities have established Catholic Studies programmes for their students. However, the majority, whilst not fully secularised, continue to resist pressures from the Church and instead follow a generalised secular path with some already within the 'accidentally pluralist' classification. In June 2005 the Vatican compiled, for the first time, an official list of Catholic religiously affiliated institutions of higher education called the *Index of Universities and Institutions of Superior Instruction of the Catholic Church*. The Vatican has not yet devised criteria of how to identify, and to measure, what might be called 'benchmarks of Catholicity'.

Mission statements – Protestant

The first Protestant evangelical colleges in the USA were founded by individual denominations with a clear sense of promoting their religious beliefs. Indeed, these Protestant denominations dominated higher education provision up until the end of the nineteenth century. Noll (1994: 110–12) details how the period 1865–1900 saw new leadership in these colleges and universities, which expanded and transformed them into research universities after the German model. He notes that it was of the 'greatest significance' that the money for these new kinds of universities did not come from the Protestant communities that had previously provided the financial support for these universities. Instead it was wealthy new entrepreneurs and then state governments that provided the funds for this expansion. Funding connected with the Churches became less and less important, and therefore these colleges and universities witnessed a decline in the Christian characteristics which had previously marked them out. An 'accommodating Protestantism' emerged that gave less emphasis to traditional evangelical convictions in the academy. As a consequence Protestant religiously affiliated colleges and universities increasingly abandoned the idea that Christians should accept the unity of all knowledge, and consequently the effort to integrate religious faith with learning was either abandoned or modified. Some Protestant colleges and universities resisted these changes, but the majority embraced them.

In a study of sixty-nine colleges and universities affiliated to the Presbyterian and Evangelical Churches in the USA, Allen Fisher (1995) found that almost all focused on values, often as an expression of their religious heritage. Since every kind of higher education institution claims to stress values, Fisher concluded that the term by itself was vacuous, and he also found that compared to other institutions these Protestant institutions offered nothing distinctive in their curriculum. There was no difference in what was being taught by them and by colleges and universities, that are not religiously affiliated. Burtchaell (1998: 239) studied the history of two Presbyterian colleges – Davison and Lafayette. His stark conclusion was that 'there is no longer either a community of sponsorship (a providing Church) or a community of mentorship (a believing faculty) or a community of discipleship (a faithful student body)'. It would appear easier to prepare a vague mission statement than actually implement it. However, a recent study of Presbyterian colleges and universities by Weston and Soden (2004) suggests that at least 11 per cent of these institutions are emphatically religious in orientation ('orthodox' or 'critical mass'), and whilst the others are largely inclusive and non-sectarian in character ('accidentally pluralist') they conclude that another 43 per cent do attempt to address their religious mission in their curriculum and campus life ('intentionally pluralist'). Burtchaell (1991) studied the process by which Vanderbilt University gradually lost its Baptist character and then, using the stages of change in Vanderbilt as a model, sought to alert Catholics to how dangerously far along the same path they had come.

At the level of mission statements resistance to the secularisation process can still be seen in a number of Protestant colleges and universities today. Northwestern College provides an education 'so our students don't just learn about the world, they learn how to live in it as Christians'. Calvin College is even more explicit about its mission: 'We pledge fidelity to Jesus Christ, offering our hearts and lives to do God's work in God's world.' Calvin College has also established the Kuyers Institute for Christian Teaching and Learning to help fulfil its mission. The majority of these Protestant colleges and universities seek to educate their students for leadership in Church and Nation. Ouachita Baptist University 'provides opportunity to experience growth in Christian ideals and character', whilst the purpose of Faulkner University 'is to glorify God'. Bob Jones University 'exists to grow Christlike character that is Scripturally disciplined', but it is often accused of being defensive and wholly sectarian in character. Oklahoma Christian University's mission is clear: 'Glorify God, Christ and the Holy Spirit while offering the Bible as the revelation of God's will.' A number of Protestant universities have been opened in Africa and Asia, in recent years, particularly by Anglicans. The Ugandan Christian University was opened in 1997 to develop lives of Christian faith and leadership. Nevertheless, all these Protestant colleges and universities are small and are not typical, in the sense that most Protestant colleges and universities are no longer as explicit about what they are in religious terms. It is perhaps why Wolfe and Heie (1993: 84), in a study of evangelical Christian colleges that was supported by the Christian College Coalition, argue that much that is claimed for Christian colleges and universities in mission statements, in recruitment literature and in brochures is not distinctive of Christian education. They believe that in many evangelical colleges their priorities simply do not match the claims by which they justify their existence. For Wolfe and Heie (1993: 12, 15) the Christian college is a community of believers, which must mentor the next generation of Christian scholars. In so doing the Christian college helps transform persons and society. As they say: 'The College extends the concern of the Church by deepening biblical understanding and complementing it with understanding from academic disciplines to form a coherent world and life view.' Therefore, Christian college slogans need to be interpreted into concrete proposals and Wolfe and Heie suggest a number of ways forward for evangelical colleges.

Calvin College is worth considering further here, as it is often said that it has been one of the seedbeds of the intellectual renaissance within American evangelism. Whilst Calvin, like many other evangelical colleges, is much more homogenous in staff and students than other Protestant institutions, it has recently established a visible presence in Christian literary scholarship, history, psychology and philosophy (see Carpenter 2002) through its first-rate scholars in these fields. The college professes its Christianity openly and explicitly and is unambiguous about what it stands for – faculty sign a covenant with the college, agreeing to these explicit religious goals. It is also a community that worships together, but above all it is a community concerned about promoting a 'faith-informed' scholarship among faculty and students alike. As Turner (1996: 12) says of the staff at Calvin College: 'while conforming to the canons of secular, mainstream scholarship, they have helped to nurture in the academy a heightened sensitivity to Christian faith as a factor important in its own right'. Faculty at Calvin have also helped found a series of academic associations that have co-operated with other Christians to revive Christianity in the life of the mind. Whilst the influence of Calvin College on secular higher education is very small, it is a significant development within Protestant evangelism.

However, Sloan (1994: 232) writes that most Protestant leaders of Church colleges and universities cannot 'avoid a constant sense of ineffectuality' in regard to their institutions' missions. He believes it is simply 'self-delusion' and even 'hypocrisy' for presidents of colleges to think that the Christian faith and values will be seriously engaged within their institutions. A more recent look at the issues by Mahoney (2001) indicates that the denominations are taking seriously the implications of their mission statements. These denominations have initiated various projects on mission and identity such as the Presbyterian Academy of Scholars and Teachers, the Teachers, the Vocation of the Lutheran College and Conversations on Jesuit Higher Education.

Modern English universities are overwhelmingly secular in origin and began with the establishment of University College London in 1826, the third oldest in England after Oxford and Cambridge. It admitted students without respect to religion and offered no religious instruction, preferring instead to welcome all students irrespective of faith. Oxford and Cambridge had of course become Anglican universities at the Reformation, and two other universities were established by the Church of England in 1829 at King's College, London, and in 1832 the University of Durham. Therefore only four universities in England until 2002 had a religious origin and every university founded since 1832 has been established as a secular university. The University of Durham was founded by the Dean and Chapter of Durham Cathedral and the students admitted were subject to Church of England religious tests. By 1871 these tests were removed and in 1907 the government removed the authority of the Dean and Chapter over the university. The university retained a number of fragments of its religiously affiliated past by making the Dean of the Cathedral an *ex officio* member of the university's Council and retaining the Bishop of Durham as the university's Visitor – a role of final arbiter in university disputes whose powers have been much reduced by government legislation and is due to disappear altogether. The university also retained some theological studies of a particularly Anglican orientation, but nothing beyond this. The university had become for all intents and purposes a largely secular university, but despite this it retains a strong Anglican flavour. King's College London followed a similar pattern and as it expanded it lost most of its traditional Anglican connections, but again retains an Anglican flavour. Consequently, the only real religiously affiliated institutions that survived into the twentieth century were the teacher training colleges.

In England, some today believe that these Church colleges of higher education, which were originally founded to train Christian teachers, have long since lost their religious rationale for existing. They claim it is difficult to detect in their current mission statements what distinctive mission they are offering society. The majority of these Church colleges, Anglican and Catholic alike, were founded in the nineteenth century with a very clear view of what they were about. They were generally highly denominational in character, single-sex and divorced from the local communities in which they were situated. The evangelical Cheltenham Training College, which was founded in 1847, had a tightly worded trust which included the following: 'It is solemnly intended and proposed that the religious education to be conveyed shall always be strictly Scriptural, Evangelical and Protestant and in strict accordance with the articles of liturgy of the Church of England as now by Law established, in their literal and grammatical sense, and that these principles should for ever be preserved as a most sacred trust at any sacrifice of pecuniary loss or temporal interest' (Scotland 1989: 27). The college was operated under a trust and the dominant ideal was that of evangelical mission, which provided deep-rooted certainties, which in turn animated this particular Christian vision of education. Admission was strict and often required a certificate of baptism, a letter of support from a clergymen, and the successful completion of a test in religion. Once admitted, students experienced a rigorous regime of compulsory services and religious courses. As Ridley (1989: 39) says: 'There would have been no question in those early years of the curriculum being influenced by Christianity. The college was the curriculum, and the curriculum was Christianity.' Cheltenham Training College began by training teachers with chapel and bible study compulsory elements of the experience. The colleges appeared to function as lay seminaries. Nevertheless, Ridley details the process of secularisation of these colleges, particularly Chester College (now the University of Chester).

Some would argue that these contemporary Anglican colleges, in common with some strands of Anglicanism, seem to have committed themselves to not being particularly distinctive. Gates (2004) outlines the frames of reference in which Anglican colleges and universities around the world operate, and they focus largely on secular and multi-faith contexts. However, these colleges have been forced to reflect the changing realities of their intakes and the changing place of religion in English society together with the influence and role of the Christian Churches in that society. They have collectively experienced a steadily diminishing recruitment of committed Christians among both students and staff, and their mission statements have been increasingly framed within a more openly humanistic tone as opposed to being concerned with explicit Christian outcomes. In the process of redefining their goals in the modern context, they have struggled with the idea of maintaining Christian distinctiveness in a climate of inclusiveness. It is not therefore surprising to discover mission statements that declare 'a commitment to sustain Christian principles and values without being exclusive . . . a faith based college for those of all faiths and none' (see McNay 2002). Some refer to their university not as a religious or faith-based university, but as a Christian 'foundation' – somehow relegating the Christian part to the past. Nevertheless, the Church of England is the only serious contender in higher education within England actively to promote a religiously affiliated university sector within a higher education system that is currently overwhelmingly secular in orientation and practice.

Cheltenham Training College went through a number of institutional transformations and eventually merged with a secular college and expanded rapidly in the 1980s to become the University of Gloucestershire in 2002. It is no longer a privately funded evangelical institution, but is largely a publicly funded university open to all. The university says that the evangelical trust of 1847 'influences the governance of the University today and provides a framework for its mission' in the curriculum and chaplaincy. However, D'Costa (2005: 69) suggests that the university is only 'thinly Christian', being really secularised. There are today no religious tests for students or staff within these Church colleges and universities or compulsory services or courses. Their intakes are entirely diverse and multicultural. Nevertheless, there are still attempts to give these new universities a distinctive flavour as some of them move increasingly towards university status. Roehampton University, for example, was established in September 2004. It had previously consisted of four former colleges, Anglican, Catholic, Methodist and a fourth constituent college founded on humanistic principles, and these institutions had experimented with each other in different institutional arrangements before successfully applying and receiving full university status. The new Vice-Chancellor thought it an ideal opportunity to review the vision of the university and decided to consult all the staff before writing this new vision. The new vision was heralded as 'one of the most radical and imaginative ecumenical projects of modern times'. However, whilst the new vision speaks of 'nurturing the human spirit', 'promoting social justice', and helping students to 'grow spiritually', there is absolutely no reference to any substantive Christian context for this vision. There is no reference to Christian scholarship or any commitment to a Christian mission. Instead, the new university is fully committed to a whole series of humanistic principles with which Friedrich Froebel, the secular educationalist who inspired the foundation of the fourth college, would have been very pleased. It could be said that the specifically Christian foundations of the three other colleges have been lost in this new vision statement.

Lord Dearing's report 'The Way Ahead: Church of England Schools in the New Millennium' (2001) highlighted the two main issues facing these Church colleges and universities: to sustain and develop their distinctiveness and ensure long-term survival. The report noted that colleges 'will have characteristics which are additional to or awarded greater importance than those found in secular institutions' (9.21), recognising their 'intentionally pluralist' status. The report envisaged some curriculum development with Christian principles and values, but all within a general humanistic perspective. There had of course been discussions about Christian identity and the Council of Church and Associated Colleges (now Council of Church Colleges and Universities) had previously promoted a number of initiatives including the support of a project, *Engaging the Curriculum – A Theological Perspective*, to explore the relationship between theology and the different ostensibly secular academic disciplines, which appear within the degree programmes of universities (see Francis 1999; Gearon 1999; Thatcher 1999). The programme's aim was 'to make available material which aims at fostering Christian insights into most of the Colleges' curricula'. The second director of the programme, Ian

Markham (1997: 3), outlined its general aim: 'The whole programme is dedicated to recovering the religious, ethical and spiritual dimension of all study. The secularisation of education diminished the task of education . . . It reduced education to the reporting of supposed "facts" in a supposedly neutral manner, and lost sight of the need to locate those "facts" in a value framework.' *Engaging the Curriculum* therefore attempted to locate learning within the Christian narrative, but its success was variable. Thatcher (1995) reported that there was not much enthusiasm among college staff to produce a curriculum that was permeated with 'theological insights'; the project was abandoned in the late 1990s. In a review of the prospectuses of these colleges, Goodlad (2002) concluded that 'Christian institutions in England take great pains to stress that they welcome students of all faiths or none. Indeed, so strongly is this message of inclusiveness purveyed that it is really quite difficult in some cases to discern from prospectuses which are Christian institutions and which are not. Even within the covers of their prospectuses, some institutions simply mention their Church roots but without indicating what the church affiliation might signify.' The Church of England established a 'Mutual Expectations' working party in 2004 to explore the mission of its colleges and universities, and in 2005 three further Church of England colleges obtained university titles in Canterbury, Chester and Winchester, together with a new joint Anglican/Catholic university in Liverpool. Over a period of time all but one of these new universities has, for varying reasons, erased their former Christian designations in order to market themselves to a broader audience. The Church of England has responded by encouraging these institutions to retain identifiably Christian aspects of their mission and ethos.

Mission statements – Muslim

Universities and colleges in majority Muslim countries can often have such a predominance of Muslim staff and students in them that they seem to fulfil the claim that they are indeed Muslim universities. They can often have a kind of Muslim ethos and try to accommodate themselves to the larger Muslim cultural system which operates in their societies, even when such universities are technically secular or under the control of the government. There appears to be little need for them to have long theological articulations of their identity or mission, as the Muslim culture is so pervasive that it is considered relevant to the life of the university, though not always to the content of the curriculum offered. In addition, there has been a debate within Muslim countries about what philosophical approach they should adopt to higher education, with many emphasising quality and excellence in research and teaching over any religious considerations. Some make absolutely no reference to Islam in their mission or goal statements. Indeed, many Muslim universities lack a clearly defined mission and do not promote the role of religion in public life. Nevertheless, there are clear tensions within Muslim countries about the appropriate role of religion in universities and there are also a number of university federations, as described in the introduction, which claim universities in majority Muslim countries as 'Muslim' or 'Islamic'.

In comparison, Muslim institutions in the West, such as the Islamic American University near Detroit, seeks explicitly in its mission statement to produce a new generation of Muslims to serve Islam, who practise Islam, and can convey it to the larger community. In the USA there are over 6 million Muslims and the Muslim American Society, which sponsored the foundation of the Islamic American University, sought the education of American Muslims in the fields of Islamic law and to develop students who are 'well rounded in Islam'. American Muslims have successfully taken a lead in the establishment of universities and have even created the Internet Islamic University which offers an alternative education for Muslims who have a limited or no choice of attending an Muslim university. American Muslims have also founded the International Institute for Islamic Thought, in Virginia, which seeks 'the revival and reform of Islamic thought' in order to regain Islam's intellectual identity. The Institute has funded a series of conferences on the Islamisation of knowledge around the world and one of its publications *Islamisation of Knowledge: General Principles and Work Plan* is perhaps the most important in the field. The booklet attempts to identify what it constantly refers to as the 'malaise'. There is a catalogue of complaints against the West and even against Muslim academics who are accused of lacking vision, and it observes 'that teachers in Muslim universities do not possess the vision of Islam and, therefore, are not driven by its cause is certainly the greatest calamity of Muslim education'.

Bilgrami and Ashraf (1985: 32–7) surveyed a number of universities within the Muslim world and concluded that most governments in Muslim states have adopted the Western model of the university with the belief that in so doing Muslim societies would make progress. The study of religion, i.e. Islam, was left largely to the mosques, private houses and the *madrassas*. They conclude that two systems were created – the Islamic system and the foreign system of university development – the latter they claim is based on a modern secular approach. Bilgrami and Ashraf (1985: 40) reject the idea that by providing some compulsory courses in Muslim studies you make an Islamic university – a practice popular in many Muslim universities. They argue that 'the aim of the Islamic university is not merely to provide "higher education" as a training of the mind or to deal with the "high" truth or to prepare for higher callings" ':

> It has to produce men of higher knowledge and noble character, enlightened with higher values, having an urge to work for the betterment of their own inner selves, and of humanity at large ... The university will aim to bring its students to a common level of peace and faith, uniting

them on the basic principle . . . one God, Prophethood and the Last Days of Judgement and making them realize their own destiny in this world through hard work and honest living.

The problem is that the Muslim community has not produced enough first-rate scholars to achieve the synthesis it seeks. Rahman (1982: 133) comments that 'the effort to inculcate an Islamic character in young students is not likely to succeed if the higher fields of learning remain completely secular'. The point being made here is that whilst there may be a general Muslim ethos in these universities, the curriculum and methods remain entirely secular in orientation. Some would argue that these secular aspects of the curriculum, including teaching methods and textbooks, promote an emphasis on Western conceptions of 'liberal education' and encourage the development of excessive critical thinking and analysis that threatens Islam. It is why some Muslims have advocated the creation of strictly Islamic universities, but what do they mean by 'Islamic'?

These new Islamic universities, mainly, but not exclusively in majority Muslim countries, have emphatic mission statements that make clear reference to Islam – for example, the International Islamic University in Islamabad founded in 1980 and located around the Faisal Mosque aims to 'to reconstruct human thought in all its forms on the foundations of Islam' and 'to develop Islamic character and personality among the students, teachers and the supporting staff in the University'. These are clear goals to form individuals with a particular religious worldview and to spread it. This university seeks an Islamic intellectual renaissance and to produce students and scholars who are imbued with Islamic learning. The university also has an Islamic Research Institute attached to it with the aim of studying the teachings of Islam in the context of the intellectual and scientific progress of the modern world. In Pakistan, government guidelines require school and university textbooks to emphasise Islam as the national ideology of the state. Conservative religious groups have thus exercised a decisive role in determining this 'ideology'. A theocratic vision of higher education has resulted, which is strongly advocated by what can only be described as 'Islamic theocrats'. General Musharraf has recently launched some liberal reforms called 'enlightened moderation' in an attempt to project a more peaceful image of Islam. This has been in response to the Pakistani government's concern at the huge expansion of *madrassas* in its cities and in the countryside, which have links with militant Islamic groups such as the Taliban, and therefore whilst supporting the development of an Islamic University in Islamabad, the Pakistani government has emphasised that it must not be militant. The university stresses therefore that it adopts a 'moderate and responsible style of discourse on the issues concerning Islam and the challenges facing Muslims'. Muslim universities range from a small number being 'fundamentalist' to most falling somewhere within Benne's other four models.

The International Islamic University in Kula Lumpur, West Malaysia, was opened in 1983 and was established by the government in collaboration with the Ministry of Education in Saudi Arabia. It is emphatically Islamic in mission and seeks to place all teaching and research within the teachings of the Koran. Its specific aim is to 'integrate Islamic revealed knowledge and values in all academic disciplines and educational activities'. It also seeks to provide leaders for the Muslim community and help students to become obedient servants of Allah. The university seeks to restore the Muslims community's leading role in all branches of knowledge. It is interesting that this university has become a role model for other Islamic universities, and yet the Malaysian people only began to be converted to Islam in the thirteenth century – after the Muslim civilisation in Arabia had reached its peak. Malaysia played no part in the historic Muslim intellectual movement. In the university students are expected to study and be examined on core aspects of Islam alongside their main disciplines and indeed attempt to integrate them. Many of these overtly Islamic universities have been inspired by the al-Azhar University in Egypt which has a missionary zeal for the 'maintenance of Islam and the advantage of Muslims'. The al-Azhar, founded as a college in 971 AD, is today considered to be the oldest Muslim university housed in a mosque; it trained its students to propagate Islam and continues to this day to exercise great influence on the minds of young Muslim students of theology. A few other Muslim universities use the title Islamic in their university designations, such as the Islamic University of Gaza, but they are not as emphatically Muslim as al-Azhar or Medina, and the two international Islamic universities mentioned above. We could also add to the list of 'ortho-dox' religiously affiliated higher education institutions the higher *madrassas* of Islam of Zeituna in Tunis and Qarrawiyin in Fez, which together with the al-Azhar are main centres for the training and instruction of scholars of religion.

The modern motivation for these specifically Islamic universities can be found in the proceedings of the First World Conference in Muslim Education in 1977. The conference set out to define the principles, aims and methods of the Islamic concept of education and sought to begin research on the ration-ale for the Islamisation of knowledge and education. Many Muslim scholars are convinced that the negative secular influences of modernisation can be mitigated through the Islamisation of knowledge. Briefly, this means to Islamise, reorganise, rearticulate and develop the academic disciplines as Islamic knowledge and promote an Islamic approach to all knowledge. The term was first used by a Malaysian scholar, Syed Muhammad Naguib al-Attas, in his book *Islam and Secularisation* published in 1978. It describes a variety of approaches to synthesise the ethos of Islam with various fields of Islamic thought. It was then promoted by the Palestinian philosopher Ismail Al-Faruqi in 1982. It involves demonstrating the relevance of each area of modern knowledge to Islam. Chapter 4 will look at this idea in more detail, but it can be noted here that there is no agreement on it among Muslim scholars. Liberal Muslims are sceptical about the Islamisation of knowledge and believe it is simply a term used as propaganda by conservative Muslims; they instead are more trusting of secular knowledge. It is also interesting that much of the movement to Islamise knowledge is led from the West, especially from Britain and the USA. It was American and Canadian Muslim communities that set up Muslim subject associations in medicine, social sciences and science. However, the influence of this movement has largely dictated the kinds of mission statements that Islamic/Muslim universities adopt. For example, as has been noted, the Islamic University in Malaysia seeks to integrate revealed and acquired knowledge in religion and secular subjects. It seeks to Islamise all branches of the sciences together with the life and culture of the university and of the students and staff. Excellence and quality in education more generally are stated as goals, but they are secondary to the first set of goals which are emphatically religious.

In Saudi Arabia there are a number of scientific universities in Jeddah that have departments of religion on the Western model. However, there are also the Islamic universities of Riyadh and Medina which are devoted to Shariah, religion and Koranic studies. Some would say that this kind of Islamic university is no more than a *madrassa*. Husain (1997: 45) helps us to understand the difference between the *madrassa* and modern university in Muslim culture. He describes the *madrassa* as having a completely different worldview and that:

> the astronomy they teach is pre-Galilean; their geology has not gone beyond the findings of medieval scholars; they reject modern historical methodology where it seems to threaten legends embedded in the consciousness of our ancestors; their logic invokes Aristotle as the last word in analysis; their hermeneutics would not at all admit the validity of modern standards of textual scrutiny and interpretation; their concept of history as a discipline would rather ignore the labours of archaeologists and anthropologists than acknowledge that what is recorded in books written centuries ago could contain errors.

However, the *maddrassa* is often the only choice or alternative in many Muslim countries to the modern university.

Jordan's first university was opened only in 1962. The Al al-Bayt University (literally the House of the Prophet University) was opened in 1992 by royal decree in Mafrag in Jordan. It is also open to all irrespective of creed, sex or race. However, it is a Muslim university and exists as an alternative to the existing universities built on the Western models. Nevertheless, it remains a liberal institution that does not attempt to promote a way of life that imposes itself on others. There is a concern in the Muslim world that the true image of Islam is being distorted in higher education and that Muslims should not leave the presentation of Islam or the personal formation of students to exclusively religious or secular institutions. The search is to combine as far as possible 'reason and science' with 'belief and spiritual values'. Muslim countries are lagging behind in terms of science and technological development and there is a search for a better form of higher education based on the Muslim tradition.

It is interesting that the Aga Khan University in Karachi, Pakistan, seeks to be a modern university but rooted in Muslim tradition by promoting Islamic civilisation and learning. The mission of the university says nothing about preparing a new generation of Muslims but instead emphasises intellectual freedom, autonomy, distinction in scholarship and even pluralism. The aims of this university simply state that the university is inspired by Islamic ethics and humanistic ideals. The idea is that Islam should benefit from modernity whilst remaining true to its tradition. It is an autonomous Muslim university open to all, without distinction of race, sex or creed. It clearly seeks to develop Pakistan and the Muslim world. The university commissioned a report by Derek Brok, president of Harvard University, in 1983, which is known as the Harvard Report. The report sought to develop 'conceptual options' for the university and concluded that Aga Khan University was and should be a model for other Muslim universities by setting an example of quality in higher education, particularly in research. The report said that the Aga Khan University could educate good Muslims as well as good and competent citizens. The emphasis in the report on quality and research reflects the principal concerns of 'first'-rate universities such as Harvard.

The Aga Khan University is therefore not solely concerned with Islamic learning but it does, in the words of the Harvard Report, try to avoid 'purely secularistic analytical positions'. In 1994 the Chancellor's Commission of Aga Khan University reported that a new Institute to study Islamic civilisations should be founded to 'strengthen research and teaching on the heritage of Muslim society in all its historic diversity'. It is interesting that this Institute for the Study of Muslim Civilisations was established in London, England so that it could be beyond any government influence or interference. It is also interesting that the word 'Islamic' was omitted from the original title and substituted with 'Muslim'. The Aga Khan University is, of course, subject to Pakistani law, which requires all universities to ensure that there are compulsory Islamic courses for all students within universities. Governments in majority Muslim countries are often alarmed by fundamentalist Islamic scholars, especially those who are free to espouse their views in the safety of Western societies. Anwar (1987: 25) notes that it was Muslim student activists based in London who denounced the Malaysian government for being 'un-Islamic'.

It is normally Arab money through the Organisation of the Islamic Conference that promotes Centres for Islamic studies in the West, and even establishes Islamic universities in Africa and Asia such as the Islamic University of Mbale in southern Uganda, founded in 1988. Islamic centres have been established in many universities in the West in order that opportunities might be provided for Muslims and non-Muslims to reach Islamic knowledge at an academic level. In Nigeria the Department of Arabic and Islamic Studies was opened in 1976 in the University of Ilorin. Some of these centres would not be tolerated within some Muslim countries or at least would have their affairs scrutinised by the state or university authorities. It is their location within Western democracies that allows them to conduct unhindered research and scholarship. By so doing, these centres are not hostage to any particular Muslim government. These centres seek to study authentic Muslim approaches to knowledge, but there can arise clashes with governments in Muslim countries which may have adopted certain Western laws and customs. Some of these governments are concerned to eradicate the rise of militant and intolerant Islam; generally governments in Muslim countries seek fully to control their higher education systems. One of the recommendations of the First World Conference on Muslim Education held in Mecca in 1977 was to establish an international centre for education, but the Saudi government insisted that this centre should be part of one of its own universities – the University of Makkah, and the government abolished it soon after its establishment. Governments in majority Muslim countries and individuals do not necessarily co-operate with each other in the provision of higher education, which again illustrates that there are many differences between them. Islam does not necessarily unite Muslims in higher education, for there are indeed many different versions of Muslim/Islamic higher education institutions and they are increasingly clashing with one another.

Mission statements – Jewish

The question that has consistently faced Jewish educators is whether the goal is the higher education of Jews or simply establishing Jewish-sponsored higher education institutions: whether the Jewish community should educate a lay community or prepare rabbis and religious teachers. Only a few within the Jewish community have objected to secular education sponsored by Jews, and have favoured the establishment of rabbinical seminaries alone. There has always been a tension between secular and Torah studies within the Jewish community. There are three Jewish higher education institutions on the East coast of America that provide an interesting contrast in terms of mission, but all three seek to prepare the leaders of the Jewish community and larger world. Two of them are ranked highly as research universities – Yeshiva and Brandeis, founded in 1927 and 1948 respectively. Both are 'critical mass' institutions according to Benne's typology. Yeshiva is the oldest and largest university under Jewish auspices in the USA and it maintains four campuses in New York, as well as affiliated campuses in Los Angeles and Jerusalem. In

1970 Yeshiva revised its charter to become, officially at least, a secular university in order to receive state and federal funding, despite vigorous student and faculty protests. Despite this, Yeshiva still seeks to advance the values and knowledge of the Torah and Western civilisation and also specifically seeks to provide active solidarity with the State of Israel. The university is ranked among the top 50 research universities in America and it seeks to integrate knowledge with 'the richness of Jewish culture and thought'. Wolfe (2002: 30) describes how universities like Yeshiva depend on their core constituencies because their identity is largely shaped by these faith constituencies. Consequently, the future nature of faith-based universities and colleges will be linked to the changing nature of their faith-based communities. In the case of Yeshiva University it is largely responding to the resurgence of orthodoxy within Judaism, but Wolfe warns that it may become isolated from the American mainstream in higher education as a result of too much orthodox influence.

In contrast, Brandeis seeks to embody the highest Jewish ethical and cultural values but states that it is a non-sectarian university open to all. The university seeks to retain a Jewish identity whilst adhering to the norms accepted at secular universities. It makes a distinction between a university supported by the Jewish community and one that is exclusively for Jewish students. It is a university that has been unclear about its identity ever since its foundation. It struggles with its identity in trying to provide a meaningful definition in the mission statement. As Fox (1993–94) says: 'One can see here the effort to separate the university from Judaism while keeping it connected to the Jewish community that is a major source of financial support, and to the "unique cultural perspective" which is ascribed to that community.' Brandeis University has therefore been viewed as suspect by orthodox Jews, who object to its non-religious Jewish identity, but its identity and purpose may eventually be altered by the growing strength and general influence of the orthodox Jewish community.

Yeshiva and Brandeis universities are private and sponsored by the Jewish community, as is the Hebrew College in Boston (there are many small private Hebrew colleges in the USA) which has a more limited curriculum and specialises in the study of Jewish religion but is again open to all. All three institutions are overwhelmingly Jewish in their student bodies and would correspond to the 'critical mass' model of a university or college. There is also the Baltimore Hebrew University which exists to promote Jewish scholarship and explore Jewish tradition, as does the Hebrew Union College in Los Angeles and the University of Judaism in California which seeks to promote Jewish heritage. There are many Jewish centres attached to various American universities, which seek to study Jewish civilisation in its historical and contemporary dimensions. Ingall (1995) has studied the goals and mission of the Hebrew College in Boston at different points in its history and concludes that it has managed to preserve its specifically Jewish purpose even with the great expansion and diversification of courses offered.

Outside the USA there are Jewish universities in Israel such as the Bar-Ilan University which is the largest and which seeks to 'develop students who bear a deep commitment to Jewish community' and also to help rebuild Jewish identity. The Hebrew University of Jerusalem was begun in 1918 and opened in 1925 as the 'University of the Jewish People'. It therefore pre-dates the foundation of the State of Israel, but is not a specifically religious university. The University of Tel Aviv has a 'commitment to Israeli society and the Jewish people'. The University of Haifa in northern Israel appears to be more pluralist and seeks to serve the interests of Israeli society, including Arabs and Jews. The Jewish University of Moscow, founded in 1991, provides detailed Jewish study programmes. There are also centres attached to mainstream universities all over Europe such as the University of Jewish Studies in Heidelberg, Germany. Not all of these centres and institutions promote a religious conception of Judaism, as some also address primarily ethnic and secular conceptions of Judaism. Nevertheless, there has been an impressive increase in religiously affiliated institutions of higher education across all three faiths around the world in recent years.

Conclusion

Whilst it can be precarious to generalise about the difference between mission statements of religiously affiliated colleges and universities today and those of around 40 years ago, it can nevertheless be said that the latter always began with a statement of faith – a theological rationale for the institution's existence. Today many Christian institutions more often than not begin with a statement of educational principles. They also, together with Jewish institutions, emphasise community involvement, the promotion of justice and service learning as unique features of their mission, but these Christian universities are not so unique. Such institutions lack a substantive definition of their religious identity and consequently their vague definitions of religious purpose lead to ambiguity and ambivalence about what they represent and how such definitions impact on every facet of their institutions. Often these kinds of religiously affiliated institutions relegate the substance of their religious identity to specific areas of university and college life, such as chaplaincy, special courses, centres or chairs. In so doing they do no more than many secular universities. There are, however, still many religiously affiliated institutions that begin with a clear statement of faith but there are clearly many more that do not. Representatives of forty-five colleges and universities – Jewish, Protestant and Catholic – have met at Valparaiso University between 1996 and 1998 for a series of conferences on religion and higher education sponsored by the Lilly Endowment. Their purpose was to clarify, strengthen and enrich the relation between religion and academic endeavour.

The conclusion of these discussions has been that the challenge for religiously affiliated universities is that they need to begin translating their religious distinctiveness into a religious institutional academic mission. Burtchaell (1998) claims that 'it is fair to say that while every one of these (religious) colleges was from the start identified with a specific church, denomination or movement, there was no manifest intensity in that identification, no very express concern to confirm or to be intellectually confirmed or critical within the particular faith or communion. There was hardly any expectation that the quality of faith in the church stood to be strongly served by the college.' The positive conclusion from the Lilly Seminars and Conferences is that Christian institutions can and should cultivate a distinct ethos together with maintaining their religious rituals and nurturing virtues and altruistic service in their students.

There appears to be some new emphasis on the integration of faith and learning as opposed to restricting questions of faith and practice to departments of philosophy and theology. A number of religiously affiliated colleges and universities of all three faiths believe it to be important for students to see the relevance of their faith commitments in each of their 'secular' intellectual areas. The University of Notre Dame in the USA requires all undergraduates to take some philosophy and theology courses. These courses are seldom doctrinal in content, but they are intended to give students some access to an intellectual culture that informs Christian understanding and faith. Notre Dame University in Australia does exactly the same and new universities in the USA, such as Christendom, St Thomas Aquinas and Thomas More College, have developed distinct religious courses which are compulsory for all students, and increasing numbers of universities in Muslim countries are doing the same. At the institutional level, religious identity is intended to serve academic goals by providing a framework for integrating disciplinary pursuits and perspectives. Nevertheless, many academics in religiously affiliated institutions are unsure or ignorant of what a religious intellectual tradition would entail for them. The debates that colleges and universities have about their religious mission are often in response to changes within the faith communities they claim to represent or echo in some way.

The reality for many religiously affiliated institutions within the Christian tradition has been that 'the religious origins of an institution neither presupposes ongoing commitment, nor necessarily makes it easy to sustain Christian visibility' (Bone 2004: 221). Within Britain, Niblett (1998) has noted that higher education and Christianity 'have more and more come to inhabit quite separate provinces'. The contrast with America illustrates that America is much less of a secular society than Britain, but there is often talk of the 'crisis of secularisation' and some religious communities respond by separating themselves from the mainstream in higher education – removing themselves from the secular arena. Neuhaus (1996) identifies several characteristics of a Christian university which include that it must have a clear identity and purpose grounded in Christian faith and that it must be affiliated to a particular denomination for immediate recognition. He believes the faculty should be supportive of the mission and that academic freedom should be seen within the search for ultimate religious truth and that those who freely choose to teach in such institutions should be encouraged to pursue this truth. He believes that these institutions should be 'communities of conviction'. Neuhaus rejects the idea that a Christian university can have a 'dual identity' both separately 'Christian' and a 'university' at the same time. He observes that whilst a Church affiliation may not make a university Christian it can help sustain Christian conviction. As he notes, *Ex Corde Ecclesiae* states that the Christian university is not a Church but it is from the Church and ought to serve the Church. Neuhaus (1996) concludes that 'A university that is not integral to the Christian mission will in time become alien to the Christian mission.' Religiously affiliated universities need therefore to maintain a distinctive profile and religious identity as opposed to becoming part of the bland uniformity which often represents the mainstream universities.

The Western system of higher education, which is so influential around the world, has drifted away from its Judeo-Christian foundations, but in some ways continues to live off the capital of this religious tradition. These secular and Western currents of thought have many of their origins in Christianity and as the secular thought of a culture is influenced by Christianity it is unlikely to be entirely secular as certain Christian ideas are preserved. Nevertheless, a more secular set of presuppositions divorced from Christianity has emerged and now guides the general direction of higher education. Christian and other faith-based institutions cease to have a meaningful religious identity when they either tacitly agree or actively pursue this kind of secular agenda. For Avery Dulles (1991) it is 'the slippery path that led from denominational to generic Christianity, then to vaguely defined religious values, and finally to total secularisation'. Is it inevitable that all religiously affiliated colleges and universities should follow this path? The long-term trend appears to suggest an erosion of an explicitly religious commitment. Many Christian higher education institutions have suffered from goal displacement as they see their originating and sustaining spirit eroded. Jewish and Muslim institutions fear the same process by which the religious values become gradually subordinated to 'academic' values, and only these 'academic values' being regarded by the secular academic community as vital to the survival and progress of university education. At the very least it results in a muted and thinned-out language for mission and identity, which is deliberately made acceptable to the secular public domain. This process, when it goes unchecked, results in a loss of the institution's *raison d'être* and renders it almost impossible to identify or determine what it means to be a religiously affiliated college or university. Ultimately, religiously affiliated colleges and universities need to look upon their sponsoring religious body or faith as the source of their identity. It may be that religiously affiliated colleges and universities are merely reflecting the quality and depth of religion found in the sponsoring religious body. They perhaps need, as Burtchaell has argued, to see themselves as an 'academic household of faith'. In the end even the most religiously inspired mission statement cannot meaningfully guide the practices and policies of a college or university if they are hopelessly out of touch with the institutional reality.

Chapter 3

Faith and governance

Introduction

The societies or gilds that constituted the early 'universities' desired and sought forms of governance that would provide them with a degree of security and sustainability. Developing well-defined administrative functions was vital. Consequently, the actions and decisions of the Church were crucial for the survival and orderly governance of these universities (see Boyd 1950: 143f.). In 1212 Pope Innocent III issued a Bull which forbade the Chancellor, a local ecclesiastic who effectively decided who could teach, to exact oaths of obedience from the masters and insisted that he should confer licences (degrees) on all candidates put forward by the masters of Paris. Pope Gregory IX subsequently issued the Bull *Parens Scientiarum* in 1231, which has been called the Magna Carta of the university. The Bull contained numerous privileges for masters including the masters' rights to organise their own course of lectures, which was defined and recognised. The masters as a corporate body could make their own statutes and compel their membership to respect them. The Chancellor's power over the masters was further reduced as were the powers of the local civil and ecclesiastical authorities. Whilst this Bull applied only to the University of Paris, other universities benefited from each other's experiences. Papal foundation Bulls provided a twofold purpose for the university: vocational education and education for its own sake. These universities also realised that their standing as academic institutions was hugely enhanced if their founding charter came from the universal sovereign – the Pope. That is why the well-established universities of Paris and Oxford sought such a charter from the Papacy after their initial foundations in the thirteenth century. By 1500, there were 79 universities in existence and the only limits on their autonomy and governance was their subordination to the Papacy. The Reformation and the Enlightenment both seriously changed this relationship of the university to the Catholic Church.

The governance of modern religiously affiliated institutions of higher education has grown and developed in response to various local situations, whether nationally or regionally. The governance of these religiously affiliated institutions are often beset with ambiguities. Therefore, there is great diversity in the external and internal governance of religiously affiliated institutions. Some are legally owned by the state whilst others are private, but subject to considerable external regulatory state authorities. In some parts of the world, governments generally lack the fiscal resources to respond to the rising demand for higher education, so they allow religious organisations to establish universities to meet this demand. For example, at the University of San Carlos in Guatemala, founded in 1676, as a Catholic university, the government provided insufficient resources for the university to such a degree that the Catholic Church decided to found Rafael Landivar University in 1966 under its own control. Indeed, it could be said that all governments, whilst attempting to control university quality and standards, encourage some form of diversity in governance within higher education. Theoretically, this allows a market in higher education in which institutions can determine their own mission and relate this to the perceived needs of students. It also allows the student freedom to choose their university and is perhaps why religiously affiliated institutions have proved popular among students. Nevertheless, the gap between costs and income in many religiously affiliated universities is causing them considerable financial strain.

It is often said that Western Europe is the most secularised continent in the world and that this very fact raises a number of problems for religious foundations. In France, for example, the legal status of Catholic universities can be difficult because the state favours a secular worldview in the public sphere and aims to confine religion to the private domain. In Germany, Spain, the Netherlands, Poland and Portugal Catholic universities and faculties are protected legally by a Concordat between the state and the Vatican. In Belgium, Germany, the Netherlands, Poland and Hungary Catholic universities are financed by the state, whilst in France and Portugal Catholic universities are private institutions and charge fees. There is also a small number of Protestant universities in Europe that are a product of the Reformation and these universities train much of the Protestant clergy, but in almost all other respects they are very similar to secular universities. In Germany there are three such universities and the German Protestant Churches are very active in these universities, but not at a governance level.

Protestant governance

The colonial colleges established in America, whether public or religious, were generally controlled by Protestant clergymen. However, there was opposition to this clerical control, which Marsden and Longfield (1992: 14f.) detail and claim was identified with classicism and amateurism. A number of Protestant reformers sought to free the colleges from clerical control and through this process there emerged a separate profession, distinct from the clergy. Marsden and Longfield (1992: 21) demonstrate how liberal Protestants allied themselves with secularism and promoted Christianity as open to all kinds of cultural responsibilities. Nevertheless, even when colleges had formally dropped any links with Christianity, they would often employ the claim that the public university had a 'Christian ethos', a phrase often merely used to exclude Jews (Marsden and Longfield 1992: 27). Marsden believes that technological advance, professionalisation of academics, and secularism combined to produce an 'aggressive pluralistic secularism' which appeared in the 1960s and questioned all religious beliefs as mere social constructs. Organised religion became peripheral to higher education. Longfield (Marsden and Longfield 1992: 146) shows how at Yale in 1899 ten clergymen still sat on the corporation which ran the university. By 1921 this had been reduced to four, and the first layman was appointed in 1899 as President. It was not until 1926 that compulsory chapel was abolished and not until the 1960s that Yale abandoned the rhetoric of being a Christian institution.

In 1990 the 69 Presidents of the Presbyterian colleges and universities issued a manifesto that raised a number of challenges they collectively faced and pointed to the religious decline in the wider Presbyterian Church. The manifesto also raised issues about competition for students, the implications of federal and state policies on higher education, changing student attitudes etc., and concluded with the bold statement that 'the Presbyterian Church could be close to the point where its involvement in higher education might be lost forever'. The legal and institutional links between Protestant denominations and their institutions of higher education were certainly eroded by the 1960s and in many cases ceased to exist in any recognisable sense. Protestant colleges and universities had traditionally a written covenant between Church and college which detailed what they could expect from each other. Some maintained this covenant, but for others, gradually and unconsciously, these mutual expectations disappeared.

Beaty and Lyon (1995) investigated Baylor University's attempt to maintain its twin identities, being religious and being academic. The university has recently attempted to correspond to the 'critical mass' model of a university. Baylor University was founded and sponsored by the Baptists of Texas and yet in 1990 a majority of Baylor's trustees voted to redefine its historic relationship to Texas Baptists by amending its charter with the state of Texas. The change established a new Board of Regents, which has sole responsibility for the governance of Baylor University. Since this change two other Baptist institutions (Furman and Samford universities) have made similar changes. Shorter College in Georgia has also attempted to break the legal and formal links between itself and its local Baptist Convention, which founded and continues to support the college. The move towards disengagement from the college's sponsoring denomination began with a dispute about appointments to the board of trustees. The college sought to appoint more liberal nominees, but the Georgia Baptist Convention vetoed them and tried to impose its own choices together with threatening to withhold $9 million in funding unless its nominees were accepted. The College Board of Trustees refused to accept the Convention's nominees and sought a court judgement about the legality of the Convention's move, and also sought to separate itself from the Baptist Convention. The court supported the college and in this way the college separated itself from the Baptist Convention and became a self-perpetuating board, independent of all outside influence. The threat of sponsors to withhold funding for religiously affiliated colleges and universities is perhaps less serious today because of other newer sources of income. Shorter College still sought legal advice to secure this funding even though it had technically become a Christian community separate from the Baptist Convention.

The Baptist Convention responded by appealing against the lower court's decision, and in March 2004 a higher court overturned the decision on the basis that the existing trustees of the college had illegally tried to remove the Baptist Convention of Georgia as the rightful owners of the college. The legal battle continues, with the college appealing against this decision. It is interesting that the college, whilst seeking total independence from its sponsoring and founding denomination, sought to preserve its general Christian (not Baptist) heritage. The Convention, on the other hand, wanted committed Baptists to serve on the Board of Trustees and was concerned that the college authorities did not rein in professors who seriously questioned Baptist doctrines in their teaching and research. The college was concerned with its academic reputation and feared that the Baptist Convention was set upon a conservative, religious takeover of the college.

There appears to be a discernible trend of Baptist colleges and universities distancing themselves from denominational sponsorship (Hull 1992). Brackney (2001) has looked at how six Baptist colleges and universities have moved from being denominationally related to being 'non-sectarian'. The reasons he gives for this 'secularisation' process is 'inadequate financial resources, paucity of qualified leadership in both administration and governance areas . . . and changed objectives of the colleges and universities'. Baylor continues to claim that it is a Christian university and as the largest Baptist university in the world its mission statement reads: 'The mission of Baylor University is to educate men and women for worldwide leadership and service by integrating academic excellence and Christian commitment . . . dedicated to Christian principles.' Nevertheless, there appears to be a trend for most Christian affiliated higher education institutions to follow the general pattern of governance in secular institutions. However, there is a sense in which these religiously affiliated institutions are on the periphery of higher education and, for some, the more emphatically religious they become, the more marginalised from the mainstream they appear. It is often this fear of marginality that acts as a powerful tool for secularisation and for the separation from their founding denominations. The question that needs to be answered is whether religiously affiliated colleges and universities face the dilemma of having to choose between a distinctive religious identity or a strong academic reputation. Mixon *et al.* (2004) are one of the few groups of academics who have researched this question, and their results suggest that this dilemma is more apparent than real. Their empirical study of over sixty colleges and universities found no evidence of religious universities losing either academic credibility or reputation through an emphasis on religious identity and that such a direction did not affect either recruitment of staff or students. They conclude (2004: 416) 'secularisation, while historically common, is not currently necessary in the pursuit of a strong academic reputation'. Consequently, those within higher education who have a tendency to equate enhanced academic quality with a secularisation process have little or no evidence to support their belief.

In England there are 15 remaining religiously affiliated colleges and universities. In the 1950s Christian perspectives on higher education retained a significant presence in public and in some academic discussions, whatever the decline in private belief and practice. Moberly's *The Crisis of the University*, published in 1949, resisted the idea of the notion of a 'Christian University' on the grounds that insights from Christianity already reinforced the 'basis of values and virtues' which ought to characterise the university's intellectual endeavour, but he recognised that external forces represented the greatest threat to this tradition. Government legislation has certainly been one of the greatest threats to this tradition, especially as such legislation on the governance and funding of higher education has been extensive. It is in a way inevitable that in a system of higher education that depends almost entirely on central government for funding for its core activities of research and teaching that the government will increasingly determine the aims and practices of higher education itself. The colleges and universities expanded and required additional resources, but the religiously affiliated institutions were even more dependent on government-funded courses and many of them closed between 1970 and 2001 – falling from 54 to 15. Legislation also shifted power away from the trustees of these surviving religiously affiliated institutions and into the hands of the governors and senior management of the colleges. The powers of the trustees, representing the sponsoring religious community, have largely been reduced to making decisions about the disposal of sites when their colleges are forced to close. However, it has been argued that the incorporation of governing bodies can potentially increase the influence of the sponsoring tradition by effectively increasing that tradition's representation on the governing body. It is not clear that all would accept this argument: Burtchaell (1998: 827) acknowledged that 'legalities illustrate but need not control the character of the college'. Changing the legal charter of a religiously affiliated institution may not then necessarily alter its religious identity or affiliation.

In England, in recent years, with the establishment of a number of universities affiliated to the Church of England, it appears that for many, in terms of governance, these institutions are very much 'accidentally pluralist', if we use Benne's (2001: 51f.) classification. They are, it could be argued, largely secular institutions where religion has been disestablished from its defining role by a long and relentless secularisation process. Christianity has become one perspective among many in the academic strategy for organising the curriculum, and the main thrust of these institutions has become the practical educational task of equipping students with skills to find jobs. Academic departments rarely relate their objectives to the Christian mission of the institution. However, these institutions continue to respect their relationship with the Church of England, and there is still representation of the vision and ethos of the Anglican tradition in the university's life and governance. Most of these institutions have an Anglican majority on the governing body. It could be said that they retain a unique and rather complex set of governance arrangements which are a result of their religious mission and foundation. The Christian presence is still guaranteed in the form of ensuring the appointment of senior management who have an Anglican connection, particularly in the appointment of the principal and chaplain who must be communicant members of the Church of England. However, this strategy is accommodated within a fundamentally secular model for defining the identity and mission of the university. The Anglican connection neither dominates nor disappears, for as Benne (2001: 52) says of the representation of the sponsoring tradition on the governing body in the 'intentionally pluralist' model: 'Sufficient numbers of persons in the educational community must continue to be convinced that representation of the sponsoring heritage is a good thing. Since a growing majority of persons in this understanding are not part of the sponsoring tradition, it may become a "hard sell" to maintain even the modest representation of the heritage.' Benne also observes that such institutions tend to establish a centre or institute 'to remind their religious constituency that the voice of faith has not been ignored completely'.

Catholic governance

Clerical control was characteristic of Catholic higher education, and this has persisted longer than in Protestant higher education. The Catholic Church is made up of individual Catholics and communities linked with one another through many diverse ecclesial relationships. Therefore a Catholic university can be established by a religious community or by individual Catholics, acting singly or in association, but also with proper ecclesiastical approval. The University of Bologna, for example, was established by a group of lay Catholics for laymen to study Roman Law. It was later recognised by the Holy See, but tensions between ecclesiastical and secular authorities and the academic autonomy of universities was common in the Middle Ages. Today, in the Church's Code of Canon Law it is for the Holy See, or a national conference of bishops or an individual diocesan bishop, to recognise the university or college as Catholic. No college or university may assume the title Catholic without the formal consent of the local bishop or competent ecclesiastical authority. However, colleges and universities were established by an impressive array of religious congregations and orders – these institutions were independent of the local Catholic bishop and claimed to be in the tradition of Benedictine, Dominican, Jesuit, Josephine, Vincentian, or other Catholic religious tradition. Often this claim to be in the tradition of a particular religious order was vaguely expressed. It was these well-organised and disciplined semi-autonomous groups that largely established, staffed and funded the beginnings of Catholic higher education around the world. The Catholic University of America was opened in 1889 by the USA Catholic bishops and was the only university they controlled directly. All the others enjoyed a considerable degree of independence from local bishops.

There appeared to be two parallel authority structures in the governance of Catholic higher education – one episcopal and the other religious communities. This resulted in no one authority being in overall control and no national strategy on the part of the Church, which inevitably led to difficulty in co-ordinating the national Catholic higher education effort. Catholic higher education is structured more independently than Protestant colleges and there has never been any centralised control or plan for Catholic higher education. Catholic higher education was nevertheless once run at the discretion of owners/trustees, who were predominantly religious orders/congregations, although this was not the case with the earliest Catholic universities. They founded colleges and universities with a particular intention or mission in line with the order/congregation's religious and educational philosophy. Their responsibilities as owners/trustees were both legal and moral. The legal basis was derived from the ownership of the college or university in two senses. First, the title of the land and buildings was registered in the name of members of the order. Second, the order or congregation owns the mission for which the college or university was established. As legal owners, the order or congregation owns the college or university in trust for the purposes (mission) to which the order/congregation is committed. Therefore the order has two distinctive and important types of responsibility in relation to the colleges and universities with which it is associated. First, to ensure that the institution, its ethos and direction, is consistent with the founding intention. Second, to ensure that the institution is well managed and funded. It is also the order/congregation's responsibility to interpret the mission of the institution in the light of prevailing circumstances by ensuring that the college or university remains true to its founding mission. This arrangement served the Church well, but did not survive the 1960s.

There has been a decline since the 1960s in the membership of religious congregations and orders, which has resulted in their physical presence in universities being visibly less in terms of the number of academic staff and administrators drawn from the religious congregation or order. Lay people increasingly became members of the governance of these universities at the invitation of the religious order and ironically there was an increase in the demands from the religious to be set free from external control exercised by religious authorities – the same religious authorities to whom they had previously vowed obedience. Catholic lay staff were also joining secular associations such as the American Association of University Professors, and this led to a number of tensions and clashes with clerical authorities who tried to oppose such moves (see Leo 1967: 193f.). Gleason (1995: 315f.) describes how the Sister President of Webster College in St Louis in 1967 announced that 'the very nature of higher education is opposed to juridical control by the Church' and how she secularised her college and continued in office without the embarrassment of being subject to religious obedience. The President, Sr Jacqueline Grennan, soon left her religious congregation, but not her post of President (Burtchaell 1998: 593). Clearly, she felt that she needed to be free of ecclesiastical control, not of her own control, but that of her immediate superiors. College presidents were now elected by their board of trustees rather than designated for this post by ecclesiastical authorities. This became the pattern for many Catholic institutions of higher education in America and in many other countries that were influenced by this American model of higher education. Webster College (now University) has since renounced any connection with the Catholic Church. In 1968 Manhattanville College renounced its 'Catholic' identity and declared itself to be 'secular'. This was partly to receive 'Bundy Money' (money provided by the State of New York to religious institutions which declared themselves non-sectarian), but the religious Sister who was President of the college argued that secularisation was part of an effort to secure more academic respect. However, the move towards greater autonomy was often associated with fears that the Vatican might intervene to exercise some control over Catholic universities.

Religious communities of priests, sisters and brothers are subject to ecclesiastical authority in the sense that they take vows of obedience to their superiors, who in turn are subject to higher Church authority. The local bishop only has an indirect influence over the governance of these religious communities. Consequently, when a religious community of Jesuits or Benedictines establishes a university, the entire enterprise, mission, property, staffing are essentially directed by the leaders of that religious community whether they are actually working in the university or not. Under this arrangement Catholic universities were still formally and legally connected to the Church hierarchy. However, religious orders and congregations began formally separating their colleges from their own communities and established instead mainly lay boards of trustees. The discretion they once enjoyed in running these colleges and universities was progressively restrained by the need for external funding and by the major upheavals after Vatican II. The University of Notre Dame transferred control to a predominantly lay board in 1967. However, it is important to note that certain forms of control were maintained. The Congregation of the Holy Cross, which owned Notre Dame, inserted certain clauses into the handover document which required that the President should be a member of the Congregation and that the very highest governing body of the university (a seven-member board of fellows), though appointed by the predominantly lay trustees, is required to have a majority of Congregation priests on it unless this requirement is overturned by the Fellows themselves. This transfer met with some limited opposition from within this particular religious community but surprisingly none from the local bishops.

The thesis appeared to be that these religious communities did not really 'own' the property of these universities and colleges, but that they were held on trust for the benefit of the general public. This thesis is highly contestable as these institutions were held in trust for the Catholic community, but this false argument effectively aided the removal of almost all Catholic colleges from ecclesiastical authority and ownership. Also in 1967 there appeared the 'Land O'Lakes' Statement on the nature of the contemporary Catholic university, made by 26 scholars and officials of nine major Catholic universities. It declared that 'the Catholic university must have a true autonomy and academic freedom in the face of authority of whatever kind, lay or clerical, external to the academic community itself'. This statement became a manifesto and a declaration of independence from the Catholic hierarchy (see Gleason 1995: 316). The emphasis on autonomy, academic freedom and independence was to mark these Catholic universities as civic institutions serving the nation and they began to lack any customary legal standing as Catholic institutions either in canon or civil law. The role of trustees also appeared to have become one of protecting the largely secular interests of their college or university. The Catholic college or university was no longer seen by many as an extension of the Church or defined as part of the apostolic work of the Church – engaged in the specialised ministry of higher education. Cuninggim (1995: 65) has suggested that neo-conservatives today are attempting 'to develop a normative account of the College–Church relationship, with the Church as the axis, or pivot, or fulcrum, and the College as a radiating arm or element'. He advocates that the college should be the pivot in the relationship. Nevertheless, there was a feeling in the 1970s that Catholic higher education had been lost to secularism and that there had been a loss of Church control. Despite these developments, colleges and universities that had legally declared themselves 'non-sectarian' and 'independent' remained on the list of official Catholic institutions contained in diocesan directories and were still recognised by the local bishop as 'Catholic', irrespective of what course they took. Consequently, Catholic foundations were able to continue as recognised 'Catholic' institutions by the mere addition of their name to a list in a directory, which seemed to be the only criterion available to judge whether they were still considered Catholic by the Church.

The Jesuits, who controlled about a third of Catholic higher education in the USA, actively encouraged other Catholic higher education institutions to disengage from their religious trusts, and in their journal *America* they argued that by separating their colleges from their order they could better 'Catholicise' them and that this could be a liberating experience for the faculty. The Jesuit definition of Catholicism appeared to include all people of goodwill. Some, e.g. Burtchaell (1998), have argued that the mission statements of these colleges, in language selected by the faculty, was no less than a cover for the real process of secularisation that was taking place below. With the decline in religious available to teach and administer, the universities began to employ lay Catholics, ex-religious and non-Catholics in larger numbers, and some colleges and universities eventually secured a majority of non-Catholics on their faculty. The idea that there should be a majority of Catholics on the faculty was dismissed as impossible and even undesirable. It is important to note that the bishops in America did nothing to prevent these developments and some appeared not to know what was happening. The Vatican did attempt to intervene in the 1970s but it was clear that neither the bishops nor the Vatican could influence developments in America at this time. Many Jesuits argued that nothing much had changed and that their universities were still Catholic, but in reality it was left to the institution itself to make itself 'Catholic' without any direction from the Church. Had Catholic property been alienated for secular purposes? This was not clear, as in the new charter documents there were often requirements that only religious should be presidents of colleges and it was unclear whether the property belonged to the religious congregation or order concerned or whether they had control over it in some way. What was clear was that property, formally held under a trust for the advancement of Catholicism and paid for by Catholics, was now being used for secular purposes.

With the decline in the number of Jesuits it was decided by them that the laity should now animate their institution with a religious Jesuit mission, but Burtchaell (1998: 714) describes this as the 'rhetoric of fantasy', since the Jesuits were effectively claiming to be applying a Jesuit spirit through the lay staff when they did not even ask questions about their faith commitments at appointment interviews. In a sense many religious congregations and orders confused the issue of Catholic identity by attempting to incorporate into the new and growing lay leadership of their universities their own particular religious charism. Lay academics were often viewed as 'more secular' and less religious and were accordingly asked to take on the charism of the particular religious congregation or order. This charism was a way to conceptualise for lay people the core values of the college or university, but it effectively avoided preparing the laity for positions of leadership on broader Catholic terms. These attempts to *impose* a Jesuit charism on the laity may have effectively denied the laity their own particular lay Catholic charism. Burtchaell (1998: 606) believes that the directing spirit for the changes that took place 'was an entrepreneurial autonomy that resisted deferring to any agenda larger than that of each president's campus'. It may also be the case that some religious congregations and orders used lay people to try and retain their own control over the college or university.

Effectively Catholic higher education saw an expansion in student numbers in the 1960s, coupled with a reduction in religious men and women willing to continue teaching within it. The Church also experienced relative turmoil as a result of the attacks upon it, which were largely led by clerics. As Gleason (1995: 306) outlines: when word broke out that the President of the Catholic University of America banned four liberal speakers – all priests, including Hans Kung – from speaking at the university in 1963, a number of Catholic bishops expressed their public disapproval of the President's action. The publicity hugely aided Kung's speaking tour of America. With a new emphasis on freedom, religious authority was undermined and resisted, particularly with a series of academic freedom cases, at the same point in time when Catholic higher education was being reorganised in a secular direction coupled with the laicisation of boards of trustees and theology departments. The religious orders were literally giving their institutions away and lay and non-Catholic faculty began to predominate. The emphasis on quality and academic excellence following Ellis's (1955) famous article in which he bemoaned the current state of Catholic intellectual life simply meant that these terms were defined by secular accrediting agencies. This process met with silence from the bishops who seemed largely to accept these new models of secular governance. Hruby (1978) captures the post-Vatican II atmosphere of the late 1970s when he called for Catholic institutions to be completely open and free, with chaplaincy teams being formed to minister to students, not only with lay Catholics doing the ministering, but with non-Catholics included in these pastoral teams. In predicting the future of Catholic universities and colleges he recognised that 'it [the Catholic college] will risk internal dissension and external criticism as it reaches out to the "People of God", but the risk of remaining exclusivist is the greater danger and, just possibly, the greater sin'. The shift to the 'intentionally pluralist' model of a religiously affiliated institution was a direct consequence of such reasoning. One other powerful tool was used to justify this secularisation process. The colleges and universities had few endowments and with their expansion money was becoming a serious concern.

By the 1970s and 1980s there was diminishing funding available from the Church and religious orders and so there was a need to increase income to fund the growing number of students. The Supreme Court in 1947, in the decision of Everson vs. Board of Education, declared that 'no tax in any amount, large or small, can be levied to support any religious activities or institutions'. This 'no-funding' principle for religiously affiliated institutions continued until the 1960s when some federal funds were made available, but on strict conditions that included the following: a religiously affiliated university could not discriminate in the hire of staff, could not have compulsory attendance at religious services, could not compel attendance at religious courses and did not indoctrinate in religion and upheld academic freedom. It seemed that religiously affiliated institutions had to declare themselves to be non-sectarian and open to all if they were to receive public funds for the 'secular' components of their courses. In New York State a law approving funds for private colleges was passed in 1968 – the so called 'Bundy money' after the Bill's author. An amendment to this Act forced religiously affiliated institutions to demonstrate that they were primarily 'institutions of higher education' and not a 'religious institution'. As a result, in Catholic institutions, religious symbolism on campuses (small chapels) and in classrooms (crucifixes) began to disappear and clergy began to disappear from trustee boards. All the mainline Churches campaigned to access federal funds on equal terms with other mainstream institutions in a manner that 'respected' the need for an appropriate separation between Church and State. Eligibility for government aid therefore varied with the amount of control exercised over the colleges and universities by the Churches. However, in the short term this policy of survival ensured that the Churches diluted their control over their institutions, but the long-term cost has been for many a serious dilution of distinctiveness with a corresponding increase in state and federal regulation. It has encouraged a secularising process, particularly in the curriculum and appointment of staff.

The establishment of lay boards separated from Church authority was only partly dictated by the need to ensure that these religiously affiliated institutions were eligible for funds. However, a number of religiously affiliated colleges have been taken or have gone to court to challenge decisions made for or against funding them by states. The Lemon-Kurtzman case in 1971 is often quoted in the literature as the one which introduced the 'pervasively sectarian' test. This requires courts of law to determine whether funding recipients are so religious that government aid is equivalent to the establishment of religion – which is contrary to the American Constitution. The Supreme Court ruled that colleges must have a 'predominant higher education mission' in order 'to provide students with a secular education'. Federal money cannot be used for funding seminarians but rather must be used exclusively for secular purposes. Catholic and Protestant institutions therefore opened their doors to all, hired staff not associated with their particular denomination, and abandoned any attempt to require attendance at either religious services or religious courses. Most court cases since have upheld the rights of religiously affiliated colleges to receive state and federal aid, although some lower courts still occasionally interpret the 'pervasively sectarian' test strictly in order to discriminate against religious institutions. However, it appears this aid was only a secondary reason for the secularisation of colleges, as there appears to be wide scope of funding and accrediting arrangements that leaves ample space for a institution to remain distinctly

Catholic or Protestant. Nevertheless, religiously affiliated institutions became ever more dependent on different forms of federal and state funding to sustain their activities and questions about whether their independence and Christian witness could be compromised have arisen since.

O'Brien (1994: 118) states three main obstacles to a clear Catholic educational vision: 'separate incorporation (giving the college a legal status independent of the Church and her agencies), professionalisation (making faculty appointments according to criteria in each discipline, following the practice of the best secular schools without much attention to specifically religious concerns), and internal diversity'. Many Catholic institutions are so diversified that it is difficult for them to have any explicit Catholic content in these courses. Therefore, Catholic colleges and universities have no common template of organisation, no common vision and differ in size, academic courses offered, and in the character of staff and students. They do all however claim some commitment to the Catholic faith, but this commitment is open to many interpretations of how it should be implemented. The severance from their legal Catholic ties now appears to have been completely unnecessary. Fordham University went to great trouble to say that the local Catholic Archbishop had no say whatsoever in the running of the college and removed the Catholic terminology from its charter. Zagano (1990) argues that the real reason for this was the desire for complete academic freedom and that a college's commitment to a particular religious view did not and does not affect funding from state or federal governments. In other words the whole episode was an internal problem within the Catholic Church. There appeared to be a desire to go beyond what was legally required to secure state and federal funding.

Paradoxically, the religious congregations and orders are currently attempting to create more control structures over their higher education institutions. They are in fact doing the opposite from what they claimed justified the changes in governance in the first place. This is taking place at a time of diminishing ability to fill faculty and administrative positions with committed members of the sponsoring religious order whose members have steadily decreased. Holtschneider and Morley (2000: 16), in a study of the governance of Catholic higher education, believe that efforts by religious congregations and orders to keep control over their institutions are inadequate and will eventually fail in the long term. Religious orders will not be able to exercise controls over their institutions as they themselves decline. They conclude that the colleges and universities will eventually shed the particular spirituality and culture that was characteristic of the founding religious order and will adopt a more broadly based Catholic character. They believe that the laity with a more 'universal Catholicism' will need to build a Catholic culture without the religious orders. The idea that religious congregations and orders are more concerned about the Catholicity of Catholic colleges and universities is no longer sustainable.

Since the publication in 1990 of the Apostolic Constitution 'On Catholic Universities', entitled *Ex Corde Ecclesiae*, 'From the Heart of the Church', and subsequent Catholic Church legislation created to help implement the text of *Ex Corde Ecclesiae*, there has been a more intense debate about who controls and what is an authentic Catholic institution of higher education. *Ex Corde Ecclesiae* has presented 'a sort of magna carta' for Catholic institutions of higher learning – a mission statement. However, the attempts by Church authorities to apply that vision through concrete juridic or legislative norms has been resisted by officials within many of the institutions they attempt to address. The Catholic Church seemed no longer prepared to cede its investment in higher education to an increasingly secular culture. Section 1 of the document outlines the theological and pastoral principles, whilst section 2 provides a series of norms to help Catholic institutions fulfil the vision of Catholic identity and mission. The issues in question are multiple and complex: institutional autonomy vs. hierarchical oversight; academic freedom vs. doctrinal integrity; scholarly credibility vs. advancement of Church teaching; competition with secular peers vs. distinctive Catholic identity. The norms that *Ex Corde Ecclesiae* set out include: Catholic universities must be approved by the Church; the governing body or trustees of the university must be Catholics committed to the Church; the president or head of the Catholic university must be a Catholic; the Catholic university must recruit Catholic staff and not allow the university to exceed 50 per cent non-Catholic staff; those staff who teach theology must have a *mandatum* granted by the competent ecclesiastical authority. The purpose of the *mandatum* is to give bishops some jurisdiction over the Catholic theology taught in Catholic universities in an effort to preserve the Catholic nature of those universities. Catholic academics in theology who teach in a Catholic institution are required to have a mandate which recognises that they teach 'in full communion with the Church'. The document recognises that the Catholic university's autonomy is 'interior', not 'exterior'. Consequently, the president and governing body must manage the institution, but since the institution is freely in and of the Church, the local bishop or bishops may make observations or remonstrations, if need be, to an individual professor, to the president, or to the Catholic public at large, whenever they consider the situation so requires it. Clearly the role of the trustees is to protect the institution from external controls, but colleges and universities are not 'autonomous' from government agency requirements or from accrediting associations and generally accept these controls without much complaint. In contrast, any hint of external ecclesiastical control is met with strong opposition.

Catholic universities all over the world have entered into discussions with their local bishops about how best to implement the goals in *Ex Corde Ecclesiae*. These discussions have focused on the crucial issues of academic freedom, institutional independence and Catholic identity. Almost all these universities have legal autonomy and their constitutions or charters are incorporated under the country in which they are located. The internal governance of these institutions is in the hands of a board of trustees, governors, directors or whatever term is used to describe the governing body. *Ex Corde Ecclesiae* recognises this and says that the governance of these Catholic institutions is an 'internal' matter. It is therefore for the governing body to establish the conduct by which the institution operates. Only regulations or laws passed by the governing body of the university will bind the institution. Consequently, in order for the norms contained in *Ex Corde Ecclesiae* to be binding on the staff of these institutions the governing body must agree formally to be bound by them and incorporate them into their constitutions. Many Catholic universities in the world claim, usually with the endorsement of their local bishops, to have 'implemented' *Ex Corde Ecclesiae* as applied to their special circumstances, but in the USA discussions seem to continue. Some Catholic universities have resisted the document and upheld very hard versions of their own understanding of autonomy and academic freedom. Others claim to agree with the aims of *Ex Corde Ecclesiae*, but not the methods. Some presidents of Catholic institutions claim that they cannot reasonably be expected to fully implement *Ex Corde Ecclesiae* because the provisions in the document are a threat to Catholic influence in the wider community. They claim that serious legal challenges may arise and that it might prevent them from recruiting the most eminent thinkers to their colleges and universities. Nevertheless, the American Conference of Bishops has published 'draft' guidelines for the implementation of *Ex Corde Ecclesiae*. In reality the Vatican is seeking to require that local bishops approve the doctrinal suitability of professors of theology, and this is very much left to the local bishop to decide. For example, the process by which a *mandatum* is granted is a private matter between the bishop and the theologian. No national criteria have been produced to award the *mandatum* other than at the local bishop's discretion in the matter. Therefore it is impossible to say how many have been awarded. The Church is clearly limiting its efforts to theology departments, but even here it has little power to effect changes. John D'Arcy (2005), the bishop of Fort Wayne-South Bend, published his personal reflections on the *mandatum* in 2005 and called for 'ongoing dialogue' with academics. He certainly had no intention of making the *mandatum* a requirement for Catholic theologians in his diocese. Marsden (1994, 1997) believes that Catholic universities are where Protestant universities were in the 1930s – on the road to secularisation.

There is concern that some Catholic universities and colleges have pursued a secular model to such an extent that their Catholic identity and mission within the Church is no longer clear. Many are simply not Catholic in the sense of *Ex Corde Ecclesiae* or the provisions of Canon Law. Marist College, New York, is one example of a college established by a religious congregation of brothers that has been declared by the Archdiocese of New York as no longer Catholic and therefore no longer connected with the Church's jurisdiction.

The college, even today, claims to be inspired by the 'Marist spirit and heritage' and that its roots are in the 'Judeo-Christian' tradition. It still has Catholic Marist brothers teaching on the staff and as members of board of trustees. However, the mission statement emphasises that the college is an independent institution that has a 'commitment to excellence in education, a pursuit of higher human values, and dedication to the principle of service'. The mission statement says nothing about what these higher human values are and omits completely to mention any connection with the Catholic Church. As I have explained already, the college was founded officially in 1946 by the Marist Brothers but in 1969 they established an independent board of trustees to ensure state and federal aid. Other Catholic colleges followed this example in the 1960s. However, today the college has a predominantly lay board which is self-perpetuating without any official Catholic Church involvement; even the Marist brothers have lost influence, having effectively given their college away. After a number of complaints to the local bishop, who has in Canon Law the responsibility to determine whether colleges can bear the title 'Catholic', the Archdiocese simply issued a press release in 2003 declaring that the college was no longer recognised by the Church as a Catholic institution.

Marymount Manhattan College, which was founded by the religious congregation of the Sacred Heart of Mary, was also removed from the Archdiocese's list in 2005. The college itself had been clear about its own identity, claiming that it ceased to be Catholic in 1961, but for some reason the Archdiocese retained the college name on its official list of Catholic institutions, despite the fact that the religious dimension of this college had slowly withered away. Marymount is the fourth historically Catholic college to be officially recognised by the Church in recent years as non-Catholic – Marist, Nazareth and St John Fisher Colleges, all in the New York area, are the others. All of these institutions had become 'accidentally pluralist'. In a sense these colleges are but the tip of the iceberg as many others in the USA and beyond, whilst forming part of the institutional structure of Catholicism, lack the inner conviction to support Catholic policy (*Ex Corde Ecclesiae*) on higher education. It appears that it is no longer a question of these institutions publicly rejecting Catholicism, but rather they do not know what Catholicism means for their institutions. Why should the Church struggle to preserve 'accidentally pluralist' institutions as part of its ministry when they are unwilling to integrate Christianity into their institution and may bring the Church into disrepute? Many have argued that the Church should drop the pretence that there are still many Catholic institutions. Instead, the Church should let them go their own way in exchange for abandoning any claim to Church affiliation.

It was Newman in his *Idea of a University* (see Turner 1996: 159–60) who argued forcefully in the mid-nineteenth century that the Catholic university cannot exist externally to the Catholic Church. He believed that the direct presence of the Church was required in Catholic universities in order to 'steady' the university, 'mould its organisation', watch 'over its teaching' and knit 'together its pupils'. He believed that Catholic universities, left to themselves, and in spite of their claims to Catholic allegiance, end up distant from what it is to be Catholic. Unbelief, he thought, is in some shape unavoidable in an age of intellect. He concluded that 'a direct and active jurisdiction of the Church over it and in it is necessary, lest it should become the rival of the Church with the community at large in those theological matters which to the Church are exclusively committed'. However, Newman also had much to say about the independence of the university and in another Discourse in the *Idea* (see Turner 1996: 25) he says: 'As to the range of university teaching, certainly the very name of university is inconsistent with restrictions of any kind.' How, you might ask, is this to be reconciled with the authority of the Catholic Church over every aspect of the university? One answer is that the idea of a Catholic university does not demand that the control of the university should be in the hands of clerics. Nevertheless, the hierarchical nature of the Church means that the bishops are bound to retain some minimum control for the securing and maintaining of its Catholic character. The degree and manner of that control will vary according to circumstances. Newman believed that the Church had no need to fear learning and whilst the basic thrust of his thesis is that the Church and Catholic university are complementary, they are also truly interdependent. This interdependent arrangement that Newman proposed was to be based on freedom and trust. However, Newman's goals for a Catholic university normally receive pious lip service from Catholic presidents. Newman's idea of a university receives numerous tributes and ritualistic praise, but his influence on policy and planning in Catholic higher education has been minimal. It is why O'Connell (1994: 236) may be correct in claiming that modern Catholic institutions are little more than 'shadowy imitations of secular institutions'. With the decline in the 'Catholicity' of these institutions, Marsden (1992: 41) supports the proposal of 'building research and graduate study centers in key fields at the best institutions in various Christian sub-cultures'. By 'best institutions' he does not necessarily mean Catholic universities and opening religious research centres in secular universities is exactly what Jews and Muslims do already.

Muslim and Jewish governance

Islamic or Muslim universities are generally established by governments or sometimes privately by certain Muslim communities or wealthy individuals. Nevertheless, whether these universities are state or privately established, Muslim governments generally do not permit universities to be totally independent of the state. The Egyptian University founded in 1908, later changed to Cairo University, was taken over by the state in 1925 after having originally been founded by a group of Muslims. The Egyptian state now appoints the President of the university. The Islamic University in Malaysia was founded by no less than eight sponsoring governments, together with the Organisation of Islamic Conference. In Palestine there are six universities, all of which are private and each has a board of trustees. However, the custom in Muslim countries has been for the government to control Islamic discourse and practice, especially in higher education. Turkey declared itself to be a secular Republic in 1923 and proscribed the teaching of religion in all state education institutions. Islam was no longer the state religion and secularism was incorporated into the constitution. In other Muslim countries the governments have kept a tight rein on activities within mosques and universities and often seek compliance to the political order. In Tunisia, which has perhaps the most radically secularist government, the President simply closed the University of Al Zaytouna, which was the only overtly Muslim university in the country. Consequently, much of the momentum of Islamic radicalism is a reaction against failing secular regimes and authoritarian governments within Muslim countries. It is ironic that the West supports many of these oppressive governments in the belief that they are advancing modernity in their own societies. This is often achieved through a complete disregard for human rights and religion, and some would argue that the elites that run these Muslim societies have simply adopted the secular mind-set of their former colonial masters. These governments have, for a variety of reasons, failed to solve the economic, social and political problems in the Muslim world. The role of Islam in public life has become an increasingly urgent issue for these governments, especially as Islam itself has become the major ideology of dissent that they face. However, the nature of authority within some expressions of Islam is, through the lenses of Christians, problematic, because there is no central authority beyond the Koran and this leads to a multiplicity of voices claiming authority and a situation that weakens the force of a united Islamic protest in higher education. Of course, to some Muslims this is not at all problematic, but simply the way Islam is.

Nevertheless, this dissent is not uniform throughout the Muslim world. There is a wide range of perspectives on faith, politics and education within the Muslim community which have ethnic, economic, political as well as religious roots. Islam is not without variation and division, and there exists within the Muslim community different intensities of commitment to Islam itself. Clarke (1988: 2) describes two faces of Islam: first, the 'official' face, which is grounded in scrupulous concern for right belief and practice; second, the 'popular' face, which is sometimes shaped and moulded as much by local culture as it is by so-called 'pure' Islam. There are clearly therefore different factions within the Muslim community, who seek different patterns of interaction with the West and different versions of Islamic higher education. Rahman (1982: 4) bemoans the 'production of 'apologetic' literature that substitutes self-glorification for reform, which, he says, is 'virtually endless' and the 'atomistic' approach to the Koran, which is too often quoted out of context. It is certainly true that many Muslim scholars caricature the West for their own purposes and have idealistic notions of reviving what they claim to be the Islamic glory of the period between the seventh and thirteenth centuries. Many Islamic and Muslim universities also, and perhaps ironically, model their administrations and organisation on American secular universities. The university in Islamabad has a President and a Board of Trustees together with a structure for faculties which is a direct copy of the modern American university. The use of the American model for university governance is pervasive and has become the norm in most Muslim institutions. The real problem in discussing Muslim higher education is discovering who or to whom a Muslim university is accountable for its religious character. Of course, I am conscious that this is a Christian question being addressed to a faith without a central authority, so the answer from a Muslim would be that accountability is to Allah, but ultimately all Christians would agree.

It has observed that Muslim traditions, customs and beliefs have dominated the pattern of governance and management in higher education in developing Muslim countries. Management culture, has often been characterised by a strict hierarchical structure which has derived its strength from stability and a dogmatic form of leadership. There is often a focus on the institution itself rather than on the community that makes up the institution, and there is much rigidity in methods, with a corresponding resistance to change. These Muslim/Islamic universities are increasingly confronted by a number of challenges that threaten their traditional management practices. These include globalisation, the development of information and communication technologies and the increased expectations of students and staff. There is also concern about the low standards in these universities. Guessoum and Sahraoui (2005) believe that there has also been a marked decline in academic quality of the higher education offered in Arab universities in the last decade. It is important to recognise that the Arab world contains over 250 universities and many other higher education institutions stretching from Mauritania to the Persian Gulf and that this region varies greatly in wealth and ethnic make-up.

Guessoum and Sahraoui (2005) indicate that there are still many within Arab Muslim societies who seek a Western education because they associate this with a higher standard of learning in areas like business studies and particularly advanced technologies which are often studied in English. This is why there has been a proliferation of American universities in Arab countries, such as the American University (AU) in Kuwait, or AU Dubai, AU Sharjah, to name but a few, as well as branches of American universities establishing themselves in various cities in the Middle East. British and European universities have also increased their presence in the region mainly as a result of the fall-off in Arab students travelling to America for their education. With these new universities come a number of practices, including transparency in administration procedures in areas such as student assessment, employment process, budgets etc. There is also the principle of shared governance, alien to many Muslim universities and a culture of democracy and free speech. Clearly there are those who would claim that these foreign universities are 'un-Islamic' and that they introduce ideas and practices that affect the beliefs and values of Muslims in a negative way. However, these universities are popular with ordinary Muslim students. Arab governments have allowed these private universities to establish themselves in their countries to meet the needs of mass higher education, but they also recognise that they represent a threat to their normally tight control over universities.

The governance of Jewish higher education is less visible, partly because of the small size and closely knit networks of the institutions and communities concerned. For example, the Leo Baeck College in London is the smallest validated academic institution in the UK. However, Jewish colleges and universities of any size share some of the same tensions and problems of other religiously affiliated institutions. For example, when the President of Yeshiva University announced his retirement, it took the orthodox Jewish community leaders three years to find a replacement. They eventually appointed Richard Joel, who in the university's 117-year-history is the first President not to be a rabbi (see Riley 2004). There were obvious tensions between religious and non-religious departments within the university, as many of those staff involved in the more secular disciplines were concerned that any new President might bring religious themes into their secular disciplines, whilst the religious department staff were concerned about the threat of secularisation with a lay President. The new President has already stated in his inaugural address to the university that he will resist the secularisation process, but he will have also to balance the tensions that exist among the faculty. Protests and tensions against the new lay President from student and faculty have largely subsided since his investiture. Funding of Jewish higher education is largely secured from within the Jewish community and it is why there is a clear majority of Jewish trustees on every Jewish institution's governing board.

Conclusion

Two kinds of ownership appear to be characteristic of religiously affiliated higher education institutions. The institution can be owned wholly by members of the religious denomination or alternatively the institution can be owned by the state, but run by members of the religious affiliation. In the first, ownership can be of two kinds: it can be owned by the main denomination or Church as a body (usually Christian) or it can be owned by a group of members belonging to the particular denomination or faith group. With Judaism and Islam it is always a particular individual or more usually a group within the faith that will own the university, but many Christian universities

are also now owned by the trustees who are simply members of a denomination or faith group and who freely declare their university to be affiliated
to a particular faith. In the second kind of ownership, the state owns the
institution but may allow the institution to declare its own mission, so long as
it is open to all who wish to attend. Universities in Israel and many Arab
countries are of this kind: they are technically 'secular', but are overwhelmingly religious in terms of student admissions and academic staff. In England
and Australia there are universities which are Church institutions paid for by
the state, and yet run by a particular denomination, but these Christian
colleges and universities are overwhelmingly non-religious in terms of student
admissions and academic staff. Ownership of the land and property comprising the physical university is not essential to the designation of a religious
institution. *Ex Corde Ecclesiae* makes this point clear – in the Catholic
Church it is for the local bishop to decide whether a college or university is
Catholic. Those that claim to be 'Catholic' from their own free choice therefore need to satisfy the local bishop that they have met the requirements
of *Ex Corde Ecclesiae*. Since bishops will no doubt differ on the understanding of these essential requirements, we can expect there to be continued
diversity in the character of these officially recognised Catholic institutions.
D'Costa (2005: 125) offers two models of ecclesial accountability for a
Catholic university – 'minimal' and 'maximal'. The minimal Catholic university sees accountability as 'variously understood forms of ecclesial authority' as part of its purpose. This could be to the local bishop, an Episcopal
conference, or to the religious congregation that founded the university. This
arrangement keeps accountability to the Church fuzzy. The maximal Catholic
university attempts to safeguard its mission integrity through a close connection with the Church. D'Costa (2005: 126), whilst refusing to judge between
them, concludes that there is no guarantee that the minimal university will
withstand the secularising process. Ultimately, it is what the institution does,
what the university community believes and what role religion is allocated
within it which will determine whether it is a Jewish, Christian or Muslim
university.

The religiously affiliated university or college requires a board of trustees
and/or governors with a substantial majority from the sponsoring faith
community. The trustees help relate the institution to the sponsoring community and they are the final institutional authority. Their role needs to
ensure that the essential religious character of the institution is upheld and
therefore they are required to lay down the general goals of the institution.
The leadership and management positions within the university, which are
delegated from the trustees, must also be committed to ensuring that the life
of the university is in accordance with the faith that sponsors it. This means
that the management and administration of the religious university must
be consistent with the stated position of the sponsoring faith community. It
also means that the right people need to be appointed to leadership positions

in these colleges and universities as is discussed later in this book. As John Dewey often said, 'a difference that makes no difference is no difference'. A number of Western governments are increasingly sympathetic to faith-based institutions, as can be seen from the Office of Faith-Based Initiatives in the USA and the recent establishment of Church universities in England. In Europe and Australia governments are also aiding the establishment of religious universities. However, the picture is rather complex as in parts of Western Europe religious institutions are being eroded under the influence of secularism from within religious faiths themselves. Some prominent Christians still make it absolutely clear that 'a university must not be confessional in any sense' (see Jenkins 1988) and therefore there are still many religious people who resist any connection between faith and the governance of a university.

Chapter 4

Belief and knowledge

Introduction

The principal goal of the first universities was to teach what was known and to train priests, administrators, doctors and lawyers as well as other masters all within a religious framework. In contrast to vocational education and training, research was not a main object of these universities, although scholarship was. These goals were accomplished within a believing community whose religion was at the core of their consciousness. Today there are increasing numbers of academics who argue that religion should have a legitimate place at the very heart of higher education. They believe that religion's place in higher education has been obscured by modernity's notion of the relationship between 'knowledge' and 'belief' and that faith commitments can and ought to play a role in scholarship. This relationship between knowledge and belief had been a central concern of universities since their foundation in medieval Europe – especially the question of how to classify secular knowledge. The new knowledge obtained from the translations from Arabic into Latin of the works of Aristotle unsettled many in Christendom, as it presented a radically non-Christian and a 'strangely systematic' outlook on the world. Scholars studied it, debated and finally Christianised this new knowledge by the use of the scholastic method: a method which contained within it a commitment to the use of reason to elucidate faith and provide it with rational content – St Augustine called it 'faith seeking understanding'. This was an ambitious project that sought to classify knowledge according to Christian principles and the master of this method was Thomas Aquinas – the great synthesiser of Christian and Aristotelian thought.

There was a strong belief among many medieval scholastic thinkers who tackled this new knowledge that nothing within it could prove detrimental to Christianity. There was a confidence that whatever was uncovered by research and study would not change Christian revelation and indeed that ultimately Christian faith could be served by new knowledge. Therefore fearful condemnations of this new knowledge were few in number in the medieval universities, and instead there was a growing commitment to the marriage of faith and reason. Every kind and branch of knowledge was open to investigation, but from a specifically Christian method and worldview. It is why *Ex Corde Ecclesiae* advocates, 'the integration of the disciplines with the aid of philosophy and theology; the dialogical integration between faith and reason, both bearing witness to the unity of truth; the unity of ethical and the scientific and the synthetic function of theology'. This call for the unity of all knowledge comes at a time when Christianity has lost its status of self-evident truth in the academy and society, and, despite the renewed interest in religion within the academy, Christianity is unlikely to gain its former position. The standing of theology as a largely secularised subject in the secular university is low down the list in the hierarchy of academic disciplines.

The roots of this loss of influence stem from the Enlightenment, which sought ultimate truth through reason alone, according no place to religious revelation. Many academics, whether believers or not, have internalised this mind-set and this in turn has transformed their self-consciousness in a largely secular direction. The standard position in any field of inquiry within the modern university involves arguments for a naturalist worldview. Even departments of theology and religion, where they have survived in the mainstream, aim at understanding the meaning and origins of religious writings and have largely ceased to develop arguments against naturalism. Academics relegated their faith commitments, if any, to their 'private lives' and excluded for the most part their theism from their publications and teaching as this theism did not meet the standards of the 'academically respectable'. The thrust of this movement was towards the irrelevance of religious beliefs for an understanding of education. Knowledge was viewed as concerned with reason and truth, whilst faith was perceived as merely passing on primitive customs and rituals. The dominant worldview within secular higher education is often opposed to religion, and the colleges and universities within it are governed by a liberal humanist elite who foster a sceptical rationalism.

A Catholic perspective

John Henry Newman's *Idea of a University* appears to continue to influence the contemporary debate in higher education, judging by the number of extracts from his book that are employed at conferences and in academic papers. However, it is not always certain that academics who employ Newman's rhetoric in support of their varying and conflicting arguments fully understand that Newman was writing primarily for the Catholic community and specifically about a religiously affiliated university. Newman's writing on education was reacting to the secularisation of his own time. Therefore, to understand Newman's conception of university education requires that it be seen within the context of his Christian worldview and his practice as Rector of the Catholic University in Dublin. The *Idea of a University* consists of a series of discourses, lectures and essays intended for the new Catholic University in Dublin of which Newman was the Rector. Newman was building and developing the Christian religious intellectual tradition of Europe in the advancement of his thesis about university education. Indeed, Newman would probably not recognise as authentic the universities of the academics who continue to quote approvingly isolated extracts from his book. Newman's idea of a university has few modern parallels within the mainstream of higher education.

Newman believed that the university was a school of knowledge of every kind and that it should be a place for the communication and circulation of thought. He defined that university as 'a place of teaching universal knowledge' and argued that all knowledge (each discipline) is connected. Newman's ideal was once everyone's ideal, but today many consider the aims and purposes of higher education to be in crisis in the modern world. In Discourse 9 of the *Idea of a University* Newman outlines what he considers to be the Christian view of knowledge in the university. He begins by stating that all branches of knowledge are of God since we cannot omit God from the quest for knowledge. If we omit God then the knowledge produced will be deficient, partial and defective. Therefore theology must be a branch of knowledge. Newman says that we need to contemplate God to reach the totality of knowledge, and consequently theology cannot be separated from the university. Newman believed that religion is a formative influence on every academic discipline and necessary for a right understanding of the disciplines, otherwise they will stumble into error. Secular knowledge is not the whole truth, as it requires revealed truth in order to fill out the wholeness of truth. Christian education is therefore a standard of measure and a point of verification for all knowledge for it gives knowledge a meaning and purpose it would not otherwise have. Newman believed that secular knowledge by itself has no moral or spiritual purpose and that it requires faith or knowledge of God to provide an essential organising and clarifying framework, otherwise it will become a tool of unbelief. Christianity is not an addendum, but the true organising principle both for the curriculum in higher education and the life of the institution, particularly the character and beliefs of the students. Nevertheless, Newman recognised that each discipline would eventually enlarge its own perspective in isolation from other disciplines. Newman insisted on the absolute integrity and unity of all knowledge and the need of the human mind to reflect on that integrity, but this knowledge was less important than faith. Newman's starting point in any discussion of the university curriculum is a religious one. He believed that knowledge and faith are indivisibly connected and that therefore there is no irreconcilable opposition between knowledge and faith. Essentially, Newman sought the ideal of a university education that combined academic excellence and personal religious commitment. It is an ideal that is not widely accepted by academics in contemporary secular and even religiously affiliated higher education. In summary, Newman was against the endless fragmentation of knowledge, the excessive rationalism within academic disciplines, the emphasis on utilitarianism in education and the movement to exclude religious knowledge from higher education.

It is often argued that once the university had a clear rationale and vision of what counted as higher education, but that this has now been lost to the fragmentation of culture and the responses of this rapidly expanding sector to external pressures. Bloom (1987: 313–24) suggests that we ought to return to the concept of higher education as the guardian of tradition, for he fears that universities have 'abandoned all claim to study or inform about value', which has led to the breakdown and fragmentation of liberal democracy. McIntyre (1990: 217) comments on this fragmentation of knowledge when he says that 'it was not merely that academic inquiry increasingly became professionalized and specialised and that formal education correspondingly became a preparation for and initiation into professionalization and specialisation but that, for the most part and increasingly, moral and theological truth ceased to be recognised as objects of substantive inquiry and instead were relegated to the realm of privatised belief'. Whilst McIntyre suggests that the only way forward is to establish different institutions committed to different forms of rational inquiry, he adds that each should be committed to a particular moral or world outlook. The religiously affiliated college or university has the potential to be such a higher education institution, committed to both tradition and to a particular worldview. However, neither Bloom nor McIntyre mentions such a possibility, even though McIntyre chooses to teach in a religiously affiliated institution – the University of Notre Dame.

However, within specifically Christian institutions many believe that there is so much chaotic fragmentation of knowledge with growing subject specialisation combined with the chorus of diverse voices in the academy, that it may well be impossible to even attempt a synthesis of faith and learning. In contrast, others continue to argue that however imperfect the attempt, it is essential that Christian colleges and universities at least make some efforts in this direction. Buckley (1998: 15) argues that the academic and the religious are intrinsically related and that they form a inherent unity, with one incomplete without the other. He defines his meaning thus: 'that the intellectual dynamism inherent in all inquiry initiates processes or habits of questioning that – if not inhibited – inevitably bear upon the ultimate questions that engage religion'. He argues that the drive of the human mind is towards the completion of the whole, and therefore the Catholic university proposes a union between the human and the divine, and between culture and faith, which will deepen the unity between the Christian faith and all forms of knowledge. It is why *Ex Corde Ecclesiae* calls for a much stronger and more concrete affirmation of the Catholic university's character, including the search for an organic unity between the gospel and culture. The actual history of the majority of Catholic efforts in the recent past has shown a shift in attitudes, mainly towards the secularisation of academic disciplines.

Roberts and Turner (2000: 121) detail how two disciplinary approaches have contributed to the exclusion of religion from higher education. They name them as methodological naturalism in the sciences and historicism in the humanities. The former 'tended to exclude religious beliefs from knowledge, historicism actually tended to explain it away'. Both Roberts and Turner do not believe that this is a conscious plot on the part of academics to remove religion from the academy but simply the secularising effects of these two disciplinary approaches. Indeed, if religious academics are so immersed in the mindset of these methods then they would not consciously think that they were in effect dissolving and re-shaping the parameters of our understanding of knowledge and belief. Turner (2003) in another publication spells out some of the contributions of the Catholic intellectual tradition to this debate. McInerny (1994: 182) believes that the Catholic faith brings with it certain understandings of things and that in considering the essential purpose of a Catholic college or university he writes: 'A university is chiefly concerned with the mind and imagination. If the faith has no influence on what goes on in the classrooms and laboratories, studies, stages of the university, the university is not Catholic.' In regard to the authority of the Catholic Church, Hesburgh (1994: 5) continues to believe that the Catholic university cannot be subject to any external authority in governance, including the magisterium of the Church, but he also believes that a Catholic perspective in the academy is still possible in such a university.

Secularisation was undoubtedly seen as an evil by the Catholic Church, but by the late 1950s there was a growing acceptance of the notion of the 'secular' as an autonomous sphere which was good in itself. In the 1960s, 'individualism', understood as thinking only in terms of oneself, apart from the community, had become a pervasive characteristic of higher education as well as of most cultures in Western societies. In such cultural atmospheres attempting to present a Catholic view of academic disciplines became increasingly difficult. Consequently, as Gleason (1967: 51–2) explains in regard to sociology, there was an attempt to create a 'Catholic Sociology' within Catholic universities and a journal called the *American Catholic Sociological Review* was founded. However, there was a growing movement to accept the autonomy of sociology independent of any religious influence, and so the journal's name was changed to *Sociological Analysis*. This process was replicated in a number of subject areas within Catholic higher education, which led Gleason to ask the question: 'In what sense is a Catholic university Catholic if it is composed predominantly of lay professors who employ, in their teaching and research, the same methods and norms as their counterparts in secular universities, and who are engaged in the pursuit of knowledge in autonomous spheres that are in no way dependent upon any over-all "Catholic position"? What in short, is the reason for being of the *Catholic* college or university.' He answers this question in the context of academics who are largely highly professionalised and secularised and who are imbued with the norms, procedures and rules of their own autonomous disciplines or professions. However, a number of Catholic colleges and universities have kept alive a rigorous commitment to a general liberal education that can challenge secular institutions who succumb more easily to the most recent educational innovation.

A Protestant perspective

Protestant philosophers also conclude that that there is a definite relationship between the intellect and the life of faith and that Christian education seeks to educate for faith as well as good character. Holmes (1987) believes that Christian higher education should promote the active integration of faith and learning and of faith and culture. He argues that what is needed is Christian scholars, not simply Christians who are scholars, and certainly not Christianity alongside the study of other disciplines but distinctive and substantive Christian education. Holmes (1987: 6–7) maintains that in pursuing the purposes of the Christian college, 'it must under no circumstances become a *disjunction* between piety and scholarship, faith and reason, religion and science'. Holmes recognises that since the Christian worldview has largely disintegrated in higher education, this will require a thorough analysis of methods, concepts and theoretical structures within higher education, but nevertheless believes that 'a lively and rigorous interpenetration of liberal learning with the content and commitment of Christian faith' is possible. Holmes (1975: 77) believes that the goal of Christian higher education is to create 'a community of Christians whose intellectual and social and cultural life is influenced by Christian values'. He speaks of 'shared values and purposes' in a community of faith and learning where 'God is always honoured in and through studies'. Therefore the integration of faith and learning remains one of the most distinctive tasks of the religiously affiliated institution. Peterson (1986: 88) also states that it is a mistake to assume that there is simply 'secular' or 'worldly' knowledge. He considers that Christian theism collapses the misleading sacred–secular distinction. God is one, and all truth stems from him and is known by him. Peterson concludes that: 'Since all truth is God's, wherever it may be found, there is no basis for insisting that only "religious knowledge" has "spiritual significance".' Holmes maintains that the Christian college curriculum should relate everything to Christian faith, especially in the humanities. He describes three types of virtue that should characterise the Christian institution of higher education: spiritual, moral and intellectual. The spiritual should characterise the unique mission of the Christian college and should include among others faith, hope, love, humility, which denote an 'unreserved commitment' to God. Moral virtues he lists as love, fairness, courage, integrity and justice. The intellectual virtues are breadth of understanding, openness to new ideas, intellectual honesty, communication and wisdom.

Nevertheless, the majority of mainstream Protestant universities have responded to the challenge of modernity by separating faith and learning. Academic disciplines are studied without any reference to each other. Sloan (1994) details how Protestants adopted a 'two-realms' approach to truth within higher education, which relegated faith to a private arena. Sloan (1994: 232) describes how the rhetoric of mainstream Protestantism sought both 'Christian faith and values' with 'academic excellence' for its colleges and universities, but in reality 'in this approach, Christian faith and values have at most a tangential relationship to knowledge, and, hence, to academic excellence. Whatever is variously concerned under Christian faith and values is, therefore, subjected to constant pressure to give way before the institutional, ideological and individual career demands of "academic excellence", which compared to "Christian faith and values" has a well-defined and agreed upon meaning.' Theology had not been well integrated with the rest of the curriculum in Protestant universities and Marsden (1997: 15) indicates that the Protestant emphasis on prayer and worship had the paradoxical effect of inhibiting the development of explicitly Christian perspectives in the disciplines. Religion became an extra-curricular activity for many and the broad Christian outlook was considered more important than integrating faith and learning. By the 1960s most Protestant universities had abandoned the quest to link Christianity to the learning process and only a few were interested in faith and learning. Hull (1992: 445) details how a number of organisations representing the role of religion in Protestant institutions of higher education simply secularised themselves. The National Committee on Religion in Higher Education, founded in 1923, became the Society for Values in Higher Education in 1975 and stated it had little concern for institutional religion. The Commission for Christian Higher Education of the National Council of Churches became the Department of Higher Education in 1965 and again distanced itself from a primary concern for Christian higher education.

Nevertheless, Marsden (1997) in his *The Outrageous Idea of Christian Scholarship* presents a Protestant case for 'faith-informed scholarship'. Marsden argues that higher education does not address first principles and is dominated by a 'secular humanism' which does not generally welcome Christian perspectives. Consequently, he proposes that all universities should be more open to the discussion of the relationship of religious faith to learning, and that Christian scholars should reflect more on the intellectual implications of their faith and bring these reflections to bear in the secular domain of academic life. Essentially, Marsden attempts to show how faith is relevant to scholarship and advocates that Christians should cease merely being Christian in private and participate fully as Christians in the public academy. Universities should accept Christian perspectives on the same basis that it accepts and promotes secular ideologies such as feminist and Marxist studies. Marsden argues that within secular universities there are no Christian schools of thought to compare with gay, ethnic, post-modern and feminist ideologies, and therefore Christianity should have an equal place alongside other worldviews. To the secular mind religious perspectives are often considered unscientific and unprofessional, and it is often thought inappropriate for academics to relate their Christianity to their scholarship. The separation of faith and learning is widely taken for granted in higher education even within many religiously affiliated universities. Many are even offended by a Christian perspective that is too explicit within a pluralist setting.

Marsden then proceeds to outline some of the ways in which Christians can combine faith and learning, but he recognises that this process is complex. He claims that his idea of 'faith-informed scholarship' also applies to Jews and Muslims and that it is possible so long as we do not lose sight of the relevant particularities of one's own faith. An obvious problem for Marsden is that within Christianity there cannot be said to be 'the Christian view', only a number of sub-traditions of Christianity which can be contradict each other. However, Marsden (1997: 47–8) says that what will make faith-based learning and scholarship distinctive will depend on the claims of revelation or sources of knowledge not shared with others in the academy. He dismisses the idea that this kind of knowledge has no place in public discourse because it is not empirically verifiable – this, he says, would exclude much else in the secular academy. He suggests that the Catholic natural law argument assists Christians to introduce some ideas from revelation into the mainstream without reference to the sources of this information. For example, arguments against war or for assisting the poor can be defended on the basis of natural law and can be accepted by all without belief in God. Therefore knowledge has a religious source but is argued for on other grounds – so what is argued for on the basis of revelation, another may accept on the basis of reason or even personal intuition. However, there are tensions in this argument, as natural law has God as its ultimate premise. Marsden's proposal is modest and designed not to offend too many within higher education. He accepts the rules of secular liberal higher education and his advice to Christians is minimal and also generally excludes any absolutist claims. The questions you are left with is what difference would it really make and will it make Christian perspectives explicit enough? The real strength of Marsden's (1997: 101) proposals are that Christian scholarship should have a strong institutional base and that Christians should build these communities and form sub-groups within secular universities, perhaps in the form of research centres. Marsden has certainly had a huge influence on evangelical thinkers who have, through many conferences and publications, attempted to develop the integral relationships which exist between faith and human knowledge within higher education. Harris (2004) is only one among many Protestant evangelical academics who has tried to explain how faith and learning can be integrated, but there is no consensus among Protestant Christians about this. Beck (1991) provides but one model of how to organise a college Christian curriculum. It is interesting that as Jacobsen and Jacobsen (2004) note, most of the literature has assumed a definition of Christian scholarship that is evangelical in orientation and associated with the phrase 'the integration of faith and learning'.

The idea of the 'integration' of faith and learning was further developed in the world of evangelical Protestantism. Jacobsen and Jacobsen (2004: 17) raise a number of questions about this approach to scholarship and detail its limitations. They outline a number of different visions of Christian scholarship and in particular contrast Protestant and Catholic approaches (Jacobsen and Jacobsen 2004: 80–1). Catholic models of Christian scholarship stress connections and continuities whilst Protestant approaches, they claim, focus more on difference, distance and opposition. The Catholic intellectual tradition is largely determined by its 'analogical imagination' that seeks similarities or unities that exist among human events. The human and the divine penetrate each other and the sacred and the secular complement each other. It was Newman who spoke loudly of the unity of knowledge which was not simply about integrating Christianity with ideas in academic disciplines, but rather about the wholeness of truth.

A Muslim perspective

In contrast to some Christian approaches, many Muslim scholars were eager to identify themselves as 'Islamic scholars' and to shape their scholarship according to Islamic principles. This applied particularly to the clerical scholars who are collectively known in Arabic as the *Ulema*, membership of which carries high status within the Muslim community. The Islamic education movement to Islamise knowledge only started in the late 1970s, partly as a reaction to the secularisation of education in Muslim countries. It was part of a discourse which advocated the Islamisation of various aspects of society and life. The modern and largely Western inspired education systems within Muslim countries appeared to divorce learning from spiritual education and Muslim scholars observed that there was a rift between faith and intellect and between knowledge based on revelation and knowledge based on acquired knowledge. Young men returning to Muslim countries after studying in the West also appeared to suggest that the secular education they had received was not beneficial to their faith, as many returned with little respect for Muslim tradition, preferring instead to follow Western mores. The educational experience of Muslim minorities in Western countries also indicated that it was difficult to provide an Islamic education that preserved the heritage of Islam intact. The First World Conference of Islamic Education in 1977 identified Western knowledge as the culprit, since it had divorced itself from spiritual education and had abandoned its links with revealed knowledge. It was a system that began and ended with man and which failed to acknowledge the Creator's role as the source of all knowledge. Some wished to disengage completely from Western thought in order to restore Islam's autonomy and independence. Others felt that Islam and Muslims needed to engage with Western ideas. The Conference wanted to avoid a superficial mix of secular and religious courses as a way forward. It therefore began with a logical statement of the nature of man, the purpose and goal of his existence, and the role of education in helping man to achieve this end (Attis 1979: v). The Islamic Universities League held an international symposium on Islamic Studies in 2004 at Dundee University in Scotland and set out a framework for the development of the study of Islam and Muslim civilisations at university level.

The Muslim concept of knowledge ultimately identifies God as the source of all knowledge. It divides knowledge into two areas: revealed and acquired. Revealed knowledge is based on the Koran and Sunnah, whilst acquired knowledge concerns itself with the social, natural and applied sciences. Acquired knowledge must be in harmony with and enlightened by faith. Muslim thought has produced a hierarchy of knowledge which begins with spiritual knowledge followed by moral knowledge, then intellectual disciplines, imaginative disciplines, and finally physical disciplines. Spiritual and moral knowledge are 'givens', whilst acquired knowledge is gained through the imaginative disciplines. No knowledge is conceivable without values and therefore it is unthinkable in Muslim education to suggest that knowledge is value free or neutral. In Islam all knowledge is sacred and should be used to counter error, prejudice and self-interest. The connection between knowledge and the virtues is consequently important in Islam in order to ensure the balanced growth of the individual in spirit, intellect, rational self, feelings and senses. The aim of this education is to infuse faith into the individual and create an emotional attachment to Islam so that they follow Islamic teaching in their lives. As Attis (1979: v) states, 'The aim of Muslim education is the creation of the "good and righteous man" who worships Allah in the true sense of the term, builds up the structure of his earthly life according to the Sharia . . . (Islamic law) and employs it to sub-serve his faith.' Ashraf (1985: 10) sums this up when he says, 'If religion is taught as one of many subjects and not as the central subject governing the approach to all branches of human knowledge, one cannot hope to reassert the moral basis of society.'

There are theoretically no limits to the acquisition of knowledge in Islam and each Muslim has a sacred task to pursue knowledge to his or her best ability. Nevertheless, with the expansion of knowledge there have appeared conflicting attitudes within the Muslim community. Some believe that knowledge pursued for its own sake is meaningless, as they claim that all knowledge must serve God. There are significant tensions between reason and revelation. The Second World Islamic Education Conference in 1980 agreed that acquired knowledge should be taught from the 'Islamic' point of view. However, in order to do this there was a need to evolve Islamic concepts of knowledge. Islamic theology was to provide the worldview for all other branches of knowledge. Theology was to provide the link to integrate all branches of knowledge, as each branch is not considered autonomous. Clearly, Muslim scholars could not practically reject all Western knowledge – the intention was rather to recast Western knowledge according to Islamic principles and constructs. This is a major objective, demanding the full intellectual resources of the Muslim community, so it is not surprising that it is not well advanced conceptually and is not without contested status within the Muslim community. The Heads of State of many Muslim countries formally subscribed to this Islamisation movement (see Ashraf 1985: 84). Nevertheless, this synthesis of faith and learning has been attempted before within Muslim education. Arab Muslims, such as al Farabi, Avicenna and Averroes, did not reject the new knowledge they found in Plato or Aristotle, but rather they assimilated it. Philosophy and science were not classified as un-Islamic but rather they were re-constructed and understood according to the teachings of Islam.

There are many tensions in trying to understand this medieval view of faith and knowledge and the contemporary interpretations of it. For example, there appears to be some similarities in Newman's view to the modern movement within Islam that seeks to Islamise all secular knowledge. However, like Newman's view, the Islamic view of knowledge is underdeveloped in practice. There is, however, a crucial difference between Islamisation and Christian integration of knowledge and this lies in the fact that Christianity in the medieval university believed in an appropriate autonomy of the disciplines, following Aristotle, but yet saw that they had the potential to be interdependent and harmonious within a Christian worldview. The contemporary Islamic view of knowledge, expressed in the movement for the Islamisation of knowledge, does not allow for this same degree in the autonomy of the disciplines.

The debate about the Islamisation of knowledge continues among Muslim philosophers and educationalists. Attis (1979: 6) speaks of the 'corruption of knowledge' in the West and how this has infiltrated Muslim minds, causing the 'de-Islamisation of the Muslim mind'. Some reject the idea that you can simply graft Islamic ideals and norms onto existing forms of knowledge (Rahman 1982). Rahman argues that it is not knowledge but its application that is the problem. It is the use of knowledge by Muslims that makes it bad or good, therefore there is nothing wrong with Western knowledge, but it is simply misused – by Muslims and Westerners alike. Rahman believes Islam simply has not kept pace in moral development with technological advancement and that the West treats religion as irrelevant to large areas of life and thought and has become thoroughly secular. There is also some misunderstanding of what Islamisation of knowledge means within the Muslim community itself. Choudhary (1993: 18) believes that the Islamic community is 'confused and doubtful about the kind of Islamisation direction to take'. Farugi (1982) has developed a method or approach to the Islamisation of knowledge which seeks to look at each branch of knowledge or academic discipline in higher education and redefine it, reorder it, rethink it and re-project it to serve the goals of Islam. Some consider this to be anti-progress, anti-science and against human development, whilst others believe that Islamisation is simply code for Arabisation. Nevertheless, institutes and universities have been established with the stated aim of the Islamisation of knowledge. Numerous books seek to outline an alternative (to Western) Muslim methodology that would be capable of responding to the social and intellectual challenges of modern Islamic societies. However, Rahman (1982: 133) comments that in trying to Islamise knowledge and education, 'this aim cannot be really fulfilled unless Muslims effectively perform the intellectual task of elaborating an Islamic metaphysics on the basis of the Qur'an'. Abaza claims that the attempt so far to invest knowledge with Islamic values has been less than negligible. He also observes that whilst the process has produced valuable insights, these are often marred by apologetic attitudes.

Bilgrami and Ashraf (1985: 40), working from the Islamic Academy in Cambridge, England, believe that the ideal Islamic university should not simply teach Islamic subjects alongside other subjects or establish institutes of Islamic Studies. Rather the aim of the Islamic university is to 'produce men of higher knowledge and noble character' who have been educated in the spiritual, not the materialistic. They subscribe to the Islamisation of knowledge and believe that the Muslim world requires a unified education system which they claim once prevailed in Muslim civilisation, 'a synthesis was brought between the rational and the spiritual approaches by the most learned scholars of the institutions, who had a complete knowledge of Islam and of modern subjects, and who with their methodology and personality brought together all knowledge into a united whole, integrating it with the unity of Truth and reality'. They suggest that this unity and integration needs to be recaptured by Muslims. Simply providing a theology faculty in a university does not aid the unity they seek. Bilgrami and Ashraf (1985: 49) recognise that this is not an easy task for the Muslim community and will require intensive research and study. They propose that Muslim scholars begin by preparing a core of knowledge and draw from the metaphysics supplied by the Koran and Sunnah to formulate a basic Islamic approach to the social, natural and applied sciences. This approach seeks to challenge the critical, secular and analytical outlook of the West by interpreting theories that underlie various disciplines from an Islamic point of view.

Bilgrami and Ashraf (1985) are clearly concerned with the negative effects of modern university education on the ideals and behaviour of the young, and they advocate Islamisation of knowledge as a partial remedy. They are careful to insist that this should not be done in a dogmatic way and that students should be trained to think for themselves. This is an important point since it would easy for academics hostile to this approach to become suspicious of institutions that promise specifically Islamic biology or even promise to give an authentic Islamic view of every subject or issue in higher education.

They may argue that this method would compromise the intellectual dignity of various disciplines in the name of religious insight, that it would demand conformity and not invite a free response, that it would simply transmit information but not cultivate critical thinking, and that it would be instruction not education. There is a distinction between teaching students how to think rather than what to think, but how we think presupposes knowing what to think. It presupposes some partisan account of the subject matter and whilst being partisan may slump into narrow indoctrination, it doesn't have to. Bilgrami and Ashraf (1985) recognise that this Islamisation project has not progressed very far beyond philosophical discussions and that Islamic scholars are only at the conceptualisation stage in formulating Islamic concepts for all the branches of knowledge. One difficulty they have is that the enterprise lacks criticism of its own tradition and often simply celebrates everything and everyone associated with Islam, whilst denigrating the West. Husain (1997: 48) recognises this point when he says that the solution is not to impose on higher education a rigid pattern of knowledge in the name of Islamisation, but rather to confront intelligently the difficulty of agreeing what the Islamic view of knowledge is. He concludes: 'preaching the theory that there exists an Islamic alternative to every branch of knowledge is not only to mislead the Muslim public but also to encourage communal suicide'.

There are many Muslim critics of the Islamisation of knowledge movement and they point to the fact that whilst there have been many critiques of the movement there have been very little concrete results in terms of an Islamic curriculum for universities (see Panjwani (2004) for a discussion of how Muslims differ among themselves on the Islamisation project). It can appear to be a vague Islamic ideology with empty rhetoric, using a simplistic approach that fails to take account of historical events. That is why a Forum on Human Rights in Cairo condemned the whole Islamisation of knowledge project. Abaza (2002: 197) comments that 'Islamisation is nothing but the monopoly of men of religion over scientific production, ending in inquisitions.' Nevertheless, Muslims continue to see Westernisation as an ideological threat to their civilisation and something that aids the educational secularisation of their higher education institutions. The response is to re-Islamise in some way this hitherto secularising Western-inspired educational project. It could be argued that secularisation is only possible when it becomes culturally acceptable, and in the majority of Muslim societies it is not acceptable.

A Jewish perspective

Traditional European Judaism avoided secular studies, focusing instead on rabbinical studies in seminaries and in the Jewish home. Jews were of course largely excluded from nineteenth-century European universities, and in America admission to colleges was much restricted, though scholarship within the Jewish community was highly respected and honoured. There was also a movement called *Wissenschaft des Judentums* for the scholarly study of history and literature in Judaism. It is interesting that the secularisation of Protestant universities in the USA facilitated the entry of many Jews to universities and assisted the appearance of Semitic studies in some of these universities. Reform Judaism adopted an inclusive approach to higher education and Ritterband and Wechsler (1994: 32) believe that it also 'rejected Jewish social distinctiveness'. The mainstream university therefore was viewed as the route to social and cultural inclusion for the Reform Jewish community. Indeed, it was believed that the mainstream university helped protect Jewish learning from insularity. This led to tensions between Jewish communal identification and academic expectations and standards within higher education. Ritterband and Wechsler (1994: 49) have observed that 'Jewish Semitists who became strongly socialised to academic norms usually declined to engage in teaching and research aimed primarily at meeting communal expectations'. The few Jewish academics within higher education appeared to stop representing Judaism within the academy. As early as 1886 Morris Jastrow at Pennsylvania University had 'rabbinics' deleted from the title of his professorship (Ritterband and Wechsler 1994: xii). A number of Jewish scholars simply abandoned communal identification. Some within the Jewish community considered mainstream universities to be too secular and heterogeneous environments for Jewish learning to flourish and favoured seminaries which presupposed religious commonality and adherence to religious tradition. This represented another tension as the seminary was concerned with transmitting extant knowledge, whilst the mainstream university was concerned with creating new knowledge.

I have already mentioned the 'continuity crisis' in Judaism which is caused by the secularisation of Jewish history, religion and heritage. In order to halt this process the Jewish community in America formed the American Academy for Jewish Research in 1920 'to stimulate learning by helpful co-operation and mutual encouragement as well as to formulate standards for Jewish scholarship'. This was a rather elitist organisation and in 1969 the Association of Jewish Studies was formed with a more liberal flavour. The Jewish people spent the last two hundred years in Europe and America trying to achieve civic and social equality, but now find themselves in a modern secular context in which many Jews have become alienated from traditional Jewish learning and values. However, there is also the problem that Jews are divided and often overtly political about education, with many subscribing to wholly secular approaches to education. Comparing a number of Jewish scholars illustrates this point. Twersky (2003) advocates that Jewish education should have an explicit religious worldview, and he uses the work of the medieval Jewish scholar, rabbi and philosopher Maimonides (1135–1204) to illustrate his point. Maimonides addressed, on behalf of the Jewish community, the perceived threats contained in the new knowledge from Aristotle's works. He was responsible for a synthesis of Artistotle's thought with Jewish learning and he combined the general scientific and philosophical ideas of his day with Jewish thought. He classified available knowledge according to Jewish principles and did not reject this new knowledge. Twersky argues that Jews, in a world that has seen a shattering of this unity in knowledge, need to re-establish the same approach to knowledge.

In contrast Brinker (2003) adopts a secular and pluralist approach to knowledge. His idea of Jewishness is more social than religious, and he defines it as those who associate themselves with the Jewish people and the Hebrew language. He believes that Jewish education is really little different from secular education in the West and should follow the same liberal-humanistic principles. This contrasts sharply with Twersky, who insists that Jewish education is about the doctrines of Jewish life and a Jewish worldview. Brinker, as an Israeli educator, is only concerned with a Zionist educational approach specifically in Israel, which is the only national Jewish community that represents a majority national culture. He argues that the Diaspora Jewish community necessarily has to have an education which emphasises the religious teaching of traditional Judaism. He believes that they (the Jews of the Diaspora) are closed to free thought and that ultimately they cannot survive secularisation. He adopts a very pessimistic view of the possibilities within the Jewish Diaspora. A third view, from Scheffler (2003: 236), presents a two-fold aim for Jewish education. First, in relation to the individual, the objective is to initiate them into the culture, history and spiritual heritage of Judaism. Second, in relation to the Jewish people, the objective is to promote Jewish survival and welfare, to interpret and communicate authentic Jewish experience, sustain and develop Jewish loyalty and honour, create living links with the Jewish past and preserve and extend this heritage for future generations. Many Jewish universities have found no difficulty in accepting these two aims. However, there is an important strand within Judaism that seeks the synthesis of the Jewish faith and learning in the world. Rosenak (2003: 186) points to the rich diversity of views on Jewish education, but from an orthodox position he argues that Jews must remain situated in Judaism even as they address the modern world – educated Jews need to translate Jewish concepts, concerns and creativity into the language of the non-Jewish civilisation.

In the Statement of Purpose and Mission of the Hebrew Union College's Jewish Institute of Religion we have a clear statement on integration from the Reform movement in Judaism. It states that the Institute seeks to develop its students by 'integrating Jewish tradition, academic knowledge and professional competence'. In the University of Judaism's mission statement there is also a commitment to integrating knowledge with Jewish civilisation. In the conclusion to Fox *et al.* (2003: 332) it is stated that there are many visions of Jewish education within a shared community and that:

Pluralism is thus the rule, not the exception. But pluralism does not necessitate an acceptance of all the visions resulting from reflection, not does it sanction a relativism that allows us to choose just any vision we like. Each of us needs to work out the principles, purposes, and practices that commend themselves to us as most sound and persuasive, while according the respect due to others who have, sharing the same task, followed a different path.

At Brandeis University there is reference to Jewish scholarship in the university's documentation, but Fox (1993–94), finds no evidence for this Jewish scholarship in a university that does not define itself by the Jewish religion. Whilst there is a Jewish atmosphere in the university that includes a wide variety of forms of Jewish expression on the campus Fox states that, 'We do nothing institutionally to help our students deal with the issues generated for religion by our whole range of academic subject matter. We do not consider the significance of the natural sciences or philosophy for Judaism.' So whilst there may be a palpably Jewish ambience on the campus, it does not translate into a serious consideration of how faculty members reconcile faith with the demands of critical scholarship. This could easily be said about many Muslim and Catholic universities.

The religious worldview and the university curriculum

The partial secularisation of both higher education and culture has resulted in the creation of a number of dualisms, including the separation of faith from learning and teaching. There has also been a separation of revealed truth from secular truth. Consequently, academics in higher education, including some Jews, Christians and Muslims, view faith and learning as contradictions that cannot coexist together – that they are two separate entities that do not fully connect. The response from many academics within all three religious faiths is that we need to reconnect all ideas, facts, and values into a unified system of Jewish, Christian and Islamic understanding. All three religions would argue that all truth is God's truth and therefore there cannot be a separation of so called secular and revealed knowledge. Secular knowledge and learning is considered incomplete and often distorted because it limits reality to the material world. The faith commitment of a person should inform all learning and a religious worldview should and ought to provide the framework of assumptions that structure and motivate the university curriculum. Such a university curriculum ought to be heavily faith-laden and value-laden. However, it is recognised that the task of integrating or reconciling faith (understanding revealed by God) and learning (understanding as discovered by man) presents an enormous challenge, not least because of the different approaches adopted by various religious academics.

And yet Jews, Christians and Muslims have addressed this challenge before, however incompletely, and each of these religious traditions can identify important figures in their history who have made outstanding contributions to synthesising faith and knowledge.

In 'orthodox' colleges and universities, such as Steubenville University, Hebrew College, Calvin College and Azhar University, there are often, in addition to mission statements, a carefully worked out curriculum statement. For example, St Thomas More College has a clear philosophy of the curriculum statement which acknowledges that the source of all knowledge is from God 'that comes to us in its intellectual form through Scripture and Tradition'. Within the different disciplines and courses offered there is also an attempt to study them in their Christian context. At Steubenville University accounting courses provide an ethical foundation for the subject, whilst economics is studied partially through the insights from philosophy and theology, psychology is studied from a Christian humanist perspective whilst sociology emphasises Catholic social teaching. Ave Maria University states in its statement of curriculum philosophy that it seeks the 'formation of men and women in the intellectual and moral virtues of the Catholic faith'. At Calvin College many of the secular courses are explicitly based on Christian insights. 'Critical mass' institutions, such as the University of Notre Dame, Baylor University, Yeshiva University and the International Islamic University in Kula Lumpar, offer compulsory courses in philosophy and theology, but apart from the faith-based centres for teaching and research, it is more difficult to see how faith is integrated into the general secular disciplines on offer. 'Intentionally pluralist' institutions, such as Raboud University, the University of Jordan, and Georgetown University may have centres to generate some Christian insights in the disciplines, but generally there is usually very little sign of faith and knowledge integrating into the curriculum on offer.

Muslim universities that could be described as 'fundamentalist' are few in number, and are generally controlled by clerics who also largely control the national government, such as in the University of Tehran. It is interesting, that these fundamentalist universities do not usually have well integrated faith and knowledge programmes, but rather emphasise an 'Islamic correctness' in which the secular disciplines like politics, say nothing to offend Islam or the state. There are of course 'orthodox' Muslim universities, but these generally focus on the study of religion and where they have medical schools or science courses they inevitably insist on compulsory Muslim studies programmes for all students. Other universities in Muslim countries follow the Western secular curriculum and could be categorised as meeting aspects of the criteria between 'intentionally pluralist' and 'accidentally pluralist', but this is only speculative. What is needed is a specific typology for Muslim universities.

How do you clarify knowledge according to your religious worldview? 'Worldview' here is understood as a set of beliefs through which one interprets all of reality. Modernity and secularisation have such a pervasive influence or impact on us and our culture that formulating a religious worldview on a curriculum-wide basis in the university presents huge challenges. The legacy of the secular approach to knowledge is still prevalent in many institutions that claim a religious foundation. This legacy includes an epistemology that has tended to limit what counts as knowledge to the production of empirical scientific investigations, eventually leading to a naturalistic worldview. This, according to many Jewish, Christian and Muslim worldviews, narrows our notion of knowledge. Postmodernism has of course made inroads into the academy and has helped destroy the dominating position of empiricism, but empiricism is still strong. Postmodernists reject any notion of determinate meaning in the academy. Harris (2004) suggests that we first need to understand how the secular academy makes knowledge claims and how its claims are shaped within the worldviews of naturalism and postmodernism. He believes this is a necessary preparation before the religious academic can proceed to connecting faith and reason to produce a religious worldview that makes a unified and coherent whole. In order for this integrative process to work, Harris argues that two conditions need to be met: first, you have an authentic religious understanding of your faith; second, the academic knowledge is true and accurate. Only then can you accept, reject, adjust new knowledge. However, there are many problems with this proposal, not least the many conflicting interpretations of what counts as religious faith and what counts as academic knowledge. There is a good deal of pluralism within all three faiths, and therefore very different ideas of how they should integrate faith and learning. There are no ready answers or procedures, simply a number of different and sometimes conflicting proposals.

There is certainly a search underway in all three faiths, but what this integration would look like and how it should be achieved is as yet still unclear. There are also acknowledged dangers inherent in the process itself for it could, depending on how it is handled, possibly stifle open and free research. For example, communist governments in Eastern Europe once enforced the teaching of Marxism through all disciplines in the university. The idea was that students would study compulsory courses in Marxism so that they would develop the ability to judge every issue and problem within their ordinary subject area from a definite Marxist viewpoint. The experiment was not a success and led to stagnation, distortion and falsification of knowledge in the university. It also led to attempts at the indoctrination of students. Today, there is a process of de-secularisation taking place in response to the rise of religiosity in former communist countries. In Iran there was an attempt to integrate traditional Islamic schools with the modern universities but this experiment has failed due to internal conflict and divisions among various religious and politically oriented factions. Clearly all three faiths need to be aware of the problems that the Marxist and Iranian experiments demonstrate. Nevertheless, a broad-minded approach characterised by the various medieval scholars (Aquinas, Maimonides and Averroes) in all three faiths is one that could be followed. They all maintained the concept of the unity of knowledge in multiplicity. They all believed that the religious dimension of human experience is central and that it is not separate from the intellectual life. This suggests a broader approach to knowledge and scholarship than the purely secular and materialistic. Religiously affiliated colleges and universities therefore have a role to promote the pursuit of truth, allowing questioning and debate, according to their traditions and in so doing they add a pluralism within higher education itself. They need to maintain in the structure of their curriculum the components of their religious intellectual tradition, not simply in theological and philosophical disciplines but in other subjects. All three faiths have clearly much to learn from each other within higher education, not least because the belief that all knowledge forms one whole is an immensely important and complex premise that cannot be resolved easily.

Conclusion

There is a strong undercurrent of individualism within Western higher education caused by the widespread influence of liberalism, which treats religion as controversial. Religious views are therefore not to be held absolutely within higher education because there is a largely subjectivist account of the nature of religious language in operation within the academy. Faith is viewed as irrelevant to the educational task in higher education, and there is no reason for considering your belief to be any more valid than that of another person. Therefore, religious beliefs can only be held in a tentative way – they must be open to revision, and this is considered the virtue of a contemporary education in a college or university. Religious beliefs are essentially to be judged by secular criteria. In contrast, other positions, such as inclusion and equal opportunity, are deemed to have an objective and non-controversial authority about them and may be believed in absolutely. Clearly, faith communities that adopt a more absolutist view of religious knowledge cannot accept this modern secularist critique of the link between faith and knowledge. The general Muslim theory of knowledge is simply that all knowledge is ultimately of God, but there is a recognition by many Muslims that human experience is another source of knowledge. The function of the university within a dominant Muslim society is to help shape that society according to Muslim or Islamic standards. The central problem many Muslims have with Western scientific and technological knowledge is how to use this knowledge for the betterment of the *ummah* without importing Western pressures of secularisation which are often closely associated with Western knowledge. It is this secularisation process that poses the main threat to Islam. Many Muslims consider Western culture to be non-religious, based upon materialistic values that represent a direct threat to the teachings of Islam. The broad secular position may value or be indifferent to the contribution of different religions to the academy, but the secularist position is clearly antagonistic to religion because it seeks to eradicate the influence of religion, except perhaps in the purely private sphere.

Nevertheless, it is worthy of note that the Society of Christian Philosophers is now the largest special interest group within the American Philosophical Association, with over 1,000 members. This has been made possible by the decline in logical positivism and the emergence of faith-based perspectives on scholarship, which have forced secular philosophers to reflect on their own presuppositions. Religious perspectives on knowledge in the academy will no doubt change some things and even have some curricular implications, but not always. And yet it is only through these concrete curricular implications that a religiously affiliated institution can demonstrate the essential connection between faith and knowledge. There is also no one evaluative tradition and so there will be Jewish, Christian and Muslim perspectives as well as a whole range of voices and understandings within each of these faith traditions. Evidence of successful integration of faith and knowledge in the curriculum of modern religiously affiliated universities is scarce and suggests that faith communities in the academy have not successfully resolved the faith/knowledge problem. There currently appear to be three options for faith communities in higher education to resolve this faith/knowledge divide. First, withdraw to within a safe fortification of revealed knowledge and reject all claims made on behalf of secular knowledge. This option would lead to a hard fundamentalism and total isolation of religiously affiliated institutions. It would mean adopting the 'fundamentalist' model of a university. Second, accommodate religious faith to what is deemed safe while refusing to recognise those elements of knowledge that are determined exclusively on non-religious assumptions. In other words, it is an approach that does not think or consider that all aspects of knowledge are theologically relevant. This option would lead to the separation of truth into secular and religious parts and could not be sustained. Third, adopt a faith worldview or integral religious vision – a synthesis of faith and reason. The main difficulty with this view is that it works at the philosophical level, but has led to a degree of superficiality in practice. Nevertheless, it is the option that religiously affiliated colleges and universities ought to follow if they are to seriously make a distinctive contribution to the advancement and pursuit of knowledge.

Chapter 5

Academic freedom

Introduction

Academic freedom has a degree of 'mystique' surrounding it and is widely used with different meanings in different cultures, but it essentially implies that higher education institutions should be endowed with certain quasi-legal rights. These rights originated in a medieval intellectual tradition in Western Europe and were established essentially to defend the autonomy of the Church. Academic rights and privileges were therefore ecclesiastical, and the university had an ecclesiastical status guaranteed by the Church. As universities established themselves, they naturally sought the protection of the Church against local and state interference. Papal recognition and confirmation of a university, often given through the issuing of a Papal Bull, gave it international recognition, together with a series of privileges and a degree of independence from local princes and rulers. When university disputes arose with the secular authorities, the Church almost always supported the university authorities. This association with the Church also led universities to claim a degree of self-government (see Russell 1993: 3–16). Thus they emphasised one vital aspect of academic freedom, namely, the freedom of the institution from external control. The modern system of university education is the direct heir of this medieval and ecclesiastical intellectual tradition, and the modern Catholic concept of academic freedom is rooted in this ancient tradition. There were of course tensions and disputes, particularly in regard to theological disciplines, with religious authorities, and some of these are detailed by Collins (1992: 26) as they occurred in the Catholic University of Leuven. At the Reformation academic freedom came under great pressure as assumptions about what was true and false underwent profound change. As Russell (1993: 16f.) demonstrates, some universities had to make a formal allegiance to the state, which could realistically be identified with allegiance to the state's religion. Morgan (2004: 112) noted that: 'There was a need for vigorous ideological control of the concentration in the universities of men devoted to the pursuit of ideas.' Universities and academic freedom now existed only at the sufferance of the state, for as Russell (1993: 22) says: 'The medieval principle demanded an extra-territorial Pope as its guarantor, and his disappearance deprived universities of a very vital protection.' The majority of universities in much of the Anglo-Saxon world are now almost wholly dependent on the state.

The nature of academic freedom

Our more contemporary concept of academic freedom originates from around 1850 in Germany, where the right of faculty within a university to teach any subject was protected by the state constitution. This was an attempt to prevent state patronage and interference in the academic affairs of universities. However, there are few such legal protections in the USA, Britain or most other countries. The idea is that these rights, conferred by the state or custom, should protect academics teaching and researching within universities from being removed or harassed because of their unpopular views or positions. These notions of rights were designed to protect academics who teach and research within their own fields of inquiry and competence – it was not about protecting just any kind of opinion. However, it would be difficult for academics to locate where these rights are actually stated. Academics are employees and generally have no other rights in law compared with any other kind of employees, but they operate largely unsupervised and there is generally a culture of tolerance of informed opinions within higher education. Universities are therefore viewed as communities of teachers and students, where controversial debates are resolved through discussion as part of the task of searching for truth. This kind of university assumes a certain type of democratic state – one that grants a degree of freedom to allow this discussion. In return the university is simultaneously responsible to the state, which gives it its charter.

There appear to be two kinds of academic freedom: individual and institutional. In the USA, the case of University of California vs. Bekke in 1978 led the Supreme Court to define academic freedom. It stated that the university can 'determine for itself on academic grounds: 1. who may teach, 2. what may be taught, 3. how it should be taught, 4. who may be admitted to study'. This definition does not really offer the professor freedom from being dismissed for espousing controversial views, as it views academic freedom as a matter of internal policy for the college or university.

In summary, there appear to be three parts to academic freedom. The first part is the freedom of academics to teach, to carry out research, and to publish it, within the context of their university mission and the law. The second part, and perhaps the most controversial part, is academic free speech, the freedom of academics to express their scholarly and non-scholarly views publicly. The third part is the freedom of academics to participate in university government and to criticise the institutions in which they do their work. A fourth part would be added by some: the freedom of students to select their own courses of study. Religious issues, including the relationship between religion and higher education, have and continue to be especially sensitive in many religiously affiliated institutions. Indeed, significant conflicts have arisen between the academic freedom of students and staff and the religious principles operative at an institutional level in religiously affiliated institutions.

Nevertheless, academic freedom is a contested concept that needs to be argued for not least because it is differently understood. It is often associated with institutional autonomy, but the simple fact that an institution is autonomous provides no guarantee of academic freedom. There is often little difference between a private university, which may be controlled by a particular group with its own worldview, which then imposes its own particular restrictions on academic freedom, and a government-controlled university which ostensibly claims to guarantee a level or degree of academic freedom in the constitution of the state. Autonomy needs to be distinguished from academic freedom. Therefore, academic freedoms can be, and often are, limited by institutional requirements, with the autonomy of the institution being used to restrict the liberty of staff and students. Shils (1991: 3–4) illustrates this point in saying that the academic is not free to absent himself from teaching or decide his own hours of work. Shils (1991: 18) believes that: 'academic freedom is justified when it contributes to the growth of the body of truthful propositions and to this body's transmission to contemporary and ongoing generations'. Even liberals recognise that academic freedom is not an unlimited freedom. However, when liberals impose certain limits on academic freedom it is referred to as the 'limits of', but if a religiously affiliated institution does the same then it is often perceived as 'limits on' academic freedom. Indeed, religious beliefs are often singled out as reasons that are unjustified or illegitimate when it comes to limiting academic freedom. However, it would appear that if the secular university qualifies academic freedom based on consensus, then the religiously affiliated university can do so on the basis of its own particular religious worldview. Secular universities are not neutral institutions and in contemporary Western society are often dominated by a rhetoric of political correctness that often hinders free discussion within higher education, students harass those with unpopular views and threats of terrorism place further constraints on academic freedom. Academic freedom is also bound by the rules of scholarly procedure and does not mean saying what you please. The methods used in Western universities are more subtle than in other kinds of societies, but they have the same effect of curbing dissident or subversive views.

In Britain the Committee of Vice-Chancellors and Principals (CVCP) issued a circular on 2 December 1987 in which they outlined what they understood to be academic freedom: 'the freedom within the law for academic staff to question and to test received wisdom and put forward new and controversial or unpopular opinion without placing individuals in jeopardy of losing their jobs'. As a definition it lacks a degree of breadth, and Tight (1988: 132) provides a more comprehensive definition, yet one that is open to interpretation:

> Academic freedom refers to the freedom of individual academics to study, teach, research and publish without being subject to undue interference. Academic freedom is granted in the belief that it enhances the pursuit and application of worthwhile knowledge, and as such is supported by society through funding of academics and their institutions. Academic freedom embodies an acceptance by academics of the need to encourage work, and of their accountability to each other and to society in general.

Strike (1982) goes further and argues that if an academic is to be free then the university cannot have an official point of view – it cannot have a mission. He believes that universities must be neutral or at least committed to neutrality, otherwise academics cannot assess the mission of a university critically because they will be either inhibited or prohibited from doing so by the university authorities. The consequence of this argument is that religiously affiliated institutions cannot really be places where truth is sought. Strike (1982: 77–8) argues that universities are required to provide reasonable security for those who express unpopular opinions, that they must not be committed to any particular doctrine, but therefore should be neutral, and that authority must be the authority of experts. In this view only the academic peers are entitled to exercise judgement concerning another academic's competence. Strike adopts a hard doctrine of academic freedom, which effectively treats all religiously affiliated or mission-driven universities as enemies of academic freedom. He believes that academics in these kinds of universities become subservient not only to the mission of their institution but also to the external authority responsible for overseeing the mission. Of course Strike could as easily be speaking of state universities with mission statements, which are controlled by the state. Modern universities are often committed in their mission statements to egalitarianism, collectivism, equality and inclusion – they are certainly not neutral.

Kirk (1955: 18) states that medieval universities enjoyed academic freedom not despite but because of the framework of Christian belief in which they operated. This framework guaranteed their liberty to pursue the truth. Kirk (1955: 31) suggests three possible policies for the Christian higher education institution: the legalistic, the libertine, and responsible freedom. He describes them as follows:

> In the eyes of the indoctrinators, the scholar and teacher are servants, hired for money to do a job. In the eyes of the Doctrinaire Liberals, the scholar and the teacher are masterless men, rather like Cain, and ought

to remain so. In my eyes the scholar and the teacher are Bearers of the Word – that is, the conservators and promulgators of knowledge in all its forms; they are neither simply hired functionaries nor simply knights-errant in their lists.

The freedom for an academic to pursue knowledge must carry with it the duty of truthfulness, as much within higher education is taken on trust. In believing that some publication or research report is accurate we depend on trust, as we are not in a position to check all the methods of academics. The academic has therefore a responsibility to be accurate in research. It is often the case that academics are relatively silent about their responsibilities and can exaggerate their claimed 'rights' to academic freedom. Academic freedom assumes that in searching for the truth academics are both competent and honest, since such freedom does not confer any exemptions from the laws of libel and slander. Universities and academics are also accountable to those who actually pay for their activities, principally teaching and research, whether it be the state or private organisations funding such activities. Academics are not free to squander public or private money in the sole pursuit of their own interests. Nevertheless, they should have sufficient resources to pursue their work. The key problem is that the state or private organisations can influence academic freedom through the amount of money they provide and for which purposes they wish research to be conducted.

The relationship between universities and religious authority, whether combined or including the power of the state, has not always been an easy one. Pertinent is the case of Thomas Aitkenhead, an 18-year-old theology student at Edinburgh University who was sentenced to death for blasphemy in 1697. His execution was a result of a repressive Calvinism which believed that any deviation in doctrine or behaviour was a mortal threat to the whole community – even under the Inquisition his life would have probably been saved. Whilst academics who are professing members of a particular faith are part of a community of believers or 'community of conviction', their scholarship may ask questions that their faith would rather ignore. Tensions are inevitable when religious authorities are involved in higher education, and this has led many to doubt the willingness of some religious believers to accept the pluralism of views in higher education. Some would argue that you need to give up a certain amount of freedom in order to belong to a nurturing, bonded community, such as in a university that emphatically declares itself to have religious gaols. The Christian Churches have used oaths of fidelity, professions of faith and mandates to try to ensure consistent and orthodox teaching in theological matters. Limitations on absolute notions of academic freedom are part of this process not in order to restrict the pursuit of truth but to affirm those higher truths that determine the religiously affiliated institution's reason for existing. Therefore, limitations or constraints are often only placed upon theological subjects within religiously affiliated institutions.

Religiously affiliated institutions sometimes specifically qualify the academic's perceived right to academic freedom by means of balancing their rights with the mission and identity of the institution. Academic freedom is therefore understood within the stated vision of the institution. This may even be inserted into the employment contracts with academic staff. In general, the freedoms often associated with concepts of 'academic freedom' need to be exercised with responsibility in order to avoid the extremes of legalism and licence, on the one hand from those who threaten to restrict academic freedom through legislation, and on the other from those who are unbridled and have absolute notions of academic freedom. Within any university there will potentially be diversity of judgement and this diversity will usually be promoted through research, debate, publication and teaching. The religiously affiliated institution will also promote academic freedom within the framework of reference to which it is committed. There is, nevertheless, the concern that if religiously affiliated institutions conceive of their religious identity too narrowly then they may restrict academic freedom as defined by secular authorities.

The American Association of University Professors (AAUP) 1940 Statement of Principles on Academic Freedom and Tenure allows for limitations on academic freedom. Exceptions are allowed for religiously affiliated institutions but the AAUP recommend that these should be stated explicitly in writing on first appointment of academic staff. Consequently, at Gonzaga University, a Jesuit university, there were in the 1960s restrictions on all members of the faculty to 'be careful not to introduce into [their] teaching controversial matter which . . . is contrary to the specified aims of the institution' (see McConnell 1990). The university reserved to itself the right to dismiss staff for 'inculcation of viewpoints which contradict explicit principles of Catholic faith and morals'. The AAUP accepted this wording in stating that 'satisfactory conditions of academic freedom . . . prevail at Gonzaga'. The AAUP position was that religious colleges and universities are entitled to depart from the AAUP statements of academic freedom so long as they clearly announce their intention to do so in advance. The 1940 statement is not an official statement of academic freedom in the sense that it has legal force, but it does have considerable authority in the context of higher education in the USA. However, it is important to state that it clearly did not require religiously affiliated institutions to adopt the statement in full.

In 1970 the AAUP produced new interpretative guidelines for its 1940 statement on academic freedom, which were more sceptical about the exceptions allowed for religiously affiliated institution. In 1988 another subcommittee of the AAUP made it clear in its discussions that it considered religiously affiliated institutions to have forfeited the right to call themselves higher education institutions if they did not subscribe fully to the 1940 statement understood according to the new 1970 guidelines. The committee made no distinction between theological disciplines and other subjects, insisting that they must be treated in the same way. Nevertheless, whilst the AAUP has censured a number of religiously affiliated institutions for limiting academic freedom, these censures are not disproportionate to the number of religiously affiliated institutions in the American higher education system. The usefulness of the AAUP statement and activities for religiously affiliated institutions has been its censure of institutions that fail to warn faculty about any limits on academic freedom. This is important since many religiously affiliated institutions depend increasingly on their mission statements, which, as we have seen, can be vague in the extreme, to preserve their identity as faith-based institutions. In this context we need to look at how all three faith traditions operate and practise notions of academic freedom within their own higher education institutions.

Catholic practices and notions

When Pope John Paul II visited the University of Leuven in 1985 he was met by the Rector who described his institution as the only medieval Catholic university to have remained true to its mission. He then described what this mission entailed in the following terms:

> The Catholic University of Leuven has a duty constantly to question inherited truths and to adapt them if necessary to modern language and thought. That inevitably brings with it conflicts between error and ortho-doxy, and sometimes the transition from error to orthodox. A Catholic intellectual, indeed any intellectual, stands at the frontier between the known and the unknown. Whatever their discipline, seekers must have the freedom to chart that unknown, to elaborate working hypotheses and to put them to the test, to integrate new findings with the already known, or to draw new conclusions about what went before. They must also have the right to be mistaken; that is one of the essential conditions for them to exercise their functions as seekers, and for the university to carry out its proper institutional function.
>
> (translated and quoted by Sayer 1999: 80–1)

John Paul's response to this claim for academic freedom is unrecorded, but if given he might have echoed Benedict Gaetani, the papal legate, civil lawyer and future Pope, who told the Paris theologians in 1290; 'You sit in your professorial chairs and think that Christ is ruled by your reasonings. Not so, my brethren, not so' (quoted in Courtenay 1989: 175–6). The welcoming speech by the Rector of Leuven outlined what many Catholic university presidents believed to be the extent of their autonomy and academic freedom in the 1980s.

Today, the Catholic University of America has an explicit statement on academic freedom which affirms its commitment to it. It declares that 'academic freedom presupposes . . . commitment to the stated mission of the university'. In particular, Catholic theologians 'are expected to give assent to the teachings of the magisterium in keeping with the various degrees of assent that are called for by authoritative teaching'. Annarelli (1987), in his critique of Catholic institutions and academic freedom, concludes that the current official Catholic interpretations of academic freedom place unnecessary constraints on these institutions. There is a real hesitancy among many religious institutions to place any limits on academic freedom mainly because they model themselves largely on secular institutions and care about how they are perceived in the secular world. Ryan (in Mastroeni 1995: 137) observes that 'The first problematic presupposition of Catholics who adopt the secular concept of academic freedom, then, is ecclesiological: they assume that the magisterium cannot be the final arbiter even of a university's specifically Catholic identity since they hold that any appeal to an external authority compromises academic freedom.' Religiously affiliated institutions with a clear mission need to have their own notions of what academic freedom means in order to justify the legitimacy of doctrinal limits on academic freedom. The AAUP report (1999) on censured administrations provides us with an example of what can arise within a Catholic college as a result of vague understandings of mission and identity. The following case is taken from the AAUP reports and concerns Albertus Magnus College in Connecticut.

Albertus Magnus is a small liberal arts college that was founded in 1925 by a congregation of Dominican nuns. It currently has around 1,500 students and a mission statement that claims that the college identifies itself as 'faithful to the Judeo-Christian tradition and its Catholic heritage'. In 1991 it appointed Professor X to its faculty of theology. Professor X had previously been vice-rector of a Catholic seminary, but in 1987 had taken permanent leave of absence from active ministry in the Catholic priesthood for what he described as 'personal reasons'. In June 1997, four months before the college suspended him and relieved him from his teaching duties, he informed the President that he was gay. He had previously attended college functions with his male partner since his appointment without any controversy and had clearly not hidden his sexual orientation. He was promoted within the college and in 1996 had requested paid leave of absence in order to complete a book on sexual ethics. As part of his application to the college authorities he stated that the book's thesis was that 'long-term sexual abstinence is harmful and . . . immoral' and that 'the assumptions that it is not harmful legitimises inhuman Church expectations that certain individuals practise long-term or life-long abstinence, most notably, gay men, lesbians, divorces and single adults'. The college authorities, including the college President, approved and funded Professor X's request. In June 1997 an article appeared in the national Catholic newspaper *The Wanderer* in which Professor X's name was linked by association to a civil suit against Professor X's former seminary. After a further article and a response by Professor X in another paper in which he claimed that he was still a priest, but on leave, the college President effectively summarily dismissed Professor X. The grounds given by the President were that Professor X claimed to be a priest and that this presented the college with a problem because of its fundamental identity as a Catholic college.

It is interesting to comment on this case further, as at no time did the college claim that Professor X's writing on sexual ethics, some of which was clearly contrary to Catholic moral teaching, concerned it. Whilst, the college's Faculty Handbook stated clearly that 'every aspect of personnel policy and practice' will be 'without regard to, inter alia, sexual orientation', the college authorities were essentially embarrassed by Professor X's claim that he was still a priest on leave and feared negative publicity for the college resulting from this claim. However, the college must have also feared for the college's public image when one of its staff was associated, if only by name, with a scandal within the Church. The college had suggested that Professor X work within another department in the college, but he refused this offer. The fact that Professor X had in both his teaching and writing departed from Catholic teaching was never an issue; indeed this departure from Church teaching seemed to have been endorsed by the college authorities. The college, if it had had a clearer idea of its religious mission, could have based its decision to dismiss Professor X on his unorthodox writing, but chose to focus instead on the status of Professor X within the Church community and dismissed him for something which was actually true – he was indeed a priest on leave. The college had employed him without fully considering the possible implications of his status, although it knew he had been ordained. For this reason an investigating committee of AAUP censured the college for dismissing Professor X. Many Catholic colleges and universities tolerate dissent on Church teaching among its faculty, arguing that academic freedom, based solely on competence and the individual integrity of the academic, protects the academic even when they are expected to respect the broad objectives of the institution's mission. Professor Daniel Maguire, an ex-priest, is Professor of Ethics at Marquette University, a Catholic university in Wisconsin, and regularly advocates at public meetings his pro-abortion views, but the Jesuit university protects him under its policy on academic freedom. There is therefore no consistent view of academic freedom within Catholic colleges and universities – each does its own thing. It might also be added that the discussion of academic freedom in Catholic circles often amounts to a crisis of faith for the individuals involved.

The two most famous cases of controversy surrounding notions of 'academic freedom' within the Catholic Church concern Charles Curran at the Catholic University of America and Hans Kung at the University of Tübingen in Germany. There are many similarities between these two cases of censured theologians. Both were Roman Catholic priests and as such members of the hierarchy of the Catholic Church. Both taught within Catholic theology departments and one within a Catholic institution – in the case of Kung he taught within a state university, but in a Catholic theology Faculty overseen by the Catholic Church in Germany and he, like Curran, held a *mandatum* – a licence from the local Catholic bishop or other ecclesiastical authority to teach in that faculty. Both priests had long histories of dissenting from or questioning Catholic teaching that began in the 1960s and both officially taught religion in the name of the Catholic Church. Curran (1990: 196) had already been removed from his post in a seminary and in 1966 he found himself trying to secure his position at the Catholic University of America after the President attempted, but failed, to remove him. Both men believed that they were protected by academic freedom to teach and publish work that questioned Catholic teaching. Both resisted the Catholic Church's attempt to remove them from their academic posts and both failed in their attempts. In both cases the Catholic Church had monitored their teaching and publications for decades as both priests had already dissented from the teachings in the encyclical *Humanae Vitae*. Curran had gone so far as to say that Catholics were not bound by the encyclical. The question for both priests was how far could they dissent from authoritative Church teaching that had not been declared infallible. The Vatican finally completed its long investigation into both priests and this resulted in disciplinary action. In the case of Kung, he had his licence withdrawn in 1979 whilst Curran had his withdrawn in 1986. The Vatican wrote to the President of Curran's university that he was neither 'suitable nor eligible to exercise the function of a professor of Catholic theology'. Kung simply taught a different subject in his university whilst Curran was dismissed from his under a separate process initiated by his university's authorities.

The controversy ignited by these cases continues to surround what counts as authentic Catholic teaching in the theological disciplines. Kung had questioned the doctrine of papal infallibility and as a consequence had been forbidden to represent himself as a Catholic theologian. Curran questioned the Church's traditional teachings governing sexuality, including homosexuality, premarital sex, divorce and remarriage. He was subtle enough not to reject Catholic teaching, but he did advocate that they were not 'exceptionless norms' – in other words whilst, for example, homosexual acts are sinful they are not necessarily so in every case. Whilst the Church withdrew his authority to teach as a Catholic theologian, the university, whose chancellor was the local bishop – Archbishop James Hickey – dismissed him. Curran took the university to court on the claim that his academic freedom to teach and research had been infringed, but the court upheld the university's decision on the grounds that the Catholic University of America has a special status as a Pontifical theological institution which accordingly limited Curran's contractual rights to academic freedom. Curran left the Catholic University to work in Southern Methodist University. It was clear that the Vatican, at least in his case, was prepared to enforce the provisions in Canon

Law that all Catholic theologians working within institutions that declare themselves to be Catholic must work under the ultimate jurisdiction of their local bishop. However, this followed a long period of failure by the Church to impose ecclesiastical discipline on some of its own priest theologians who dissented from Church teaching. This failure meant that a few priest 'dissenters' had effectively scored a practical victory for their understanding of academic freedom at every level. In a sense they sought, as Newman warned would be the case, to establish the functions of a Catholic university or faculty as a rival Church, pitting the dogmas of their own relativism against the dogmatic teachings of revealed religion. For Newman, the Catholic university is ancillary to the church and academic freedom is therefore grounded in the authority of the Catholic Church. Ratzinger's (1997: 133) comment on Luther is worthy of note here: 'Luther had exchanged his priestly robes for the scholar's gown, in order to show that Scripture scholars in the Church were the ones who had to make the decisions.' Curran and Kung failed and even refused to accept that authority in the Catholic Church is determined externally to the local irregularities they found themselves creating, however competent they believed themselves to be as theologians. This is why Newman insisted that the Church, through its bishops, should have a 'watch over' role in relation to the theological disciplines in a college or university.

To what extent should the mission of the religiously affiliated university affect the practices of a given subject or discipline? In some subjects the potential for conflict is small whilst in others it can be wide, especially when academic staff embrace secular academic standards and methods that are potentially hostile to religion. The fact that the Church appears to focus on theology is no surprise when you consider, for example, the Catholic Theological Society of America's publication on Human Sexuality from 1977 (see Kosnick 1977: 214–15). This document, written by Catholic academics in Catholic universities, stated that no definitive grounds existed to condemn practices such as contraception, sterilisation, masturbation and homosexuality. In *Ex Corde Ecclesiae* it is stated that the Catholic university 'possesses that institutional autonomy necessary to perform its functions effectively and guarantees its members academic freedom, so long as the rights of the individual person and the community are preserved within the confines of the truth and the common good'. The Church seeks to maintain a balance between institutional integrity and academic freedom. *Ex Corde Ecclesiae* would seem to indicate that theology in Catholic higher education institutions is not in the same position as other subjects. The document insists that the local bishop must be involved in the theological discussions of the Catholic college or university, but not necessarily in the governance of these institutions. Academic freedom is connected to the nature of truth and for a Catholic institution this will involve the Church's teaching authority and the Catholic person together with the understanding of human nature. Therefore a Catholic notion of teaching and research in theology does not accept a wholly secular version of what academic freedom should mean. That is why Dulles (1991) says that Catholic theologians cannot teach or research in ways that are contrary to the teaching authority of the Church and at the same time represent the Church in some official teaching capacity. Therefore, the autonomy of the Catholic higher education institution together with the academic freedom of staff needs to be balanced against fidelity to the Church's teaching. Students have the right not to be led astray or confused in their faith. Academics in Catholic colleges and universities therefore ought to have a commitment to both scholarly and ecclesiological accountability. If they do not, then they cannot claim to be putting forward ideas on behalf of the Catholic Church. Within a Catholic university academics can and do engage in some forms of private dissent from Catholic teaching, but when they use their public positions as academics to undermine the credibility of the teachings of the Church they are effectively putting their own judgement on a par with the Church's teaching authority. The dilemma is often presented in the following terms – can Catholic academics follow the argument wherever it leads in the firm belief that it will ultimately lead to the truth or can they defend freedom of thought only insofar as it does not contradict Catholic doctrine? Some would argue that this second proposition does not truly allow for academic freedom, but the important distinction here is that theology in a Catholic institution is an essentially ecclesiastical discipline, and as Dulles (1995) argues, the freedom of the theologian must not be absolutised over and against the community of faith and the mandate of the ecclesiastical magisterium.

However, it could be argued that it has been the case that a few radical members of the Church, often led by priests, religious sisters or brothers, demand for themselves the greatest amount of academic freedom, but whilst espousing their own views show limited respect or toleration for the Church's official teaching. The same small number of religious readily recognise the authority of external academic agencies – no matter how secular – while rejecting the authority of the Church to whom they have formally pledged obedience or loyalty. These priest and sister theologians who are in reality employees in Catholic institutions often see themselves as 'partners' with the local bishop and often act out of their professional competence as modern theologians, but not always in the name of the Church. Consequently, their own self-definition necessarily excludes the right of the Church to evaluate their work. In such cases their students may be given distorted versions of what the Church actually teaches. This is not surprising when they often claim for themselves exaggerated and absolutist versions of academic freedom and negatively critique other Catholic institutions that seek to balance the rights of academic freedom with their mission. They simply do not accept that current secular models of academic freedom require some modification before being applied to Catholic institutions.

In 2003 the Catholic College of St Catherine in Minnesota banned speakers from the Freedom from Religion Foundation, who had been invited to a meeting at the college by a group in the college called the St Catherine Secular Society. The President banned the speakers on the basis that they brought into question the fundamental values on which the college was founded. The President of Xavier University in Ohio cancelled a controversial production of *The Vagina Monologues*, as did many other Catholic institutions, whilst the Baptist College of William Jewell in Missouri allowed the play to be performed on the grounds of protecting academic freedom, but the college was severely criticised by the Missouri Baptist Convention, which sponsors the college. There were calls from within the Baptist Convention to withhold $1 million from the college. These presidents were setting the parameters of academic freedom understood within their own religious traditions and life within their institutions. Another example is provided by Georgetown University (see O'Neil 1997: 208–9), which is a Jesuit and Catholic institution that refused to recognise and provide access to university facilities to two gay student groups. The District of Columbia had instituted an ordinance prohibiting all educational institutions from discriminating on the basis of sexual orientation. Georgetown, however, claimed that the ordinance infringed on its religious freedom, that by recognising and supporting the student groups (through the use of facilities) it would be forced to endorse (at least implicitly) forms of sexual behaviour that Catholicism prohibited. The courts eventually ruled against Georgetown, claiming that the gay rights law did not compel the university to accept the sexual behaviour of these groups but simply to allow them the freedom to express themselves within the academic community – a right that Georgetown grants to many other groups. This judgement appears to ignore the freedom of the university to restrict its facilities and other resources in accord with its declared identity. If students or staff wish to organise a lecture or meeting fundamentally hostile to the aims of the university then they can do so, but it seems reasonable to conclude that they have no right to use the facilities of the university, which is opposed to such hostile views. The new President of the University of Notre Dame, Fr John Jenkins, has recently said that events that are inconsistent with Catholic values should not be allowed on the campus. He said that because of the distinctive character and aspirations of Notre Dame it may be necessary to establish certain boundaries, while defining the appropriate exercise of academic freedom. If these presidents and institutions had adopted wholly secular notions of academic freedom, then they would effectively be extinguishing any claim to distinctiveness in intellectual life. Religious freedom, both at the individual and institutional level, is necessary within a democracy for religiously affiliated institutions to make a contribution to society precisely because of their religious identity and tradition which ought to help all members of a society broaden their horizons and deepen their appreciation of different cultures and ethical positions. Fr Jenkins has subsequently reconciled free speech rights with the mission of his Catholic insitution in favour of the former when he stated that he now sees 'no reason to prohibit performances of *The Vagina Monologues* on campus' or restrict the Notre Dame Gay Film Festival.

However, if bishops intervene or comment on matters of academic freedom or issues within higher education, then they need to make clear from what position of authority or competence they are speaking. Protection against dismissal or censure for views held or research completed can be accomplished through a contract between the professor and the university. Marsden (1994: 442, note 10), whilst supporting religiously affiliated institutions, found that dictatorial rule was often too common among Catholic higher education institutions. Kadish (1969) details how St John's University had an unprecedented purge of 31 members of its faculty, which resulted in the first major strike by professors in American higher education. The religious community that ran the university considered these faculty members to be religiously unorthodox. At the heart of the dispute was an attempt to eliminate the relationship between the university and the Catholic Church, and the university authorities stood alone in insisting that the university would remain emphatically Catholic in orientation. Whilst Catholic universities must find ways to institutionalise criticism, as criticism is essential to academic inquiry, they need to achieve this within a Catholic framework of values and purposes.

Protestant practices and notions

In 1960, the Board of Governors of Waterloo Lutheran University (WLU) in Canada adopted a document on academic freedom that imposed significant restrictions where issues of religion were concerned. Almost half the faculty resigned. In 1962, the governors imposed 'a statement of university philosophy' calling for 'a faculty that as a whole openly and unapologetically avows the Christian perspective in and out of the classroom'. Not every professor needed to be a Lutheran or even a Christian, but everyone had to 'honour the Christian character of this institution, and co-operate in its programme of Christian nurture'. Seven more faculty members resigned. At Acadia University, a Baptist institution, a dispute broke out in 1965 between the Board of Governors and the Baptist Convention of the Atlantic Provinces as to who should control the institution. Key issues with implications for academic freedom included whether it was appropriate for the university to employ non-Christian professors, and what, on the subject of religion, were the appropriate limits on professorial free speech. An incident that disturbed some members of the Baptist Convention was a debate at Acadia in early 1965, sponsored by the Student Christian Movement, on the 'Necessity of Religion', in the course of which two faculty members had reportedly said that in its current form religion did more harm than good (see Horn 2004).

There are also examples of disputes about academic and institutional freedom from within other Protestant institutions of higher education. A German Professor of the New Testament at the Protestant Faculty of Theology in the University of Göttingen, Gerd Ludemann, declared in 1998 that he was no longer a Christian. The university responded by appointing him to a new chair, specifically created for him, rather like the situation with Fr Kung. The Ludemann case ended up in a German court whose decision in 1999 was that a professor is a civil servant but in the case of professors within denominational faculties of theology in German universities they have an additional condition that they belong to the denomination in question and are acceptable to the Church. In other words, professorships in these faculties are reserved for members of the particular denomination approved by their Church.

In another case the Dean of the Protestant Faculty of Theology in the State Ruhr University Bochum began the appointment of a new theology professor in 1993 which led to conflict within the Evangelical Church of Westphalia, which was responsible for largely determining the theological tone of the faculty. Some details of how appointments are made to confessional theology faculties is needed here. The faculty is responsible for drawing up a shortlist of three candidates, placing its first preference as number one on the list. This list is then approved by the university and sent to the local state ministry responsible for the formal appointment. In Germany the faculty, Church and State each has a role in the appointment of theology professors to confessional faculties, but the boundaries of authority are sometimes ambiguous. In the case of Erich Gildback, who was the Dean's number one choice, the ministry declared that it was willing to approve the appointment on condition that the President of the Westphalia Evangelical Church had no reservations about the candidate's 'confession and teaching'. The Church did have reservations as Professor Gildback was a Baptist and therefore not a member of the Evangelical Church, and it was worried that in his teaching in the chair of systematic theology he might teach against infant baptism – a practice Baptists do not accept. The faculty responded first by trying to rename the chair to make it less objectionable to the Church and to make Gildback's appointment 'confession free'. The faculty also informed the Church that its rejection of Gildback would cause public scandal if it was made public. The Evangelical Church responded by agreeing to re-name the chair and it insisted that Gildback sign a statement not to teach against the Evangelical confession, which he agreed to do. There are clearly similarities here with the methods the Catholic Church uses. However, his appointment was delayed by two years, which demonstrated that the Churches in Germany continue to hold the power to appoint professors of theology. It is why many Protestant theologians in Germany are eager to disentangle the Church from appointments altogether (see McDaniel and Pierard 2004).

Religious institutions often incorporate into their articles of governance certain conditions concerning academic freedom and the following example is from an Anglican Church university in England. In its Articles of Government it is stated that

> In view of the fact that X institution was established as a Church of England College and continues to be so, no member should at any time undermine the ethos of the College or the code of conduct based on that ethos. Subject to the above qualification, the Governing Body shall ensure that academic staff of the College have freedom within the law to question and test received wisdom, and to put forward new ideas and controversial or unpopular opinions, without placing themselves in jeopardy or losing their jobs or any privileges they may have at the College.

The ethos of an institution is difficult to define or measure and so determining whether someone has breached it could be difficult if not impossible. Universities in Britain are all legally autonomous institutions, they are not owned or controlled by the government, and are not part of any public service in education. Nevertheless, they are all dependent on government funding and regulation whether they are religiously affiliated or not.

Muslim practices and notions

Whichever way you understand the idea of academic freedom, its practice in Islamic, Muslim and secular universities within majority Muslim countries has been a mixed affair. Indeed, some would argue that the concept of academic freedom is largely non-existent in Muslim countries, whilst others see discrepancies that can be explained away (Taha-Thomure 2003). There has been a series of cases in which Muslim academics have been discriminated against or abused within Muslim universities. In the University of Nablus in Palestine an academic, Suliman Bashear, was thrown from a second floor window by his students for arguing that Islam developed as a religion gradually rather than emerging fully formed from the Prophet's mouth (see Stille 2002). Human Rights Watch list a number of cases of Muslim academics being subjected to government intimidation, physical abuse and imprisonment in order to silence them. Indeed, most of the cases of violation of academic freedom it highlights are in Muslim countries. Research and teaching is censored in a number of Muslim universities by both authoritarian governments and fundamentalist Muslim clerics. Dr Walid Ma'ani, Head of the Centre for Strategic Studies in the University of Jordan was removed from his post as a result of government influence on the university authorities. In Kuwait, Dr Almad Al-Baghdadi, chair of the department of political science, was imprisoned on 4 October 2004 for a month. His crime had been writing an article for the university student magazine claiming that the prophet

Muhammad had not successfully converted all non-believers during his period in Mecca. A number of clerics objected to his 'association' of failure with the Prophet's work. Scholars for Academic Freedom is another international group that monitors academic freedom around the world and again alleged abuse of scholars in Muslim societies appears to feature prominently.

The World University Service (WUS 1990–1995) has monitored the state of academic freedom in a number of countries and has raised a number of concerns, particularly in Islamic states. In the Sudan the University of Science and Teaching insists that every student, whether Muslim or not, must receive four hours of compulsory Islamic instruction each week (WUS 1993: 125). The question is, would the WUS raise the same concerns about Catholic universities that also provide compulsory religious courses – it seems not. The Islamic government in the Sudan has also dismissed academic staff who do not or are unwilling to conform to its Islamisation of knowledge programme (CODESRIA 1996: 149). In Iran academics are not allowed to 'philosophise' about how to determine right and wrong in government policy, as the role of the university is to translate and popularise the Islamic state's decisions. Clerics were appointed to key positions in universities and those not considered loyal to the Islamic Revolution were dismissed. The Constitutions in Muslim countries do not refer to academic freedom but some claim that they guarantee freedom of belief (Egypt 1971, Syria 1973, Jordan 1952), some talk of freedom of conscience (Algeria 1989), some of freedom of thought and opinion (Mauritania 1991). In Muslim countries under strict Islamic law Christians and Jews are second-class citizens, whilst non-believers are rejected. However, speaking against Islam is still considered a crime punishable by death so it is unlikely that a tolerant and liberal Islam will arise in the Muslim cultures presently in Iran or the Sudan. Esposito and Tamimi (2002: 4) says, 'The degree of one's intellectual sophistication and objectivity in academia was often equated with a secular liberalism and relativism that seemed antithetical to religion.' Each Arab country has experienced an Islamic resurgence in different ways and some have deliberately tried to suppress this resurgence such as Syria, Turkey, Algeria and Tunisia, whilst others have embraced it, such as Iran, Sudan, and Saudi Arabia, whilst yet others prefer an uneasy co-existence, such as Egypt. It seems ironic that the greatest abusers of academic freedom in the Middle East are secular governments.

In Egypt the al Azhar University acts on behalf of the state as censor for books and media. Consequently, if a committee of religious academics (*Ulama*) in this university decides that some publication does not concur with Islamic doctrine, it can order it to be banned. The university dismissed Dr Ahmed Subhi Mansour for writing a thesis on the Prophet which they considered 'non-Islamic' and even 'hostile to Islam'. Dr Mansour was imprisoned for six months (CODESRIA 1996: 140). In March 2004 Dr Matrous al Feleh and Dr Ali al Domaini were arrested in Riyadh in Saudi Arabia and imprisoned for 'using Western terminology in demanding political reform'. Dr Matrous had taught political science at King Saud University, but was banned from teaching by the state authorities. Clearly, academic freedom is understood and imagined differently from one culture to another. In Muslim countries the academics' understanding of academic freedom needs to be set alongside the culture in which they operate. Human rights within Islam are really seen as a set of obligations connected with God and the fear of God. There are powerful forces within Muslim countries that seek to maintain Islam and guard it against secular ideologies, including the proclaimed rights to 'academic freedom'. Muslim conservative forces see their role as defending the ultimate truth and so academic freedom is seen as a sort of Western individualism concerned with self-expression that undermines religion and society. Debates about notions of academic freedom within Muslim societies take place within this all-pervading religious framework and idiom.

It is a framework that concerns itself with the perceived moral decay of society and one readily attributed to the negative influence of Western ideas on Muslim education, or more generally, modern, secular forces. Western ideas of a liberal education that aim to strengthen the critical faculties of students and academic staff alike are not without their own critics within Islam. It is increasingly believed in many Muslim societies that liberal forms of education lead students to challenge traditional beliefs and conventional thought, encouraging so-called Western ways of thinking, judging and believing. The exercise of criticism which liberal education sponsors is often directed at political and religious practices and tends to question the legitimacy of institutions and beliefs. There is a powerful movement against raising such questions in Muslim countries. Western ideas of academic freedom are overwhelmingly concerned with protecting the rights of individuals, whilst the Islamic emphasis is on maintaining political order and protecting the stability of the community. In such an atmosphere, human rights, far less academic freedom, have a limited standing. Therefore Western notions of academic freedom have difficulty in taking root within Islamic cultures – the priority in these societies is given to traditional community life through adhesion to given religious laws and morality. The true function of academics, according to conservative clerics and the state, is to be largely concerned with maintaining the social, political and religious order of society, even if this means sometimes assisting in the imposition of a degree of conformity in thought and behaviour. However, the basic order of a Muslim society rests on a core of values that are generally shared by society's members and are embodied in the institutions of society, including within the thinking of colleges and universities. Academic freedom is therefore a highly contested concept and problematic within Islamic culture, as it is largely seen as a Western individualistic conception of human freedom.

The small minority of Muslims who promote a 'rights culture' in academia are often labelled as individualists because they champion autonomy and freedom and challenge the consensus in society. They do so in societies that largely share a commitment to certain explicit values which can clash with individualist expressions of rights. It could be argued that the overwhelming majority of people in Muslim countries believe in Muslim values of some kind, but they are not generally forced to comply with these values. This is why Islamic conservative forces within these societies can appeal to the people for support for their policies and views. These systems of Islamic belief held by members of society set limits on what other members can do. Academics are increasingly therefore expected to recognise, respect and promote traditional Islamic culture and exercise a vital role in keeping order – many accept this role. Muslim academics also have to function within societies that are not democracies and have strong governments, normally unelected, and therefore they have to accept severe limitations on their academic freedom for some higher political or religious goals. Dictates of political or religious values consequently take priority over considerations of academic freedom. Another way of looking at it is that Muslim scholars are free to teach and research so long as they choose God's way as interpreted by diverse conservative forces in society.

However, the alternative view is that academic freedom is meaningless within a society or university dominated by religious scholars or clerics who totally control what can be published and are themselves the litmus test of orthodoxy. This raises questions about what kind of Islam ought to be followed and who the interpreters should be. Academics who take a stand against the abuse and arbitrary exercise of power by either the state or clerical authoritarianism or question the legitimacy of the overall framework are certainly brave individuals as they understand more than anyone what they are doing. The case of Professor Hashem Aghajari illustrates the point (see Hashemi 2004). Professor Aghajari was a history professor in Tehran's Tarbiat Modares University, but was arrested in November 2002, secretly tried and sentenced to death on a charge of insulting religious figures and leaders. His crime was to give a lecture entitled 'Islamic Protestantism' in which he called for a re-interpretation and renewal of Islam and he criticised the blind imitation of religious clerics in Iran. When the case was eventually leaked to the public there were huge public protests against this trial, which indicated that a more liberal interpretation of Islam is popular in some circles. The government was forced to declare a mistrial and asked the Islamic judges to reconsider the case. In June 2004 Professor Aghajari was sentenced to five years' imprisonment for insulting Islamic values. As Hashemi (2004) says, rights are not simply handed down to people from documents or imposed upon them, but rather must be struggled for within a context of conflict and diversity. However, it is difficult to see that any struggle will provide a balance between rights and religious duties in Muslim societies, as compromise is a feature of Western democracies not Muslim dictatorships. Abdel-Motall (2002), a former President of Egypt's Menoufia University, claims that academic freedom is enjoyed by Egyptian academics, but recognises that this is often constrained by the way national priorities are defined and determined as well as the lack of sufficient research facilities. All these impose limitations on academic freedom, as does close government oversight and supervision exercised through government policy.

Another difficulty for the idea of academic freedom in Muslim universities is that many of these institutions are characterised by rote-learning. Tibi (1990: 110) refers to them as rote-learning institutions and argues that this is the main reason why they are the bottom of international tables of university quality in research and teaching. The purpose of Islamic education is to socialise young Muslims by transmitting to them a specific Islamic orientation, which in itself does not prepare them for change but rather for what conservative religious academics call *stabilisation*. Some would argue that it simply leads to stagnation. Tibi (1990: 113) makes the distinction between a university and a madrassa in 'the madrassah cannot yet be understood as a university, inasmuch as the latter serves the unrestrained free pursuit of truth and inquiry into the nature of the world by means of human reason, but not solely the handing-on of already existing sacrally determined knowledge'. The self-image of many conservative Muslims as forming a superior community also hinders the possibility of change, as the reality of Islamic universities does not correspond to the self-image of some within the Muslim community. Many within Islam reject Western notions of academic freedom, which they claim are largely predicated on a view that knowledge is best advanced by the freedom of individuals to criticise and adopt sceptical stances in their academic analysis. In contrast, Islam understands knowledge to require academics to make reference to and respect religious authority, community and faith. Western notions of academic freedom cannot therefore be universalised. Dulles (1992: 65) claims that the secular model is narrowly based on a theory of knowledge more suited to the empirical sciences than to theology, which rests primarily on divine revelation. Thus, the secular model of academic freedom requires considerable modification before it can be applied to religiously affiliated institutions whether Jewish, Christian or Muslim. Some Muslims would reject it completely. The extent of this modification will depend on the mission and context of the institution.

Jewish practices and notions

In Israel academics participate in political debates through articles in newspapers and appearances on TV and are therefore very much part of an open and free public debate. However, their diverse critiques, particularly of the Israeli–Palestinian situation, has caused some to believe that those who advocate opinions criticising the Israeli State are likely to be subject to discrimination. The Bar Ilan University is Israel's only emphatically religious university and its Centre for Strategic Studies specifically aims to present alternative views to those academics at the more liberal Yaffe Centre for Strategic Studies at Tel Aviv University. The distinction between facts and opinions is not always made clear in these debates, but the attempts to censure academics have come from within academia itself and from political circles who many believe target, label and attack left-wing academics to prevent them from speaking out. For example, in recent years the Israeli Minister of Education, Limor Liuriat, wrote to the President of Ben Gurion University to inform him that she would not be attending the meeting of the Board of Governors since the university continued to employ faculty who were, she argued, anti-Israel. She singled out one academic, Dr Lev Gringerg, who had published an article in Belgium in which he criticised the Israeli government for its policy of targeted assassination of Palestinians. The actions of the Minister aroused considerable hostility from many within Israel's academic community. Jewish universities seek to protect academic freedom, but like most other Western universities need to take account of the political environment in operating policies on academic freedom. These kinds of debates and tensions change over time.

Conclusion

We have seen that there are questions over Islam's compatibility with the Western concept of academic freedom. But there are also questions for Christians and Jews to answer, not least that freedom has many meanings in the Western cultural tradition, but only one kind is being promoted within academe – absolute individualism and autonomy. The freedom that St Paul spoke about was understood as perfect servitude in the service of Christ. Extreme individualism and absolutist notions of academic freedom reject commitment, discipline and duty, and appear to lack balance between individual freedom and the good of the community. Whilst Muslim countries have been subject to extensive criticism from international human rights organisations and UN rights bodies, religious groups within Western countries have also faced criticism over human rights. Marthoz and Saunders (2005) argue that 'points of divergence are growing between religion and human rights' and they identify the cause as fundamentalism, meaning of course religious extremism. This view is simplistic since there is, as they recognise, a great deal of convergence between human rights activists and faith groups. Nevertheless, they are right in identifying the growing uneasiness between religious faith and certain human rights that have perhaps become a rival or alternative 'secular faith'. Marthoz and Saunders (2005) point to the increasing coalition between the Holy See and the International Islamic Conference on population issues and women's rights as evidence of this traditionalist backlash against the rights culture. They recommend that activists should oppose pressures from religious groups that seek to dilute or eliminate certain 'rights' and warn that 'the human rights movement should not sacrifice its most valued principles and objectives in order to protect its good relations with religious communities'. In relation to universities there is a lack of consensus about how academic freedom is understood and practised. Academic freedom is also limited by contractual relations, by the methods of academic disciplines, and also by the underlying worldview of institutions and individuals, whether religious or otherwise. This worldview can be seen as a paradigm of intellectual and moral presuppositions through which one processes and interprets the experiences of life and by which one reaches conclusions and forms opinions. The Jewish, Christian or Muslim worldview begins by affirming a set of beliefs just the way that the secular position does.

Dulles (1995) maintains that the secular model of academic freedom is based on a theory of knowledge more suited to the empirical sciences than to theology, which rests primarily on divine revelation. In conclusion, absolute notions of academic freedom can diminish a religiously affiliated institution's ethos and actually encourage the advocacy of ideas that undermine its religious mission. In contrast, if academic freedom is severely limited then the religiously affiliated institution's ability to search for the truth is impaired. A balance is required, but a religiously affiliated college or university that limits academic freedom in order to preserve its religious identity can be considered a university in the full sense of the term. Since there is no such thing as academic freedom without limits, it is essential that all institutions, including those which are religiously affiliated, should state clearly what those limits are in their own cases.

Chapter 6

The secularisation process

The process and history of secularisation in Christian institutions, except in the case of Catholic higher education, did not happen suddenly. The accumulated and incremental decisions of those within religiously affiliated institutions or of their sponsoring religious bodies or even of the state authorities combined to encourage the drift to secularisation. Indeed, as society and some religious communities drifted away from their Christian moorings and became more influenced by secular thought it was inevitable that higher education would follow suit and encourage it at times. Any religious higher education institution is most likely to become more secular in orientation not through some deliberate decision of the trustees, governing body, staff or by changes in the character of students, but rather through a degree of 'erosion'. This is not consciously intended – there is usually no public institutional decision to abandon the religious principles upon which the college or university was founded. Nor is there a single act or cause that brings about this secularisation, but rather it is achieved through incremental steps and inadvertence. However, the process is aided by members of a faith tradition becoming much more influenced by a secular culture than by the precepts of their own faith tradition. Many of the established universities in Christian countries once set out to be religious but ended up far wide of that objective. Paris, Bologna, Oxford, Cambridge, Glasgow, Harvard, and Chicago all had a religious foundation, but that fact of their past has no bearing on their functioning in the present, even if they retain some vestiges of their religious roots. George Marsden (1994: 8) believes that their secular existence today was a result of the 'unintended consequences of decisions that in their day seemed largely laudable or at least unavoidable'. In short, most religiously affiliated colleges and universities did not initially recognise that they were entering upon a process of secularisation.

James Burtchaell (1998: 827) claims that secularisation only becomes inevitable 'the moment when the sponsoring church was removed from college governance'. Essentially, if the sponsoring religious body is no longer looked upon as the source of mission for the institution, then secularisation is the only alternative. Philip Gleason (1995: 320) believes that Catholic institutions are now crippled by 'a lack of consensus as to the substantive content of the ensemble of religious beliefs, moral commitments, and academic assumptions that supposedly constitute Catholic identity, and a consequent inability to specify what that identity entails'. Newman (see Turner 1996: 153) captured this whole process when he wrote: 'It is not that you will at once reject Catholicism, but you will measure and proportion it by an earthly standard. You will throw its highest and most momentous disclosures into the background, you will deny its principles, explain away its doctrines, re-arrange its precepts, and make light of its practices, even while you profess it.' Newman's prediction has certainly come to pass and it needs to be recognised that a small minority within these colleges and universities actively sought and led a conscious secularisation of their institutions.

The main pressures on Western religiously affiliated institutions that led to this secularisation process could be summarised as follows. First, the need these institutions have for survival through security of funding. The lack of adequate funding from the sponsoring religious body in the majority of religiously affiliated institutions resulted in greater dependence on the state and on external funding bodies which had their own criteria, usually secular, for the distribution of funds. Indeed, the poverty and financial crises within many religiously affiliated institutions meant that many of them believed that there was nothing at stake in disavowing their denominational ties. The temptation of state money in the USA caused many to depict themselves as secular in order to qualify for these funds; the same could also be said of a number of Catholic European universities. Second, pluralism and diversity within society and also within the sponsoring religious communities eroded the common religious language in each of the Christian denominations. The concern for minorities, for issues of gender and race, and for multiculturalism have all placed pressure on institutions to make changes to their understanding of their mission and purpose. Consequently, religiously affiliated institutions sought to change their public image. Third, the desire for independence from religious authority, especially from those authorities that are increasingly viewed as 'external' to the institution. This has led, in some cases, to absolutist notions of autonomy and academic freedom advocated by staff within religiously affiliated institutions. Fourth, the reduction in the number of clergy directly involved in religiously affiliated institutions. There was a demand that religiously affiliated colleges and universities required a more professional approach to academe and management. 'Experts' were needed, not clerical amateurs. Fifth, the desire to be accepted by the secular establishment in higher education as true academic colleges and universities. As Neuhaus (1996) says, there was a desire to move beyond 'sectarianism, parochialism, and Church control in the direction of greater acceptance in the scholarly community'. These five issues represented the main forces that pushed for a more secularised higher education system, which has also led to a more standardised and uniform system, since there are enormous pressures towards secular conformity. Neuhaus (1996) sums it up pessimistically when he said that these colleges that 'had been born Christian, that had stayed Christian, that had assumed they would always remain Christian, suddenly awoke to find they were no longer Christian, or were so far down the road past Christian identity that it was too late to recover'.

The reasons for the changes in religiously affiliated institutions could be made to appear reasonable and necessary, especially if they were phased in over a period which served to weaken opposition to them. A variety of justifications were also given. There was thus no need for a rhetoric of rejection of Christianity in higher education or any explicit praise of secularisation. Secularisation is a subtle process and, as Norman (2001: ix) observes, it usually occurs because of a 'lost habit' as opposed to an attack by any particular ideology, including secularism. The claim and the belief of many was that the Christian college or university would remain religious in orientation after any 'lost habits'. However, it is clear that any institution made up of very independent minded scholars would necessarily be less answerable to its sponsors if it gained financial independence or became legally detached from its sponsoring tradition. There were others who did not want the patronage of the Church and sought to be completely free from any control other than that of their own. Other academics simply viewed the Christian Churches as far too authoritarian, reactionary, confining, and narrow to have a place in higher education. These ideologically motivated academics had a presence on the religiously affiliated campus and shared with their secular colleagues elsewhere the belief that Christianity could and often had an oppressive effect on learning. This view has a long pedigree, which makes Christianity a target of contempt from academic cultural elites in Western societies. The majority, though, do not recognise secularisation as a hostile ideology or as a force that marginalises religion and so, as Norman (2001: 152) says, they engage in 'dismantling the walls of the building with all the best intentions'. Therefore, it is the adoption, whether conscious or not, by members of the Christian churches of secular thought that erodes the distinctiveness of religiously affiliated institutions. Members of the religiously affiliated university become almost completely integrated with the assumptions that sustain acceptance of the secular society. That is why the majority of Christian religiously affiliated universities and colleges have made the shift from 'orthodox' and 'critical mass' institutions to 'intentionally pluralist' and 'accidentally pluralist' institutions. Sociologists, it appears, are unable to fully account for the fact that many religiously affiliated institutions continue in their path of secularisation, whilst there is a general resurgence in religious movements.

In Muslim institutions the main cause or pressures for secularisation came from the state. Whilst a number of private Islamic or Muslim universities have been established in recent years, the greatest influence over Muslim higher education remains the state. Consequently, the character of higher education will legally depend on whether the state is pro-Western at one end of the spectrum or radically Islamic in orientation at the other end. Two examples illustrate the ends of each spectrum: Turkey's higher education system is legally 'secular' whilst Iran's is legally 'Islamic' in character. What this means in reality in each country can be confusing, since the strong pervasive influence of Islam on individual Muslims tends to resist the secularisation process.

The secularisation process

The following outlines the various steps in the secularisation process that can and have been taken by the majority of Christian institutions of higher education. Of course no institution has taken all of these steps and a few have only taken a small number. These steps, as they accumulate, have had the effect of secularising the institution even when the individual decisions by themselves could be otherwise justified in the particular circumstances. This is why many of the outcomes and results of these decisions were often unforeseen. For some it meant that they were no longer identified with a particular Christian Church, whilst for others it meant a looser affiliation with their sponsoring and founding denomination. However, it is clear that many higher education institutions went well beyond what was reasonable or necessary to secure a degree of independence or external funding, to such an extent that some have called it 'death by incremental secularisation'. The process of secularisation itself simply reduced the influence of religion on the particular higher education institution by emphasising only human values and de-emphasising religious values. Some of these steps have also been taken by Muslim and Jewish colleges and universities. The following five areas include a series of decisions or steps which aid the secularisation process and they indicate that multiple elements are at work in secularising higher education. The five areas are: mission and identity; leadership and governance; the curriculum; religious life and ethos of the institution; and community: staff appointments and student selection.

Mission and identity

Mission and identity is vital to any university, but particularly a religiously affiliated institution. The kind of decisions that will erode any intensity in the religiously affiliated institution's self-identification as a Christian sponsored part of higher education could be summarised as follows:

*   Remove the designations of Catholic, Baptist, Presbyterian etc. in the mission statement and replace it with 'Christian'. This erodes the religious uniqueness of the particular denomination's contribution.
*   Insert references to 'Judaeo-Christian values', 'gospel values', 'Jesuit tradition', etc. into mission statements. The words 'tradition' and 'values'

are largely abstract and vague and essentially replace 'Church', which is a living community and has a membership with particular beliefs and practices. Make vague contextual references to religious heritage and background.

- Remove references to the 'formation' of students in any of the particular *mores* or customs of a Christian denomination. Focus instead on student support services and provide programmes for volunteering and community service.
- Explicitly emphasise that the university primarily serves a particular region and/or the country as whole. No references should be made to serving the Church community.
- State that the central purpose of the institution is teaching and research. Play down or remove any references to teaching Christianity and prioritise academic excellence above all else.
- Use a new language in the mission statement that is vague; emphasise what is shared in common with other religions and particularly with secular society in general. The institution can now employ a humanistic vocabulary that all might agree on. Use objectives that can be derived from Christianity but are not exclusive to it.
- Encourage competing discourses within the institution, together with encouraging a range of academic and personal identities that are distant from the core religious mission.

Leadership and governance

How the institution is connected to the sponsoring religious body and how it governs itself are two vital areas for the continued survival of religiously affiliated institutions. The following list of decisions erode that connection by removing influence and 'control' over the institution, this renders the ability of the sponsoring denomination to protect, far less advance, the institution's religious identity, meaningless:

- Persuade the sponsoring religious body to give up its proprietary rights on the basis that this will free the religiously affiliated college or university to secure greater funding and become more efficient, without endangering the religious identity of the institution. The result of this decision is that the religious sponsoring community will divest itself not simply of land and property, but also of the juridical control and management of its college or university. It is done in the belief that the institution would still remain and only appoint those sympathetic to the foundational religious aims and purposes of the institution. In reality it has often resulted, when changes are made without guarantees, in Church property and land being used for secular purposes.
- It follows that the college or university will need to change the constitution

or legal basis of the institution to ensure that no external body to the institution has authority to appoint members to the board of trustees. In other words, disconnect the sponsoring religious body from the legal documentation that founded the institution.

- This will inevitably result in an increase in the number of 'expert' lay-people to be appointed, whilst decreasing the number of clergy or religious. The trustees are no longer answerable to any outside authority, so whilst they may still claim they have some religious affiliation this affiliation will have no legal or any other authority within the college or university.
- The college or university becomes legally a 'secular' institution – emphasising its non-ecclesiastical, non-denominational, and non-sectarian status with certain audiences, whilst emphasising that there is still a religious presence in the college or university to members of the previous sponsoring community. The institution is declared autonomous and independent.
- Appoint more trustees who are not primarily sympathetic to or even members of the religious sponsoring community. Some institutions appoint a president who is not a member of the former sponsoring religious community. The majority of trustees on some boards are also not of the 'sponsoring' denomination. The trustees are no longer obliged to appoint a president from a particular denomination or indeed of any religious faith.
- Invest in the trustees the power to elect future trustees without reference to any other authority. They have become effectively a self-perpetuating body.
- Obtain from largely secular sources financial funding that secures the independence and sustainability of the institution. Funding from alumni and from other sources dictate the direction of the college or university by gaining for them representation on the board of trustees. The university is viewed as a business and the administrators are primarily concerned with being businesslike, without serious consideration for the mission of the institution.

The curriculum

The intellectual life of the institution in terms of its teaching and research is another vital area, one would assume, for the religiously affiliated institution. However, a number of decisions taken by these kinds of institutions has shifted them in a secular direction.

- The institution moves towards ideas of academic excellence as defined by secular universities and academic subject associations. There is no attempt to integrate religion into all subjects and consequently no attempt at a synthesis of faith and reason. Achieving academic respectability is considered more important than affiliation to the tenets of a particular denomination.

- Adopt secular notions of academic freedom.
- Theology is seen as divisive and sectarian – courses in theology are rewritten to include broader Christian and other faith perspectives. Religion is seen as an ordinary discipline and no special status is given to it within the institution. The methods of theology are secularised and academics are loyal to the secular norms within their respective disciplines.
- Any compulsory courses in religious or ethical subjects are ended. There is a new emphasis on the study of secular subjects with new centres and departments opened resulting in what Newman called the 'unmeaning profusion of subjects'.
- Research is perceived as objective and rational without reference to any religious concepts. A new emphasis is given to open and free inquiry with every opinion or view given equal status. The college or university adopts no normative position – Christianity loses its privileged position.
- There is a new critical approach to religion, particularly Christianity, and all kinds of dissent are tolerated and indeed promoted through academic publications sanctioned by the college or university.
- The secular values of academe replace the theological values of the sponsoring religious body. Professional courses for the world of work predominate and career advancement is given emphasis without reference to the ethical precepts of the sponsoring tradition.
- Student and staff handbooks are amended to emphasise the secular nature of the disciplines on offer and to emphasise that the university seeks to meet the needs of all students.
- The demand is for academic excellence and inclusion within the secular intellectual mainstream, which means relegating the institution's religious intellectual tradition largely to extracurricular activities.
- The curriculum is completely detached from the university's or college's declared mission and talk of integrating faith and knowledge is discouraged.
- Increase the range of disciplines and particularly the courses, units and modules taught, so that there is a plurality of missions in the one institution.
- Establish numerous centres and research units that sit uneasily in relation to the core mission of the institution.
- Establish firm alliances and collaborations with secular institutions and organisations and emphasise the importance of external accountabilities – particularly in the quality of teaching and research through accreditation by professional bodies.

Religious life and ethos of the institution

The role of religion in the wider life of the college or university is another vital consideration. Some religiously affiliated institutions have located their religious commitments outside the curriculum. Does the institution attempt to develop the denominational faith of the members of the community? How does it affect the ethos of the institution.

- All compulsory chapel or religious services are abolished. All religious symbols or symbolism are either removed, neglected or understood differently. Any religious holidays are removed from the calendar and replaced with a new emphasis on civic holidays.
- The institution no longer presumes religious commitments in its student body – the emphasis is now on responding to individual needs, not to the whole community. Students are seen as free to make their own decisions and life choices and no moral or religious considerations are accepted as part of the rules of the university – political correctness and the language of inclusion are the new controls. Faith becomes a private matter to the enterprise of the college or university and the *in loco parentis* role is abandoned.
- There is a greater emphasis on social activism outside of the college or university based on humanistic principles – the use of religious doctrine is excluded from overtly justifying service to neighbour on the grounds that it is divisive and not sufficiently inclusive.
- The college or university facilities are opened up to the larger public, and any chapel or church on the campus grounds is either sold or turned into an auditorium for teaching.
- Chaplaincy provision focuses on therapy and counselling methods and becomes another 'service' to students.
- Speakers are invited to the campus to 'challenge' the students with postmodernist ideas and to advocate moral views completely contrary to the teachings of the religious community that founded the university.

Community: staff appointments and student selection

The community that makes up a religiously affiliated college or university is yet another central factor in considering the role of religion in higher education. It is often assumed that a critical mass of believing individuals is needed for a religiously affiliated institution to continue in any authentic way, and that the staff are important bearers of the Christianity of the institution.

- The number of professing Christians of the particular denomination that sponsors the institution declines, partly as a result of a more open approach to admissions and appointment of academic staff. There is a corresponding increase in members of other Christian denominations and non-Christians in both the student body and faculty. Heterogeneity is promoted. No preference is given to members of the sponsoring denomination for admission or appointment. Admissions are to be as cosmopolitan as possible.

- Policies are constructed to ensure there is no discrimination in recruitment of staff or admission of students. Questions should not be asked of a person's religious affiliation in interviews, and any information that might be seen to be prejudicial in nature is removed from the interviewing process. The process has gone from being 'committed' to being 'sympathetic' to 'familiar' with, the sponsoring religious tradition. Being 'hostile' is a fourth stage that some may reach after appointment.
- Contracts should have no clauses that bind staff to any religious or moral position. Instead, academic freedom is given emphasis. An overriding value is placed on academic qualifications and publications in selecting staff.
- Marketability is central, whilst questions of securing a meaningful affirmation of religious identity are played down.

If what is being taught is not significantly different from secular institutions, then there is a problem with identity. Some colleges and universities have even withdrawn from national and international religious associations to complete the secularisation process. Religion's role or presence in the religiously affiliated college or university become co-ordinate, especially when the university's ties with the original sponsoring body become largely cultural and when faculty and students become no longer conscious of these ties. For example, a meeting in a religiously affiliated college or university might once have begun by a specific prayer distinctive to the sponsoring denomination, but this would have changed to a simple prayer that all Christians could share, then later to a period of silence or now nothing at all. Advocating pluralism has become the new rhetoric for justifying change, but as Donovan (1993: 217) argues, pluralism is coercive for it does not allow others to simply be themselves. He says:

> To play the pluralist game properly, parties are expected to countenance quite radical reinterpretations and amendments being made to their own positions as well as those of others. Pluralism presupposes liberalism, which involves compromise, accommodation, and the dismantling of distinctive traditional convictions. The common features and agreed truths it purports to arrive at, though embracing a wide range of viewpoints, are in fact simply reinforcements for the political and economic interests of a dominant ideology.

Muslim scholars have identified this 'ideology' as Westernisation and many

Christians perceive it to be secularism. In this context, the pluralistic vision of education evades explicit substance and has a rhetoric of vagueness that is used to encourage uncritical participation and avoid conflict. However, if 'pluralism' is truly taken seriously, it can mean supporting different intellectual traditions, including those based on faith.

Other Christians believe that the above paints too negative a picture and that there has never been a 'golden age' of vibrant Christianity in higher education. O'Brien (1998: 41f.) argues that many of the religious courses once offered in Christian colleges and universities were poor and superficial, and that those who advocated an integration of theology and reason were often isolated idealists. He emphasises that religiously affiliated institutions have a shared responsibility for the wider secular society and that their presidents often had a noble vision in trying to make their colleges serve society. In regard to Catholic institutions, O'Brien believes that these presidents made the decision to trust the Church and its people by transforming their boards of trustees and faculties into lay dominated bodies. He argues that to try to mandate some identity or integration of reason and faith is impossible and that what needs to be done is to persuade academic staff of the worth of the Christian case. He omits to say who should do the 'persuading' and openly assumes that faculty in a Catholic institution need to be so persuaded of the worth of Christianity. He rejects the idea of reaffirming a distinctive Catholic identity as this, he concludes, is too sectarian and will only lead to trouble. However, he also admits that the Catholic university is far too diverse and pluralistic today for it to make a strong case for articulating a specifically Catholic vision for higher education. In other words, he is saying that it appears difficult to justify a Catholic higher education institution today.

The development and resurgence of Jewish, Christian and Muslim universities should not be seen as the revival of fundamentalism or the restriction of academic freedom of thought and action. The real question is what is the fundamental *raison d'être* of religiously affiliated institutions of higher education? Much of the issue surrounds the ideological problem related to the secularisation of education. Religious affiliated institutions do not set out deliberately to be pluralist institutions; rather they have been largely forced by a variety of circumstances to have a strong potential for pluralism in practice. Cochran (2002: 232) adopts a firmly institutional approach to religiously affiliated colleges and universities, as he debates the role institutions play in embodying meaning, sustaining it in the people who belong to them, mediating it in new members, and manifesting it to the larger world. Cochran believes that Catholic institutions in particular must witness to the Catholic faith and become icons of Christ. If a university or college is only a place for teaching, learning and research, then it has become a mere shell. Religious affiliated institutions must be icons of distinctive religious meaning. Cochran (2002: 137) lists a number of ways a religiously affiliated institution might do this. These include fostering places for reflection on the institution's tradition and its implications for the curriculum and internal community life. It also includes examining the academic disciplines with a theological perspective and promoting character formation and community service from a distinctive religious worldview. The University of Steubenville in eastern Ohio was once known for its liberal approach to Catholic education, but under a new President in 1974 this Franciscan university transformed itself into an 'orthodox' model of a Catholic institution. It simply reversed many of the forces of secularisation – it could be said that it de-secularised itself, which proves it can be done despite the view that once something is secularised it is irreversible.

In regard to the Muslim world, Esposito and Tamimi (2000: 9) believes that the 'secular presuppositions which inform our academic discipline and outlook on life, our Western secular and worldview, have been a major obstacle to our understandings and analysis of Islamic politics and have contributed to reduce Islam to fundamentalism and fundamentalism to religious extremism'. In terms of higher education Davutoglu (2000) describes the institutional dimensions of secularisation. We have already seen that in terms of academic freedom, the Muslim community is often viewed by secularists as a retrogressive religion inhabited by the illiterate and uneducated. In reality, many of the leaders of what some call fundamentalist education movements are well-educated professionals. Secularisation is seen by many Muslims as separating religion and education and indeed anti-religious in itself, and therefore Islam challenges secularisation. However, in the Middle East there are Muslim countries which are dedicated to the secular principle of separation of religion and state – Turkey and Tunisia. There are others that are self-proclaimed Islamic states, such as Saudi Arabia, Sudan, Pakistan, Iran etc. The latter group also sees secularisation as not simply an attempt to separate religion and politics, but as anti-religious in itself. It is viewed as an alternative religious doctrine with the explicit aim of destroying religion. Even in Turkey there has been a resurgence of Islamic feeling among the people that is challenging the secular status of the nation, particularly in educational institutions of all types.

The Jewish response, aided by a resurgence of orthodoxy within the faith, increasingly treats the Jewish Enlightenment of the nineteenth century with scorn. It was an Enlightenment that aimed at enriching Jewish culture by opening it to secular influences. The forces which encouraged the movement towards secularisation are today being challenged by Jews, Christians and Muslims. Many religiously affiliated institutions no longer fear presenting themselves as authentic religious institutions and they are taking steps to stop the dilution of their mission. Students who operate within the educational market of higher education appear to be attracted to such institutions. Some academics, trained in secular disciplines, are also increasingly thinking about what Christian scholarship means. We need to look at the ways religiously affiliated colleges and universities, who wish to take seriously their mission, respond to the process of secularisation and where they find themselves in that process. In order to move, for example, the 'intentionally pluralist' to a 'critical mass' institution will require strong and determined leadership coupled with a commitment to a conscious de-secularisation process.

Chapter 7

Religious renewal

Rhetoric or reality?

Today there is still vague talk of the 'post-secular society' or the 'secular succession', but religious beliefs and values have shown an amazing capacity not only to survive but to re-emerge and flourish. Whether religion is retreating or returning is a contemporary debate, because the secularisation thesis has only proven partially right, as religion has not become so personal and privatised that it is irrelevant to public life. University academics who remain privately religious, but publicly secular in their decision-making and actions, simply fail to critique their academic role from their faith perspective. Different subgroups within Judaism, Christianity and Islam differ in their relationship with and critique of modernity. It is generally assumed that Islam is anti-modern and that Christianity and Judaism accommodate and indeed promote modernity. The picture is clearly more complex than this. Judaism, Christianity and Islam are religions that can encompass the whole individual life of a person and therefore the private and the public, the individual and the communal, necessarily include a faith perspective. Sometimes religious scholars experience the cultural and legal enforcement of the separation of religion and the academy, but religion cannot be left to the private conscience of the individual. If it were, then our religious convictions would become effectively muzzled and religious faith would become merely a matter of opinion.

Religiously inspired scholarship has a legitimate place in contemporary public debate and religiously affiliated institutions ought to provide for this role in the public arena. However, within higher education the situation is perhaps clearer. Berger (1999: 10) identifies an international subgroup composed of Western inspired academics in higher education, especially within the humanities and social sciences, who have almost been completely secularised. He identifies this tiny globalised 'elite' culture as the principal 'carrier' of progressive secular ideas and values. Whilst it is indeed a tiny minority of people, they have enormous influence since they control access to and the content of higher education. The colleges and universities in which they work provide the official definition of reality and they are similar all over the world. It seems therefore that colleges and universities are one of the main bastions of secularism. Berger seems to be suggesting that what needs to be explained is not the endurance of religious beliefs, but the secular culture that still dominates most of higher education. Others believe that secularisation never took place and religiously affiliated colleges and universities simply adopted different cultural expressions of what they sought to achieve. Others are arguing for the de-secularisation of higher education; which implies changing things over time with the eventual re-emergence of religion after a period of absence or quiescence. The degree to which a religiously affiliated college or university is secular is not simply a quantifiable matter of the extent to which religious concepts are employed in the institution. There is often confusion because there can be seen both continuity and discontinuity of religious traditions in these institutions.

It is without doubt that religiously affiliated colleges and universities of all three faiths have significantly contributed to the ethical, cultural and intellectual life of their societies. Religiously affiliated colleges and universities remain important vehicles for shaping and transmitting fundamental human values, and they justify themselves largely by asking questions that are not often asked elsewhere in higher education. This in itself is a good reason for maintaining them, as they search for truth from a different angle and provide a different worldview from the general naturalist position. There is also the case for diversity and pluralism, but as has been discussed already current understandings of diversity and pluralism can force faith-based universities to adopt a bland conformity to mainstream institutions. A truer argument from pluralism in higher education would emphasise the value in maintaining distinctive faith-based institutions that reflect the different intellectual traditions of faith-based communities. This enriches higher education and society, but only if what is being taught is significantly different from secular institutions. If there are only superficial differences between religiously affiliated institutions and mainstream secular institutions, then there can be no distinctive contribution. We need to ensure a space in the public domain for different kinds of commitments in higher education, including the religious worldview. However, religiously affiliated institutions need to demonstrate their religious mission in concrete and measurable ways.

A religiously affiliated college or university is by nature one that is supported, morally and financially, by a religious community. This religious community begins with a theological worldview approach to the search for knowledge. The religious academic community connects religion to the academy by supporting intellectual discussions among scholars and exposing its students to religious traditions, so that a special kind of knowledge, often not recognised elsewhere, can be produced and preserved. In this context students and staff choose a religiously affiliated college or university for diverse reasons many of which may have nothing to do with religion. However, there can be religious reasons and among these reasons may be included:

- the institution offers an holistic approach to knowledge that attempts to integrate the life of faith and learning;
- the religiously affiliated institution is often a small community that emphasises pastoral care and character-formation opportunities for its members;
- the institution offers opportunities for worship, fellowship and intimate community and is concerned with all persons within it;
- the institution offers opportunities for community involvement and service of neighbour;
- there is a strong and pervasive value framework underpinning the whole institution;
- the institution has a strong theology department and cross-curricula institutes of religion and philosophy;
- the institution endows chairs in religious themes and provides a mentoring facility for students and staff to induct them into its aims and activities;
- staff development is a regular feature and there is a focus on the vocation to teach and serve.

The possibility of the de-secularisation of religious colleges and universities means that it is increasingly recognised that the secularisation process is not irreversible. Whilst many point to the reasons why a college or university is unable to maintain its vitality and distinctiveness as a religious institution, it is the case that new leadership can change this. Today, the practices of professionals and academics are increasingly challenged by religious groups seeking accommodations to their beliefs and practices. With liberal sensitivity to minority faith groups they often accommodate these religious practices, which in turn press towards some degree of de-secularisation. The rise of religious beliefs and practices in the world has provided a powerful movement of de-secularisation, as well as making religion an increasingly potent political force. At the beginning of the twentieth century we saw the widespread secularisation of education by progressive governments and secularly educated elites, whilst at the start of the twenty-first century we witness the de-secularisation of education systems in Eastern Europe and the Middle East. Religion is clearly no longer peripheral, even if Western Europe appears to be the exception to this general de-secularisation trend. Alan Wolfe (1997), a sociologist and 'secular academic', believes that the 'rediscovery of religion' is an important new direction for the university.

Benne (2001: 211f.) has shown that colleges and universities that have almost completely secularised themselves can still revive a meaningful connection to their sponsoring religious tradition. He suggests a number of strategies for renewal and believes that those partly 'secularised' colleges and universities could actually make their religious affiliation carry some meaning. Whilst this is acknowledged as a great challenge, I believe that Benne provides some excellent advice, for, as he concludes (2001: 214): 'A tradition, in the words of G. K. Chesterton, is a democracy in which the dead have a vote. Perhaps it is time for those partly secularised colleges to hear those ancient voices, take responsibility for the cause they championed, and reconnect with the heritage of those who have gone before and those who enliven that heritage today'. Burtchaell (1991), who is rather sceptical of any hope of changing things, advocates that there could still be a revival of Catholicity in Catholic higher education. He suggests the establishment of new orthodox Catholic institutions and the reform of older ones. He insists that there must be a critical mass of Catholics in both faculty and students – the overwhelming majority in both cases. His conditions include compulsory religious courses, worshipping together as a community and integrating the institution with the Church. It is entirely possible for a religiously affiliated college or university to become a prestigious academic institution, as measured by secular standards, without giving up any of its distinctive religious character. In order to make these reconnections I offer five headings that could be of some use to Jews, Christians and Muslims in higher education and particularly to those institutions that have a religious affiliation to one of these faiths. These five themes largely give the religiously affiliated institution its distinctive character and they are the same themes addressed in Chapter 6: mission and identity, leadership and governance, curriculum, religious life and ethos of the institution, and community: staff appointments and student selection.

Mission and identity

To take any college or university's claim for mission at face value would be both naïve and simplistic. The mission has to be evidenced in the decision-making and policies of an institution, in particular in the actions and commitment of senior management. Any religiously affiliated institution can sever its connections or freely choose to move towards a stronger identification and connection with the religious heritage of its sponsoring religious tradition. In this sense many state universities in Islamic or majority Muslim countries consider the religious heritage of their society to be the sponsoring religious tradition of their university community, even when the university or college is technically 'secular'. As long as Islam is a living influence on education and society there is, it appears, little need for articulating a concept of Islamic education in explicit mission statements. Mission statements, founded on a faith perspective, that are weak or highly diluted, can be strengthened and vague language about religious values, which is often not understood by members of the university itself, can be eliminated from these statements in favour of much clearer words of commitment and intention. The religiously affiliated institution must be guided by a vision founded on a religious world-view, and all three faiths can provide their own distinctive theological world-view. Therefore, to argue that such a distinctive worldview is divisive and out of place in a pluralist society is to misunderstand both the purpose of a religious institution and the meaning of pluralism. Identification with a religious faith, its mission and character, remains the principal grounding for the existence of a religiously affiliated institution. A religiously affiliated college or university therefore ceases to be seriously affiliated to any tradition if it pursues the same mission as secular universities, and of course pluralism requires distinctiveness for pluralism itself to exist within higher education.

Religiously affiliated colleges and universities need to identify themselves communally and institutionally with their own particular religious tradition. This should be done consciously and explicitly in order to ensure a clear sense of purpose that clarifies the very nature of the institution's existence. In an ideal sense, the personal mission and identity of both staff and students should be linked to the institution's mission as the values and beliefs of individuals need to be represented in the mission. In reality, the mission has to be communicated to staff and students, after consultation, and also to the wider external community. This does not mean that the mission should be written solely by senior managers, but it does mean that the core values and beliefs of the religious foundation should be incorporated into the mission. If this is impossible because of the values and beliefs of the current management and staff of the college or university then it may be that the institution decides to abandon any claim to a religious mission. If there is still some commitment to the religious mission of the institution, then a clear mission statement will aid future planning and decisions that are consistent with the mission.

Leadership and governance

Leadership is perhaps the second most important area for the success of any reconnection between faith and the academy. It needs to be a leadership endowed with vision and one with the authority to make changes that facilitate the reconnection. Clearly, the leader of such an institution will need to be a believer who remains loyal to the mission. In other words, leaders need to be committed, believing and practising, people who pray in faith and accept their faith's authentic teaching. They will also need to understand the nature and purpose of their faith's philosophy of education, be able to articulate this vision, inspire others with it, and have the ability and courage to establish and sustain that faith identity in their college or university. In a sense, they need to be leaders not only of their college or university, but leaders in some sense of the faith community as well. They will consequently insist that religion has a central place in the life of their institutions and will help build a community in which the faith development of all is integrated into the ethos and curriculum. The religious dimensions of their leadership will never be seen as additional, but central to their task of leading.

It can be difficult in institutions where former presidents are still active to make serious changes to the identity of a college or university. Nevertheless, strong-willed leaders who can take effective steps to change their institutions, and who are able to push things through despite angering others with their decisions, are clearly needed and there appears to be no shortage of role models: for example, leaders such as Robert Sloan, former President of Baylor University, who strengthened his university's academic excellence profile whilst successfully strengthening its Christian mission. Fr Michael Scanlan, former President of the Franciscan University of Steubenville, after his appointment in 1974, restored the university's dynamic orthodoxy after a period of serious identity crisis. Fr Joseph Cahill, President of St John's University in New York City, campaigned for authentic Catholic higher education throughout the 1970s and 1980s. These leaders of religiously affiliated institutions of higher education successfully strengthened their universities' Christian commitment, not in a defensive sectarian way, but in a positive way, and thus against an imposing secular culture coupled with some opposition from within their own universities.

The curriculum

The philosophy and practice of the curriculum in a religiously affiliated institution is another vital ingredient of what makes up a genuine reconnection with the sponsoring religious tradition. Whether the institution talks about dialogue, integration or synthesis of culture and faith, colleges and universities need to stop thinking of the curriculum merely in terms of course content and structure, as this inevitably treats knowledge as a product for consumption. Academic staff are often so immersed in current secular theoretical approaches to their subjects that it could be impossible to implement a curriculum philosophy that attempts to diffuse religion and its values throughout the entire curriculum. It seems reasonable to expect religiously affiliated institutions to provide foundation components to all degree courses, whether professional or solely theoretical, introducing appropriate worldviews from their faith perspectives. Contemporary educational thought and practice in higher education is increasingly dominated by 'competences', 'skills', 'outcomes', 'raising standards', 'techniques for sharing good practice', 'effectiveness', 'usefulness', and what the lecturer and student 'can do'. Contemporary educationalists have in response not been slow to critique these new terms in education with a passionate conviction that they are wrong or misguided but they invariably replace them with a rhetoric of the need for 'critical thinking and reflection', but often nothing more substantial than that. Little attention is given to questions of purpose and meaning and indeed to what the student might become. There is an educational dominance that rejects that which cannot be easily packaged as factual knowledge and easily measured. Religiously affiliated colleges and universities have an opportunity, some would say duty, to challenge this instrumental approach or 'academic secularism', precisely as part of their faith mission. That is why academic freedom must be conceived within the particular faith mission framework.

The establishment of centres and institutes to support and promote the stated mission of the institution is one strategy that is popular among all three faiths. Centres or departments that promote arguments for the particular religion have been established in religiously affiliated institutions and within secular universities all over the world. Institutes that attempt to link faith in an authentic way to contemporary culture are also a modern feature of many religiously affiliated colleges and universities. These institutes are marked by a commitment to integrate faith and learning within the context of contemporary culture, and they adopt interdisciplinary approaches. Simply teaching religion does not make the institution religiously affiliated. Margaret Steinfels described those characteristics of the Catholic intellectual tradition, which could apply to other faiths. The list she provides, Gallin (2000: 186) argues, represents the non-negotiables for Catholic colleges and universities, whatever their cultural context or needs of the time. They include:

(a) in this tradition reason and faith are not seen as antagonistic or unconnected; (b) the tradition takes philosophy and philosophical thinking seriously; (c) it challenges the belief that facts come in pristine form – no baggage, no assumptions, no language that fills it with meaning; and (d) it resists reductionism; it does not collapse categories; we do not deny reason in order to profess faith nor deny faith because we trust reason. Both are part of the picture.

Religious universities therefore cannot sacrifice these fundamental elements – ultimately they need to understand through the eyes of faith.

Religious life and ethos of the institution

The religious ethos or the climate of an institution expresses itself in a range of ways. However, the integration of a community in learning and living in the light of its faith tradition is and should be a distinguishing feature of a religiously affiliated institution. Any secular institution can and does have active religious societies, designated places for religious worship, volunteering opportunities to serve the wider community, debates and discussions on campus about religion, and a few have all this and a rich range of religious symbolism concretely expressed in their architecture. However, this does not provide the college or university with a complete religious ethos – more is needed and only the religiously affiliated institution can provide this.

Benne (2001: 61–2) provides positive examples of how religiously affiliated institutions can develop their ethos and religious life. In regard to the provision of worship, Benne talks about 'public' worship being openly sanctioned and encouraged as part of the 'orthodox' and 'critical mass' college or university. This public worship is fully integrated into the institutional life of the religiously affiliated institution. In an 'intentionally pluralist' institution, specific times are designated for worship for specific groups, but only a small percentage attend. In such institutions, Benne says, 'worship is not a public habit of the institution', but it retains some importance. 'Accidentally pluralist' institutions have chapels, but these are also used for other purposes and such institutions may even be hostile to worship on campus. Benne's detailed categorisation of ethos in each of his models of religiously affiliated colleges and universities provides an excellent way of viewing the ethos of these institutions and, more important, a way of fostering such an ethos. Benne warns that changing the ethos of a university is more difficult than changing the character of the academic staff. He warns that student culture in secularised colleges and universities is resistant to any limits on freedom, especially if these limits are religiously inspired. Therefore, he recommends that it is better to work from the bottom up.

Community: staff appointments and student selection

The community that comprises the religiously affiliated college or university can vary from 100 per cent drawn from the religious tradition to less than 5 per cent. There is a debate about what percentage represents a 'faith community' or 'community of believers'. If the community is made up principally of non-believers, then it is legitimate to ask to what extent can they share in the mission of the institution. Some argue that a 'critical mass' is necessary, and that this requires institutions to recruit staff and students of their sponsoring faith, who are committed to the college or university as a faith-based institution. An 'orthodox' religiously affiliated institution with a clear ethos will regard the beliefs and conduct of its academic staff as vital, because it will see their work as vocational rather than merely functional. It will not separate 'religious function' jobs from 'secular function' jobs in the academic community. Staff will be expected to engage in religious duties or provide a role model dimension of their work for students. That is why it is important to recruit distinguished scholars who combine faith with their scholarship. However, many other colleges and universities operate where their 'religious ethos' is much less pronounced, and may choose not to give preference to candidates for employment who simply follow the religious beliefs of the foundation.

In most countries religiously affiliated institutions are subject to laws prohibiting religious discrimination in employment. Nevertheless, whilst most religiously affiliated institutions will share the intellectual and scholarly objectives common to public institutions of higher education, there is the question of the faith dimensions of the college or university that should be explored at interview with all candidates. no matter what level of post. The religiously affiliated institution needs to help discern a potential candidate's views of the institution and its mission in order to identify the extent to which his or her values are consistent with that of the institution's mission. Therefore, it is right to ask each candidate what aspects of the mission statement appeal most to them and to enquire whether any aspects of the mission cause them some concern – anything they might have difficulty with, anything they have questions about. The religiously affiliated institution will also wish to consider the thoughts of candidates for academic posts on the relationship between faith and reason in the academic environment. This helps highlight the fact that the institution assumes that there is a distinctive and positive relationship between religious faith and human reason. Whilst the religiously affiliated institution may not require or ask that you believe a particular faith it will want to be reassured that each and every candidate for employment will show respect for the sponsoring faith. If the candidate's response is qualified, then the interview can explore the reasons given.

Religiously affiliated institutions routinely claim that being a practising Jew, Christian or Muslim is a 'genuine occupational qualification' for a particular academic or administrative post within a college or university. Applications to certain or even all posts within a religiously affiliated college or university may be by reason of the nature of the activities or their context reserved for those who profess the institution's sponsoring faith. This means that a person's religion or belief constitute a genuine, legitimate and justified occupational requirement of the college or university's religious ethos. However, the religiously affiliated institution needs therefore to define its ethos clearly. The *Oxford English Dictionary* defines ethos as 'the characteristic spirit, prevalent tone of sentiment, of a people or community; the "genius" of an institution'. An institution in which religion permeates everything will have a particular way of doing things based on its shared values. The institution will be infused with a religious mission and the more orthodox the institution, the more those who join the institution will be expected to sign up to a Statement of Faith and be invited into membership. The college or university would in these circumstances constitute a community of faith or believers and form a religious community in which relationships are just as important as the academic role tasks. This would be at one end of the spectrum of religiously affiliated institutions, but as you move towards the other end, institutions need to determine to what extent are members of the college or university expected to participate in the religious mission of the institution. In pluralistic religiously affiliated institutions it may be that only the religious faith and practice of the principal or chaplain are considered as 'genuine occupational qualifications' and that the rest of the staff have no extra dimension to their duties and therefore can largely ignore the wider religious issues that exist in the religiously affiliated college or university.

No matter where the religiously affiliated institution is located on Benne's typology, from 'orthodox' to 'accidentally pluralist', each college or university with a faith dimension to its mission needs to determine what kind of 'religious ethos' is relevant and whether particular posts within it require 'genuine occupational qualifications' based on religious belief and practice. Benne suggests that religiously affiliated institutions should consider religious criteria for entrance for some students in order to make the Christian presence on campus more visible. No college or university wishes to appoint those who are fundamentally opposed to or at odds with the religious goals and practices of the institution. In order to achieve this, the following areas of each institution should be considered and reviewed: statements made in the trust deed, articles of government, or founding documents; statements made in the contracts of employment or staffing policies; the extent to which the religious ethos of the college or university is explained and publicised; the proportion of posts within the college or university filled (or should be filled) by academics who identify with the particular faith; and the extent to which staff are required to exercise judgement and act in conformity with the religion or beliefs in the exercise of their duties. Even though the college or university may be providing services parallel to those provided by a secular institution, becoming in part a public service institution, it still retains and requires a religious mission in some form. Whilst I agree with Gates (2004) when he says that 'the rationality and moral sense found in secular higher education can be affirmed as divinely resourced, even if that is denied or nor overtly acknowledged by the institution itself', religiously affiliated institutions need to make this claim explicit. If there is little shared understanding between the community that makes up the college or university and the wider religious community that supports and gives its name to the institution, then tensions will abound.

Conclusion

Religiously affiliated institutions need to integrate actions with authentic beliefs and values within the religious tradition. There has clearly been a time of uncertainty and ambiguity in religiously affiliated institutions, but they need to move to a more philosophically coherent position, a position where culture and faith intersect and where a much needed diversity is brought to mainstream higher education. Religiously affiliated institutions need to ask whether their courses really reflect their mission. It is often said that universities and colleges may understand the characteristics or features of the environment within which they find themselves, but are largely unable to do much about these features. Indeed, the complexity of the relationship and forces through which institutions move is such that they are often hardly in control of their own identity (Barnett 2003: 25). I do not hold that religiously affiliated higher institutions cannot be other than what they currently are. A religious conception of the religiously affiliated institution is a normative notion, and thus it is not a question of describing what its contemporary characteristics or features are, nor what they were when it was founded. It is rather a matter of working out what these characteristics *ought* to be and what they ought to be must be something they realistically could be. At the same time, it is important to avoid a completely utopian view of the religiously affiliated college or university, which cannot realistically take root. Ultimately, each religiously affiliated institution needs to conduct a strategic review, which positively encourages a collective identification with the values and principles of the institution's mission. This is far more likely to occur if the large religiously affiliated institution decentralises itself by creating small residential colleges within the university.

Chapter 8

Conclusion

Religiously affiliated colleges and universities are coloured by the effects of history, culture and religion and will have their own distinctive relationship with their founding body or religious community. There is therefore no ideal form of relationship between a university and its sponsoring tradition. It is also recognised that there is always a tension between the goals of religiously affiliated institutions and the shortcomings of their institutional form. There is no consensus about which religious beliefs ought to shape the identity and mission of religiously affiliated institutions, and no shared academic mission between or within each of the three faiths discussed in this book. Almost all these colleges and universities, especially in the West, are concerned about widening access, providing lifelong learning, making a contribution to the economic progress of their societies, emphasising applied research, and reducing social exclusion in the community. They clearly have multiple and complex functions and a variety of important roles and largely operate within an imposing secular and humanistic culture and ethos, which has a strongly secularising influence on Western culture. Some will even hail these largely secular concerns and functions as their true religious mission while others will be unwilling, or unable, to implement identifiably religious initiatives in higher education. Differences in assumptions about their mission and identity mean that any attempt to define them often hides important differences in approaches to their relationship with their sponsoring religions or denominations. Thus, a complex picture emerges since faith and secularisation are controversial concepts principally because of the various levels of analysis, which in turn provide different definitions and evaluations. Identity and mission in these circumstances become fluid entities, with different expressions arising out of particular religious traditions. Nevertheless, it appears increasingly that the threat of the 'secular' in many religiously affiliated institutions has now become, for some, the threat of the 'religious', understood pejoratively as dogmatic and authoritarian influences in higher education. The religiously affiliated university does not claim a value-free stance, as it ought openly to acknowledge its adherence to certain religious values. It must have something to say to the modern world that only it can articulate. Indeed, as we have seen, secular institutions are not free from an 'ideological' bias or stance.

However, it seems that a number of religiously affiliated institutions need to be more honest and perhaps sever their ties with their funding religious sponsors. After all, many are happy to answer to the wider society for what they do, rather than to their religious tradition. In answer to the question 'Is this a religiously affiliated institution?' too often the answer depends on the audience and the purpose of the questioner, as well as the particular view of the speaker. The answer is invariably marked by uncertainty and ambiguity. Religious sponsors of higher education also need to review their association with their colleges and universities and decide whether they should continue to invest in them and allow their 'trademark' to be used by these institutions. The mission of many religiously affiliated institutions makes no difference to the operation or curriculum of these universities and colleges, as what they actually do is often at variance with their mission. Alternatively, many religiously affiliated colleges and universities have the option to renounce their supposed secular 'neutrality' and embrace without apology their own religious heritage and discipline. There is a place for such institutions within the complex world of higher education. The religiously affiliated institution of higher education should stand in marked contrast and even opposition to the secular model, for religion provides its purpose and direction. Because of the diversity within, say for example, Catholicism and Protestantism, it is often difficult not to see one's own particular tradition as orthodox and normative, and all the others as heterodox, but an orthodox tradition is more likely to produce distinctive ways of viewing the world. It is the particular theistic traditions in Judaism, Christianity and Islam that ultimately provide the 'distinctiveness' and 'uniqueness' of a college or university.

This book has shown that religiously affiliated institutions in all countries develop very different ways of relating to governments and societies. Religiously affiliated colleges and universities have faced conflict between their often newly acquired traditions of secular excellence and autonomy and the demands of mission accountability. Increased funding of higher education from central governments and from industry began to replace the goals of Christian religiously affiliated institutions with a non-denominational perspective, but this in turn developed into a militant secular humanist stand in which universities were marketed as in some sense neutral in respect to particular cultural and religious values. Many religiously affiliated institutions have responded in the last decade by defending their Christian perspectives on higher education against attempts to integrate them into the liberal secular outlook, which they view as incompatible with their perspective. They also believe this secular outlook is neither neutral nor universal. Indeed, the religiously affiliated institution challenges the myth that institutions of higher learning can be value-free. Jewish, Christian and Islamic scholars need to engage in critical public dialogue that is facilitated by the religious underpinnings of their institutions. In doing so they are able to account for their particular vision of education by answering the criticisms of secular academics, whilst also offering a potential alternative vision. Religiously affiliated institutions with a weak religious worldview will be unable to contribute much in the way of an alternative vision, whilst institutions holding inflexible worldviews will make critical dialogue impossible. This is why it is important that religiously affiliated universities and colleges explore ways of promoting understanding by learning about 'the other', whilst at the same time nurturing their own religious integrity – in other words belonging to one faith tradition without separating completely from other traditions.

In examining the role of religion in higher education, we have clearly been dealing with many different thinkers and complex ideas in varying contexts. Invariably there are tensions between the fundamental beliefs and principles in Judaism, Christianity and Islam and the often diluted or exaggerated versions of these principles found when they are applied to many religiously affiliated institutions of higher education. It is clear that we cannot always expect to find a sense of religious coherence in the operation of religious colleges and universities. Whilst all three faiths seek to interpret their institutions around specific religious aims by prescribing the values they ought to aspire to and exhibit, it is important to stress that the operations within contemporary secular higher education more often than not can compromise these aims and values. In response, some advocate dogmatic solutions in an attempt to maintain religious purity within a secular environment, which can so easily degenerate into crude propaganda. Others simply jettison the religious aims and values they feel are uncomfortable or irrelevant to their perceived task in secular higher education. A realistic approach is one that is loyal to and is in solidarity with the authentic beliefs and principles of faith, but which is also internally self-critical and open to dialogue. Those who interpret their faith narrowly in authoritarian and rigid terms present a misleading picture of what a religiously affiliated college or university is and can be, but so do those who shift and weave in and out of their faith. The selected beliefs of the latter group represent the main reason why many religiously affiliated institutions have lost their *raison d'être*.

There are many differences between the three great faiths discussed in this book that should not be ignored and yet there are also many similarities. All have large colleges and universities that privilege in some way the voice of Judaism, Christianity or Islam and yet can be diverse in membership. However, these umbrella-type institutions do not integrate faith and secular knowledge, but rather allow them to co-exist with each other. Institutions that have a normative or foundational theological statement that guides every aspect of the institution are rare in all three faiths. The affirmation of a religious identity should not conflict with serious scholarly aspirations. There should not be an assumption that there is only one model for academic excellence, namely that represented by the secular university. It is often said that religions evolve through continued absorption of new and often foreign ideas and practices and so with higher education there ought to be some cross-fertilisation of ideas and practices between all kinds of religiously affiliated institutions. Intensifying dialogue within and between different religious traditions, between believers, in order to identify and widen areas of common ground in higher education is critically important. As the great ninth-century Arab philosopher al Kindi said: 'We ought not to be ashamed of applauding the truth, nor appropriating the truth from whatever source it may come, even if it be from remote races and nations alien to us.' The questions remain: How can we embrace the religious and the secular simultaneously in the academy? How can we navigate between the dangers of secularisation and isolation? The religiously affiliated institution of higher education ought to be ideally placed to make a contribution to the answers.

Bibliography

AAUP (American Association of University Professors) (1940) *Statement of Principles on Academic Freedom and Tenure*, Washington, DC: AAUP.

AAUP (American Association of University Professors) (1999) *Report on Censored Administrations – Albertus Magnus College Report of Investigating Committee*, Washington, DC: AAUP.

Abaza, M. (2002) *Debates on Islam and Knowledge in Malaysia and Egypt*, London: Routledge/Curzon.

Abdel-Motall, M. B. (2002) 'Academic Freedom and Civil Society: Some Personal Reflections', *Higher Education Policy*, 15, 4, pp. 365–70.

Abramson, G. and Parfitt, T. (1994) *Jewish Education and Learning*, London: Harwood Academic Publishing.

Alexander, H. A. (2003) 'Jewish Education in Extremis: A Prolegomenen to Postmodern Jewish Educational Thought', *Religious Education*, 98, 4, pp. 471–94.

Allen, J. (2005) *Opus Dei*, London: Penguin Books.

Allen, M. (1988) *The Goals of Universities*, Milton Keynes: Open University Press.

Annarelli, J. J. (1987) *Academic Freedom and Catholic Higher Education*, New York: Greenwood Press.

Anwar, Z. (1987) *Islamic Revivalism in Malaysia*, Salangar, Malaysia: Pelanduk Publications.

Arthur, J. (1995) *The Ebbing Tide: Policy and Principles of Catholic Education*, Leominster: Gracewing.

Arthur, J. (2001) 'Changing Patterns of Church College Identity and Mission', *Westminster Studies in Education*, 24, 2, pp. 137–44.

Ashraf, S. A. (1985) *New Horizons in Muslim Education*, London: Hodder and Stoughton.

Astley, J., Francis, L., Sullivan, J. and Walker, A. (2004) *The Idea of a Christian University*, London: Paternoster Press.

Attis, S. M. (1978) *Islam and Secularisation*, Senegal: Muslim Youth Movement of Malaysia.

Attis, S. M. (ed.) (1979) *Aims and Objectives of Islamic Education*, London: Hodder and Stoughton.

Barnett, R. (2003) *Beyond all Reason: Living with Ideology in the University*, Milton Keynes: Open University Press.

Batfield, T., Klein, J., Dunn, S. and Cairns, E. (1981) 'Trends in Jewish Education Today', *British Journal of Religious Education*, 3, 4, pp. 131–7.

Beaty, M. and Lyon, L. (1995) *Religion and Higher Education: A Case Study of Baylor University*, A Prelininary Report Prepared for the Lilly Endowment, Inc. Waco, TX: Baylor University.

Beck, W. D. (1991) *Opening the American Mind: The Integration of Biblical Truth in the Curriculum of the University*, Grand Rapids, MI: Baker Book House.

Benne, R. (2001) *Quality with Soul: How Six Premier Colleges and Universities Keep Faith with their Religious Traditions*, Grand Rapids, MI: Eerdmans.

Berger, P. (1969, republished 1973) *The Social Reality of Religion*, London: Penguin Books.

Berger, P. (ed.) (1999) *The Desecularisation of the World: Resurgent Religions and World Politics*, Grand Rapids, MI: Eerdmans.

Berleur, J. (1995) *Analysis of Mission Statements or Similar Documents of Jesuit Universities and Higher Education Institutions*, Faculties Universitaires Notre-Dame de le Paris Namur, Belgium. Available online at <http://www.info.fundp.ac.be/~jbl/mis-stat/index.htm>.

Bigongiari, O. (ed.) (1953) *The Political Ideas of St. Thomas Aquinas: Representative Selections*, New York: Hafner.

Bilgrami, H. H. and Ashraf, S. A. (1985) *The Concept of An Islamic University*, London: Hodder and Stoughton.

Bloom, A. (1987) *The Closing of the American Mind*, Harmondsworth: Penguin Books.

Boardman, F. (1977) *Institutions of Higher Learning in the Middle East*, 2nd edition, Washington, DC: The Middle East Institute.

Bone, J. (2004) *Our Calling to Fulfil: Westminster College and the Changing Face of Teacher Education 1951–2001*, Bristol: Westminster College Oxford Trust.

Boyd, W. (1950) *The History of Western Education*, London: A. & C. Black.

Brackney, W. H. (2001) 'Secularisation of the Academy: A Baptist Typology', *Westminster Studies in Education*, 24, 2, pp. 111–28.

Brighton, T. (1989) *The Church Colleges in Higher Education*, Chichester: West Sussex Institute of Higher Education.

Brinker, M. (2003) 'Jewish Studies in Israel from a Liberal-Secular Perspective', in Fox, I., Scheffler, I. and Maron, D. (eds) *Visions of Jewish Education*, Cambridge: Cambridge University Press.

Brok, D. (1983) *Possible Courses for Development of Aga Khan University*, Cambridge, MA: University of Harvard.

Buckley, M. J. (1998) *The Catholic University As Promise and Project: Reflections In a Jesuit Idiom*, Washington, DC: Georgetown University Press.

Burtchaell, J. (1991) 'The Decline and Fall of the Christian College', *First Things*, April, pp. 16–29 and May, pp. 30–8.

Burtchaell, J. (1998) *The Dying Light: The Disengagement of Colleges and Universities from the Christian Church*, Grand Rapids, MI: Eerdmans.

Carpenter, J. (2002) 'The Perils of Prosperity: Neo-Calvinism and the Future of Religious Colleges', in Dovre, P. J. (2002) *The Future of Religious Colleges: The Proceedings of the Harvard Conference on the Future of Religious Colleges*, 6–7 October 2000, Grand Rapids, MI: Eerdmans.

Casanova, J. (1994) *Public Religions in the Modern World*, Chicago, IL: Chicago University Press.

Chadwick, O. (1990) *The Secularisation of the European Mind in the Nineteenth Century*, Cambridge: Cambridge University Press.

Chazan, B. (1984) *The Language of Jewish Education*, New York: Hartmoure House.

Choudhary, M. A. (1993) 'A Critical Examination of the Concept of Islamisation in Contemporary Times', *Muslim Education Quarterly*, 10, 4, pp. 3–30.

Clarke, P. (1988) *Islam*, London: Routledge.

Cobban, A. B. (1975) *The Medieval Universities: Their Development and Organisation*, London: Methuen and Co.

Cochran, C. (2002) 'Institutions and Sacraments: The Catholic Tradition and Political science', in Sterk, A. (ed.) (2002) *Religion, Scholarship, and Higher Education: Perspectives, Models and Future Prospects*, Lilly Seminar, Notre Dame, IN: University of Notre Dame Press.

CODESRIA (1996) *The Study of Academic Freedom in Africa*, Senegal/Oxford: Dakor.

Cohran, J. (1986) *Education in Egypt*, London: Croom Helm.

Collins, R. F. (1992) 'Academic Freedom – American and European Contexts', in Worgul, G. S. (ed.) (1992) *Issues in Academic Freedom*, Pittsburgh, PA: Duquesne University Press.

Conrad, C., DeBerg, B. A. and Porterfield, A. (2001) *Religion on Campus*, Chapel Hill, NC: University of North Carolina Press.

Courtenay, W. J. (1989) 'Teaching Careers at the University of Paris in the Thirteenth and Fourteenth Centuries', in *Texts and Studies in the History of Medieval Education*, Vol. 18, Notre Dame, IN: University of Notre Dame Press.

Cox, H. (1965) *The Secular City*, New York: SCM Press.

Cuninggim, M. (1995) *Uneasy Partners: The College and the Church*, Nashville, TN: Abingdon Press.

Curran, C. E. (1990) *Catholic Higher Education, Theology and Academic Freedom*, Notre Dame, IN: University of Notre Dame Press.

D'Arcy, J. M. (2005) *Achieving the Goals of Ex Corde Ecclesiae*, Fort Wayne-South Bend, IN: Fort Wayne-South Diocese.

Davutoglu, A. (2000) 'Philosophical and Institutional Dimensions of Secularisation', in Esposito, J. L. and Tamimi, A. (eds) (2000) *Islam and Secularism in the Middle East*, London: Hurst and Company.

D'Costa, G. (2005) *Theology in the Public Square: Church, Academy and Nation*, Oxford: Blackwell.

Dearing, Lord (2001) *The Way Ahead: Church of England Schools in the New Millennium*, London: Church House Publishing.

Diekema, A. J. (2000) *Academic Freedom and Christian Scholarship*, Grand Rapids, MI: Eerdmans.

Donovan, P. (1993) 'The Intolerance of Religious Pluralism', *Religious Studies*, 29, 2, pp. 217–30.

Dovre, P. J. (2002) *The Future of Religious Colleges: The Proceedings of the Harvard Conference on the Future of Religious Colleges*, 6–7 October, 2000, Grand Rapids, MI: Eerdmans.

Dulles, A. (1991) 'Catholic Identities in Institutional Ministries: A Theological Perspective', unpublished paper, Conference on the Future of Catholic Institutional Ministries, Fordham University, New York, 21 April 1991.

Dulles, A. (1992) 'The Teaching Mission of the Church and Academic Freedom', in

Worgul, G. S. (ed.) (1992) *Issues in Academic Freedom*, Pittsburgh, PA: Duquesne University Press.

Dulles, A. (1995) *The Craft of Theology*, New York: Crossroad, pp. 175–7.

Dunbabin, J. (1999) 'Universities c1150–c1350', in Smith, D. and Langslow, A. K. (1999) *The Idea of a University*, Higher Education Policy 51, London: Jessica Kingsley.

Ellis, J. T. (1955) 'American Catholics and the Intellectual Life', *Thought*, 30, Autumn, pp. 351–88.

Esposito, J. L. and Tamimi, A. (eds) (2000) *Islam and Secularism in the Middle East*, London: Hurst and Company.

Evans, M. (2004) *Killing Thinking: The Death of Universities*, London: Continnum.

Farugi, R. (1982) *Islamization of Knowledge*, Herndon, VA: International Institute of Islamic Thought.

Fisher, A. (1995) 'Religious and Moral Education at Three Kinds of Liberal Arts Colleges: A Comparison of Curricula in Presbyterian, Evangelical, and Religious Unaffiliated Liberal Arts Colleges', *Religious Education*, 90, 1, pp. 30–49.

Fortna, B. C. (2002) *Imperial Classrooms: Islam, the State, and Education in the Late Ottoman Empire*, London: Oxford University Press.

Fox, M. (1993–94) 'Jewishness and Judaism at Brandeis University', *Cross Currents*, pp. 464–9.

Fox, I., Scheffler, I. and Marom, D. (eds) (2003) *Visions of Jewish Education*, Cambridge: Cambridge University Press.

Francis, L. J. (ed.) (1999) *Sociology, Theology and the Curriculum*, London: Cassell.

Gallin, A. (2000) *Negotiating Identity: Catholic Higher Education Since 1960*, Notre Dame, IN: University of Notre Dame Press.

Gates, B. (2004) 'The Credibility of the Anglican Model of a Christian University in a Secular and Multi-Faith Society', Colleges and Universities of the Anglican Communion.

Gearon, L. (1999) *English Literature, Theology and the Curriculum*, London: Cassell.

Giddens, A. (1999) *Runaway World: How Globalisation is Reshaping Our Lives*, London: Profile Books.

Gleason, P. (1967) 'American Catholic Higher Education', in Hassenger, R. (ed.) (1967) *The Shape of Catholic Higher Education*, Chicago: The University of Chicago Press.

Gleason, P. (1995) *Contending with Modernity: Catholic Higher Education and American Culture*, New York: Maryknoll.

Goodlad, S. (2002) *Christian Universities and Colleges: A Conceptual Enquiry*, The St Matthias Lecture, 12 September 2002.

Guessoum, N. and Sahraoui, S. (2005) 'The Role and Impact of American Universities in the Arab World', Paper at the Conference on Higher Education in Developing Countries, Aga Khan University, Institute for the Study of Muslim Civilisation, London, 24–25 February 2005.

Hadden, J. and Shape, A. (eds) (1989) 'Secularisation and Fundamentalism Reconsidered', *Religion and Poltical Order*, Vol. 3, New York: Paragon.

Harris, R. A. (2004) *The Integration of Faith and Learning: A Worldview Approach*, Eugene, OR: Cascade Books.

Harvanek, R. F. (1989) *The Jesuit Vision of a University*, Chicago, IL: Loyola University.

Hashemi, N. (2004) 'The Relevance of John Locke to Social Change in the Muslim World: A Comparison with Iran', *Journal of Church and State*, 46, 1, pp. 39–53.

Hashmi, S. M. (1989) *Muslim Responses to Western Education (a Study of Four Pioneering Institutions)*, New Delhi: Commonwealth Publishing.

Hassenger, R. (1967) (ed.) *The Shape of Catholic Higher Education*, Chicago, IL: University of Chicago Press.

Henle, R. J. (1979) 'The Pluralism of North America and the Catholic University of Today', in *The Catholic University: Instrument of Cultural Pluralism in the Service of the Church and Society*, Paris, International Federation of Catholic Universities, pp. 54–72.

Herbert, D. (2003) *Religion and Civil Society*, Brookfield: Ashgate Publishing Company.

Hesburgh, T. M. (ed.) (1994) *The Challenge and Promise of a Catholic University*, Notre Dame, IN: Notre Dame University Press.

Holmes, A. (1975) *Faith Seeks Understanding: A Christian Approach to Knowledge*, Grand Rapids, MI: Eerdmans.

Holmes, A. (1987 ed) *The Idea of a Christian College*, Grand Rapids, MI: Eerdmans.

Holtschneider, D. H. and Morey, M. M. (2000) *Relationship Revisited: Catholic Institutions and their Founding Congregations*, Occasional Paper No. 47, Washington, DC: Association of Governing Boards of Universities and Colleges.

Horn, M. (2004) 'Academic Freedom', *History of Intellectual Culture*, 4, 1.

Hossain, S. M. (1979) 'A Plea for a Modern Islamic University', in Attis, S. M. (ed.) (1979) *Aims and Objectives of Islamic Education*, London: Hodder and Stoughton.

Hruby, N. J. (1978) 'The Future of the Small Catholic College', *Religious Education*, 73, 1, pp. 35–41.

Hughes, R. and Adrian, W. B. (eds) (1997) *Models for Christian Higher Education: Strategies for Success in the Twenty-First Century*, Grand Rapids, MI: Eerdmans.

Hull, W. (1992) 'Christian Higher Education at the Crossroads', in *Perspectives in Religious Studies*, 19, 4, pp. 441–54.

Hunt, T. C. and Carper, J. C. (1996) *Religion in Higher Education in the US: A Source Book*, New York: Garland Publishing.

Husain, J. (1995) 'A Critical Review of Makdisi's work: The Rise of Colleges in the Islamic World', *Islamic University Quarterly*, 2, 1, pp. 37–47.

Husain, S. S. and Ashraf, S. A. (eds) (1979) *Crisis in Muslim Education*, London: Hodder and Stoughton.

Husain, S. S. (1997) 'Islamising the University Education: Problems and Prospects', in Sarwar, G. *et al.* (1997) *Issues in Islamic Education*, London: The Muslim Educational Trust.

Ingall, C. K. (1995) 'Hebrew College and Normal Schools', *Religious Education*, 90, 1, pp. 50–70.

Jacobsen, D. and R. H. (2004) *Scholarship and Christian Faith: Enlarging the Conversation*, New York: Oxford University Press.

Jenkins, D. (1988) 'What is the Purpose of a University?', *Studies in Higher Education*, 13, 3, pp. 239–47.

Kadish, S. H. (1969) 'The Strike and the Professoriate', in Metzger, W. P. (ed.) *Dimensions of Academic Freedom*, Champaign, IL: University of Illinois Press.

Kazamias, A. M. (1966) *Education and the Quest for Modernity in Turkey*, London: George Allen and Unwin.

Kepel, G. (1994) *The Revenge of God: The Resurgence of Islam, Christianity and Judaism in the Modern World*, Cambridge: Polity Press.

Ker, I. T. (1976) *The Idea of a University*, Oxford: Clarendon Press.

Ker, I. T. (1994) *The Achievement of Newman*, Oxford: Clarendon Press.

Ker, I. T. (1999) 'Newman's Idea of a University: A Guide for the Contemporary University', in Smith, D. and Langslow, A. K. (1999) *The Idea of a University*, Higher Education Policy 51, London: Jessica Kingsley.

Khan, M. W. (ed.) (1981) *Education and Society in the Muslim World*, London: Hodder and Stoughton.

Kirk, R. (1955) *Academic Freedom: An Essay in Definition*, New York: Greenwood Press.

Kosnick, A. (ed.) (1977) *Human Sexuality: New Directions in American Catholic Thought: A Study Commissioned by the Catholic Theological Society of America*, New York: Paulist Press.

Leo, J. (1967) 'Some Problem Areas in Catholic Higher Education: The Faculty', in Hassenger, R. (ed.) (1967) *The Shape of Catholic Higher Education*, Chicago, IL: University of Chicago Press.

Levy, D. C. (1985) 'Latin America's Private Universities: How Successful Are They?', *Comparative Education Review*, 29, 4, pp. 440–59.

McConnell, M. (1990) 'Academic Freedom in religious Colleges and Universities', *Law and Contemporary Problems*, 53, 3, pp. 303–24.

McDaniel, C. and Pierard, R. V. (2004) 'The Politics of Appointments to Protestant Theology Faculties in Germany: The Case of Professor Erich Gildback', *Journal of Church and State*, 46, 1, pp. 54–82.

McInerny, R. (1994) 'The Advantages of a Catholic University', in Hesburgh, T. M. (ed.) (1994) *The Challenge and Promise of a Catholic University*, Notre Dame, IN: Notre Dame University Press.

McIntyre, A. (1990) *Three Rival Versions of Moral Enquiry*, London: Duckworth.

McLoughlin, R. J. (1999) 'The Catholic College: At the Crossroad or at the End of the Road', in McInerny, D. (ed.) *The Common Things: Essays on Thomism and Education*, Washington, DC: Catholic University of America.

McNay, I. (2002) 'Governance and Decision-Making in Smaller Colleges', *Higher Education Quarterly*, 56, 3, pp. 303–15.

Mahoney, K. (2001) 'Religion: A Comeback on Campus', *Liberal Education*, 87, 4, pp. 1–5.

Makdisi, G. (1981) *The Rise of Colleges: Institutions of Learning in Islam and the West*, Edinburgh: Edinburgh University Press.

Malloy, E. A. (1992) *Culture and Commitment: The Challenges of Today's University*, Notre Dame, IN: University of Notre Dame Press.

Manet, P. (1994) *An Intellectual History of Liberalism*, Princeton, NJ: Princeton University Press.

Markhan, I. (1997) *Bulletin of Engaging the Curriculum*, 5, Spring, p. 3.

Marsden, G. (1994) *The Soul of the American University: From Protestant Establishment to Established Belief*, New York: Oxford University Press.

Marsden, G. (1997) *The Outrageous Idea of Christian Scholarship*, New York: Oxford University Press.

Marsden, G. and Longfield, B. J. (eds) (1992) *The Secularisation of the Academy*, Oxford and New York: Oxford University Press.

Marthoz, J. and Saunders, J. (2005) *Religion and the Human Rights Movement*, Human Rights Watch World Report, 2005.

Martin, D. A. (1969) *The Religious and the Secular*, London: Routledge and Kegan Paul.

Martin, D. A. (1978) *A General Theory of Secularisation*, Oxford: Blackwell.

Martin, D. A. (2005) *On Secularisation: Towards a Revised General Theory*, Aldershot: Ashgate.

Mastroeni, A. J. (ed.) (1995) 'The Nature of Catholic Higher Education', Proceedings of the 18th Convention of the Fellowship of Catholic Scholars, Minneapolis.

Meijer, W. A. (1999) 'Islam Versus Western Modernity: A Contrast in Educational Thought', *British Journal of Religious Education*, 21, 3, pp. 158–66.

Metzger, W. P. (1969) (ed.) *Dimensions of Academic Freedom*, Champaign, IL: University of Illinois Press.

Mixon, S., Lyon, L. and Beaty, M. (2004) 'Secularisation and National Universities: The Effect of Religious Identity on Academic Reputation', *Journal of Higher Education*, 75, pp. 419–40.

Moberly, W. (1949) *The Crisis of the University*, London: SCM.

Mohamed, Y. (1991) 'Knowledge in Islam and the Crisis of Muslim Education', *Muslim Education Quarterly*, 8, 4, pp. 13–31.

Mohamed, Y. (1993) 'Islamization of Knowledge: A Comparative Analysis of Faruqi and Rahman', *Muslim Education Quarterly*, 11, 1, pp. 27–40.

Morgan, V. (2004) *A History of the University of Cambridge*, Vol. II, Cambridge: Cambridge University Press.

Murphy, J. P. (1991) *De Paul University: Vision and Values in Catholic Higher Education*, Kansas City, MO: Sheed and Ward.

Nakosteen, M. (1964) *History of Islamic Origins of Western Education AD 800–1350*, Boulder, CO: University of Colorado Press.

Neuhaus, R. J. (1996) 'The Christian University: Eleven Theses', *First Things*, 59, pp. 20–2.

Niblett, W. R. (1998) *Higher Education and Christian Believing*, Audenshaw Paper 175, The Hinksey Network.

Noll, M. A. (1994) *The Scandal of the Evangelical Mind*, Grand Rapids, MI: Eerdmans.

Norman, E. (2001) *Secularisation*, London: Continuum.

O'Brien, D. J. (1994) *From the Heart of the American Church: Catholic Higher Education and American Culture*, New York: Orbis Books.

O'Brien, D. J. (1998) 'A Conversation with a Friend', in Buckley, M. J. (1998) *The Catholic University As Promise and Project: Reflections In a Jesuit Idiom*, Washington, DC: Georgetown University Press.

O'Brien, D. J. (2002) *The Idea of a Catholic University*, Chicago, IL: University of Chicago Press.

O'Connell, M. R. (1994) 'A Catholic University, Whatever That Means', in Hesburgh, T. M. (ed.) (1994) *The Challenge and Promise of a Catholic University*, Notre Dame, IN: Notre Dame University Press.

O'Hara, A. (1997) 'Fordham's Catholic Mission', *Current Issues in Catholic Higher Education*, 17, 2, pp. 19–22.

O'Keefe, J. M. (ed.) (1997) *Catholic Education at the Turn of the New Century*, New York: Garland Publishing.

O'Leary, De L. (1948) *How Greek Science Passed to the Arabs*, London: Routledge and Kegan Paul.

O'Neil, R. B. (1997) *Free Speech in the College Community*, Bloomington, IN: Indiana University Press.

Osmer, R. R. and Schweitzer, F. (2003) *Religious Education Between Modernization and Globalization, New Perspectives on the United States and Germany*, Grand Rapids, MI: Eerdmans.

Pacaci, M. and Aktay, Y. (1999) '75 Years of Higher Religious Education in Modern Turkey', *The Muslim World*, 89, 3–4, pp. 389–413.

Pace, C. R. (1972) *Education and Evangelism: A Profile of Protestant Colleges, Carnegie Commission on Higher Education*, New York: McGraw Hill.

Panjwani, F. (2004) 'The "Islamic" in Islamic Education: Assessing the Discourse', *Islam and Education*, 7, 1, December 2004.

Peterson, M. L. (1986) *Philosophy of Education*, Leicester: InterVarsity Press.

Petrenko, K. I. and Glanzer, P. L. (2005) 'The Recent Emergence of Private Christian Colleges and Universities in Russia', *Christian Higher Education*, 4, 2, pp. 81–97.

Plantinga, A. (1994) 'Christian Scholarship', in Hesburgh, T. M. (ed.) (1994) *The Challenge and Promise of a Catholic University*, Notre Dame, IN: Notre Dame University Press.

Prins, M. H., Janssen, J. A. P. J., Uden, M. H. F. and Halen, C. P. M. (2003) 'Cultural Diversity in a Catholic University', *International Journal of Education and Religion*, 4, 2, pp. 168–85.

Rahman, F. (1982) *Islam and Modernity: Transformation of an Intellectual Tradition*, Chicago, IL: University of Chicago Press.

Ratzinger, J. (1997) *Milestones: Memoirs 1927–1977*, San Francisco, CA: Ignatius Press.

Razek, A. A. (1925) *Islam and the Origins of Government*, Cairo: Dar al Maanef.

Ridley, S. (1989) 'Theological Perspectives Over 150 Years', in Brighton, T. (1989) *The Church Colleges in Higher Education*, Chichester: West Sussex Institute of Higher Education.

Riley, N. S. (2004) 'A More Public Yeshiva', *First Things*, 139, January, pp. 17–20.

Riley, N. S. (2005) *God and the Quad: How Religious Colleges and the Missionary Generation are Changing America*, New York: St Martin's Press.

Ritterband, P. and Wechsler, H. S. (1994) *Jewish Learning in American Universities: The First Century*, Bloomington, IN: Indiana University Press.

Roberts, J. and Turner, J. (2000) *The Sacred and the Secular University*, Princeton, NJ: Princeton University Press.

Roche, M. W. (2003) *The Intellectual Appeal of Catholicism and the Idea of a Catholic University*, Notre Dame, IN: University of Notre Dame Press.

Rosenak, M. (2003) 'Educated Jews: Common Elements', in Fox, I., Scheffler, I. and Maron, D. (eds) *Visions of Jewish Education*, Cambridge: Cambridge University Press.

Rosenthal, F. R. (1975) *The Classical Heritage in Islam*, London: Routledge.

Russell, C. (1993) *Academic Freedom*, London: Routledge.

Sack, D. (1997) 'Struggling for the Soul of the American University: Studies in Religion and Higher Education', *Religious Studies Review*, 23, pp. 35–39.

Safi, L. (1996) *The Foundations of Knowledge: A Comparative Study in Islamic and Western Methods of Enquiry*, Kuala Lumpur: International Islamic University Malaysia Press.

Sanyal, B. C. (2005) 'Governance and Management of Higher Education in the Developing Countries With Focus on Muslim Contexts: Successes and Lessons', Paper at the Conference on Higher Education in Developing Countries, Aga Khan University, Institute for the Study of Muslim Civilisation, London, 24–25 February 2005.

Sarwar, G. *et al.* (1997) *Issues in Islamic Education*, London: The Muslim Educational Trust.

Sarwar, G. (1997) 'Islamic Education: its Meaning, Problems and Prospects', in Sarwar, G. *et al.* (1997) *Issues in Islamic Education*, London: The Muslim Educational Trust.

Sawatsky, R. J. (2004) 'Prologue: The Virtue of Scholarly Hope', in Jacobsen, D. and Jacobsen, R. H. (2004) *Scholarship and Christian Faith: Enlarging the Conversation*, New York: Oxford University Press.

Sayer, J. (1999) 'Linking Universities Across Europe', in Smith, D. and Langslow, A. K. (1999) *The Idea of a University*, Higher Education Policy 51, London: Jessica Kingsley.

Scheffler, I. (2003) 'The Concept of the Educated Person: With Some Application to Jewish Education', in Fox, I., Scheffler, I. and Maron, D. (eds) *Visions of Jewish Education*, Cambridge: Cambridge University Press.

Shils, E. (1991) 'Academic Freedom', in Altbach, P. G. (ed.) *International Higher Education: An Encyclopaedia*, Vol. 1, New York: Garland.

Scotland, N. (1989) 'The College of St. Paul and St. Mary Cheltenham', *History of Education Society Bulletin*, 44, pp. 26–30.

Sloan, D. (1994) *Faith and Knowledge: Mainline Protestantism and American Higher Education*, Louisville, KY: Westminster/John Knox Press.

Smith, D. and Langslow, A. K. (1999) *The Idea of a University*, Higher Education Policy 51, London: Jessica Kingsley.

Sobrino, J. (1997) 'The University's Christian Inspiration', in O'Keefe, J. M. (ed.) (1997) *Catholic Education at the Turn of the New Century*, New York: Garland.

Stanton, C. M. (1990) *Higher Education in Islam: The Classical Period AD. 700–1300*, Lanham, MD: Rowman and Littlefield.

Stark, R. (1999) 'Secularisation R. I. P', *Sociology of Religion*, 60, pp. 249–73.

Sterk, A. (ed.) (2002) *Religion, Scholarship, and Higher Education: Perspectives, Models and Future Prospects*, Lilly Seminar, Notre Dame, IN: University of Notre Dame Press.

Stille, A. (2002) 'Scholars Are Quietly Offering New Theories of the Koran', *New York Times*, 2 March, p. A1.

Strike, K. (1982) *Liberty and Learning*, Oxford: Martin Robertson.

Sultan, T. (1997) 'The Role of the Islamic Universities in the Islamization of Education', *Muslim Education Quarterly*, 14, 3, pp. 57–72.

Taha-Thomure, H. (2003) *Academic Freedom in Arab Universities: Understanding, Practices and Discrepancies*, Lanham, MD: University Press of America.

Tamimi, A. (2000) 'The Origins of Arab Secularism', in Esposito, J. L. and Tamimi, A. (eds) (2000) *Islam and Secularism in the Middle East*, London: Hurst and Company.

Taylor, C. (1998) 'Modes of Secularism', in Bhargava, R. (ed.) *Secularism and its Critics*, Delhi: Oxford University Press.

Thatcher, A. (1995) 'Engaging the Curriculum – A Theological Perspective', *Journal of Further and Higher Education*, 19, 3, pp. 109–18.

Thatcher, A. (ed.) (1999) *Spirituality and the Curriculum*, London: Cassell.

Tibi, B. (1990) *Islam and the Cultural Accommodation of Social Change*, Boulder, CO: Westview Press.

Tight, M. (ed.) (1988) *Academic Freedom and Responsibility*, Milton Keynes: Society for Research in Higher Education/Open University Press.

Turner, F. M. (ed.) (1996) *The Idea of a University by John Henry Newman*, New Haven, CT: Yale University Press.

Turner, J. (2003) *Language, Religion and Knowledge*, Notre Dame, IN: Notre Dame University Press.

Twersky, I. (2003) 'What Must a Jew Study – and Why', in Fox, I., Scheffler, I. and Maron, D. (eds) *Visions of Jewish Education*, Cambridge: Cambridge University Press.

Uddin, J. (1992) 'Problems of Islamization of the University Curriculum in Indonesia', *Muslim Education Quarterly*, 10, 3, pp. 5–22.

United States of America Conference of Catholic Bishops (2003) Draft Application of the Apostolic Constitution on Catholic Universities (*Ex Corde Ecclesiae*), http://www.usccb.org/education/excorde.htm

Young, R. B. (2001) 'Colleges on the Cross Roads: A Study of the Mission Statements of Catholic Colleges and Universities', *Issues in Catholic Higher Education*, 21, 2, p. 65.

Watt, W. M. (1945) *The Influence of Islam on Medieval Europe*, Edinburgh: Edinburgh University Press.

Weston, W. and Soden, D. (2004) *The Presbyterian College Ideal: A Proposal*, Presbyterian Academy of Scholars and Teachers, www.apcu.net

Wilson, B. (1966) *Religion in Secular Society*, London: Penguin Books.

Wolfe, A. (1997) 'Religion in the Academy', *Chronicle of Higher Education*, 19 September.

Wolfe, A. (2002) 'The Potential for Pluralism', in Sterk, A. (ed.) (2002) *Religion, Scholarship, and Higher Education: Perspectives, Models and Future Prospects*, Lilly Seminar, Notre Dame, IN: University of Notre Dame Press.

Wolfe, D. L. and Heie, H. (1993) *Slogans or Distinctives: Reforming Christian Higher Education*, Lanham, MD: University Press of America.

Worgul, G. S. (ed.) (1992) *Issues in Academic Freedom*, Pittsburgh, PA: Duquesne University Press.

World University Service – *Academic Freedom*, Vol. 1 (1990), Vol. 2 (1993), Vol. 3 (1995) London: Zed Books.

Zagano, P. (1990) 'Sectarian Universities, Federal Funding, and the Question of Academic Freedom', *Religious Education*, 95, 1, pp. 136–49.

Zaman, S. M. (1985) 'The Concept of the Islamic University', *Muslim Education Quarterly*, 2, 4, pp. 28–36.

Index